Discovery Travel Adventures

SCUBA DIVING

Susan Watrous
Editor

John Gattuso
Series Editor

D0573414

INSIGHT GUIDES

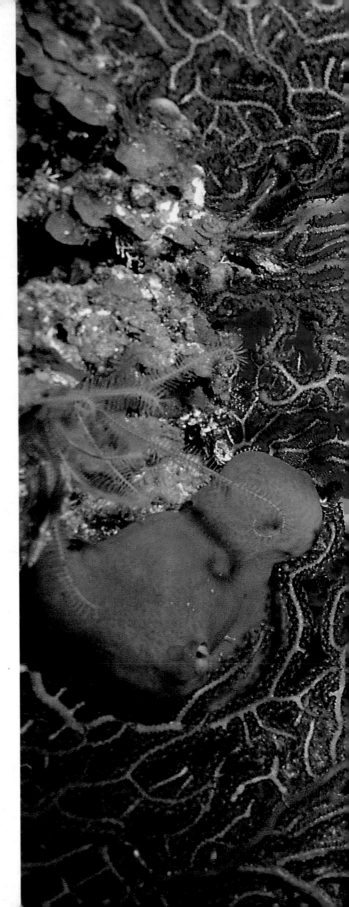

Discovery Communications, Inc.
John S. Hendricks, *Founder, Chairman, and Chief Executive Officer*
Judith A. McHale, *President and Chief Operating Officer*
Michela English, *President, Discovery Enterprises Worldwide*
Raymond Cooper, *Senior Vice President, Discovery Enterprises Worldwide*

Discovery Publishing
Natalie Chapman, *Vice President, Publishing*
Rita Thievon Mullin, *Editorial Director*
Mary Kalamaras, *Senior Editor*
Maria Mihalik Higgins, *Editor*
Heather Quinlan, *Editorial Coordinator*
Chris Alvarez, *Business Development*

Discovery Channel Retail
Tracy Fortini, *Product Development*
Steve Manning, *Naturalist*

Insight Guides
Jeremy Westwood, *Managing Director*
Brian Bell, *Editorial Director*
John Gattuso, *Series Editor*
Siu-Li Low, *General Manager, Books*

Distribution
United States
Langenscheidt Publishers, Inc.
46–35 54th Road
Maspeth, NY 11378
Fax: 718-784-0640

Worldwide
APA Publications GmbH & Co.
Verlag KG Singapore Branch, Singapore
38 Joo Koon Road, Singapore 628990
Tel: 65-865-1600. Fax: 65-861-6438

Discovery Communications produces high-quality nonfiction television programming, interactive media, books, films, and consumer products. Discovery Networks, a division of Discovery Communications, Inc., operates and manages the Discovery Channel, TLC, Animal Planet, Travel Channel, and Discovery Health Channel. Visit Discovery Channel Online at www.discovery.com.

Although every effort is made to provide accurate information in this publication, we would appreciate readers calling our attention to any errors or outdated information by writing us at: Insight Guides, PO Box 7910, London SE1 1WE, England; fax: 44-20-7403-0290; e-mail: insight@apaguide.demon.co.uk

Printed by Insight Press Services (Pte) Ltd, 38 Joo Koon Road, Singapore 628990.

Library of Congress Cataloging-in-Publication Data
Scuba diving/Susan Watrous, editor.
    p.cm. — (Discovery travel adventures)
    Includes bibliographical references (p.) and index.
    ISBN 1-56331-927-6 (alk. paper)
    1. Scuba diving — United States — Guidebooks.
    2. Scuba diving — Caribbean Area — Guidebooks.
    I. Watrous, Susan, 1956- II. Discovery Communications, Inc. III. Series.
GV838.673.U6 S38 2000
797.2'3 — dc21   99-054277

Scuba Diving combines the interests and enthusiasm of two of the world's best-known information providers: **Insight Guides**, whose titles have set the standard for visual travel guides since 1970, and **Discovery Communications**, the world's premier source of nonfiction entertainment. The editors of Insight Guides provide both practical advice and general understanding about a destination's history, culture, institutions, and people. Discovery Communications and its website, www.discovery.com, help millions of viewers explore their world from the comfort of their home and encourage them to explore it firsthand.

About This Book

This book reflects the contributions of dedicated editors and writers familiar with the top diving and snorkeling destinations in North America and the Caribbean. Series editor **John Gattuso**, of Stone Creek Publications in New Jersey, worked with Insight Guides and Discovery Communications to conceive and direct the series. Gattuso called on **Susan Watrous**, a Santa Cruz, California, editor and writer, to serve as project editor. Formerly with a dive travel magazine, the native Californian has lived by the Pacific all her life. "I always feel as if I am going home to the sea whether I snorkel, poke around in tidepools, or simply watch the moon sink into the waves."

The watery places of our planet have inspired the other contributors, too. **Jean-Michel Cousteau**, who wrote the introduction, has spent his life exploring the world's oceans and is an eloquent spokesman for the environment. Son of the late ocean explorer Jacques Cousteau, Jean-Michel has produced 65 documentary films, many award-winning, and founded Ocean Futures Society, a nonprofit organization dedicated to uniting the world's people in a global effort to halt marine devastation.

"I've been snorkeling since I was five and diving since 14," says **Pierce Hoover**, an avid cave diver who divides his time between writing and teaching. The combination made Hoover an ideal choice for the training and equipment chapters. Science writer **Robert Mazurek**, who explains the various forms of specialty diving, got certified at age 16 in Lake Michigan. "In fact," he says, "I got my driver's license and my C-card within three weeks of each other."

San Francisco Bay Area writer **Blake Edgar** gives a wide-angle view of life beneath the surface and covers the kelp forests of Monterey Bay, where he took his first open-water dives. Venturing beyond the usual haunts – and choosing the right destination when she does – is the expertise of **Susan Wilmink**. The former publisher of two dive magazines has been on nearly every continent – "just Antarctica and Australia yet to go" – and still travels regularly from her home in Chicago.

After letting a banded coral shrimp scour her teeth off Maui, **Aryn Kelly** was finally convinced that the Valley Isle really does have it all. Trained in Monterey Bay, she made her first tropical dive in the Maldives and has been keen on warm-water destinations ever since. Kelly also contributed to Travel Tips. Elsewhere in Hawaii, science writer **Mary Miller** took a warm-weather break from her home in the San Francisco Bay Area to gather tropical tales from the Kona Coast.

Coral reefs, kelp forests, and pelagic waters are all familiar to writer and photographer **Brandon Cole**, who has logged some 4,000 dives from pole to pole. He brings this considerable experience to his chapter on the San Juan Islands. **Heather Cantwell**, a writer and diver based in Santa Cruz, California, covered Cabo San Lucas at the southern tip of Baja California. Cantwell has traveled extensively in Latin America and the Caribbean but enjoys "breaking out my diving gear or surfboard and exploring the kelp forests a mile from home."

Writer and scuba instructor **Tom Morrisey** contributes to travel magazines when he's not penning adventure novels. While the lure of wreck diving has taken him around the world, his favorite dive spot is Lake Superior's Whitefish Point near his Michigan home. "I don't feel completely natural in the water," says Morrisey, "unless I'm wearing a dry suit." Freelance writer **Theano Nikitas**, another cold-water veteran, earned her certification exploring shipwrecks in the Northeast. She warms herself with a yearly pilgrimage to North Carolina's Outer Banks, known as the Graveyard of the Atlantic for the abundance of shipwrecks on the seafloor.

Writer and photographer **Bob Friel** has been diving for more than 25 years and holds a degree in marine science. When he's not under the water, Friel is soaring above it. "I use an amphibious ultralight plane that allows me to scout sites, shoot aerials, even land on the water and jump in when I see something really interesting." Based in South Florida, he covers his home surf in the Florida Keys chapter, then ventures beyond to the Turks and Caicos and to Belize. Another Florida resident, **Bill Belleville**, has more than 20 years of scuba experience and is now a documentary filmmaker and environmental writer. His book, *River of Lakes: A Journey on Florida's St. Johns River*, was published in 1999. "Diving allows me to be in solution with another environment," he says, "an exotic world."

Keith Phillips, who writes about the U.S. Virgin Islands and Grand Cayman, made his first Caribbean dives off St. John in 1992. "That's where I got hooked on dive travel and decided to make a career of it." He now serves as a senior editor at *Rodale's Scuba Diving* magazine. Another Rodale editor, **Nick Lucey**, has crisscrossed the planet in search of great diving spots. He profiles one of his favorites, the British Virgin Islands.

Jesse Cancelmo, based in Houston, Texas, has traveled the marine world from Indonesia to the Carolina coast. His hometown reef, the Flower Garden Banks, remains a favorite place for spotting rare pelagic species. **Michael Menduno** had just made his first journey to Cozumel in 1988 when he decided to become a freelance writer, and he returns to the island often. In 1990, he founded *aquaCORPS*, the scuba industry's first technical diving magazine. These days, he resides in Santa Cruz, California, where he writes about technology, health care, and underwater exploration.

Thanks to Steve Manning of The Nature Company and the many park rangers, naturalists, dive operators and instructors, and tourism liaisons who reviewed the text. Thanks also to Jerry Burke, Natasha Fraley, Steven Stewart, Clara Weygandt, and the members of Stone Creek's editorial team: Judith Dunham, Edward A. Jardim, Michael Castagna, Enid Stubin, and Nicole Buchenholz.

Sponges (above) look like plants but are actually simple animals. They draw water through their bodies, filtering out oxygen and nutrients.

Jack mackerel (opposite), found on the West Coast, often form large schools near kelp forests. The fish are from two to 24 inches long.

Mola mola (below), also called ocean sunfish, weigh up to 3,000 pounds and sometimes bask on their sides at the surface.

A diver in Cozumel, Mexico (previous pages), examines a sea fan, a type of coral.

Christ of the Abyss (following pages) stands in 25 feet of water off Key Largo, Florida.

Table of Contents

MAPS

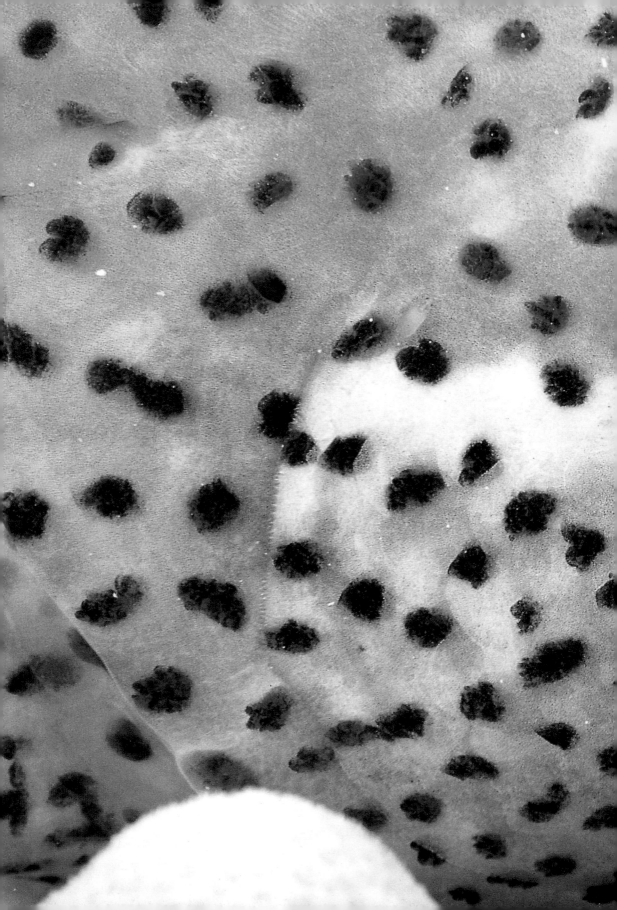

Into the Sea

INTRODUCTION
by Jean-Michel Cousteau

"If there is magic on this planet, it is contained in water." So wrote naturalist Loren Eiseley, and anyone who has swum beneath the waves knows it to be true. A dive mask opens a magical world far beyond the imagining of surface dwellers, and nowhere are dive sites more accessible or diverse than in North America and the Caribbean. Divers here frolic with sea lions in the kelp beds of California, marvel at the blue holes of Belize, probe wrecks in the Great Lakes, and thrill to the vibrancy of coral reefs in warm Caribbean waters. ◆ For North Americans, these sites are like gems found unexpectedly in one's own backyard. For visitors from faraway shores, they are wonders on a par with better-known destinations such as the Grand Canyon and Yellowstone. All are precious and terribly fragile, and whether we like to admit it or not, we leave evidence of our presence every time we visit. It's essential that we minimize this impact, lest we do irreparable damage to the places we love so well.

Divers are stewards of the sea. They must protect what they love and encourage others to do the same.

That's why this guidebook shows you not only how to reach your destination but how to be a more environmentally responsible diver once you get there. ◆ The dive mask is a window through which we discover new worlds. But it is also a mirror, reflecting our understanding of nature. Relatively few people engage in diving. We are the only ones who know this environment firsthand. As the undersea eyes of humanity, we have a responsibility to protect the sea. Our stories and photographs expand everyone's awareness of the underwater world just as the words and pictures in this book will expand yours.

A scuba diver descends into the indigo waters of the U.S. Virgin Islands.

Previous pages: Snorkeler and Atlantic spotted dolphin, Bahamas; blacknose hawkfish, Hawaii; wreck of the R.M.S. *Rhone*, British Virgin Islands

Preparing to Dive

A scuba-diving class is your ticket to underwater adventure. With proper gear and training, you can explore historic shipwrecks, submarine caves and canyons, and a fascinating array of marine life at dive sites throughout North America, the Caribbean, and Hawaii.

Waterborne

Before we walked, we swam. ◆ From the first creatures that slithered ashore 310 million years ago to the liquid-filled wombs where we take shape, humans are born of water. Water makes up more than two-thirds of our bodies and blankets 71 percent of the planet. More than 95 percent of the biosphere, the life-sustaining zone of the Earth, is in the sea. No wonder that we have always longed for a way back in. But how? ◆ In 2450 B.C., Babylonian divers plunged into the Persian Gulf and remained underwater for almost four minutes, but without an external source of air there was no way to exceed the limits of a single breath. Legend tells of Alexander the Great having himself lowered into the ocean in about 350 B.C. in what was probably the first diving bell – a glass barrel, perhaps, or a wooden cask with a window. Like a glass inverted in a sink filled with water, the bell trapped a pocket of air below the surface.

Scuba diving and snorkeling take us on a journey back to our watery origins.

Centuries later an Italian inventor designed a bell that allowed divers to look for sunken barges in a lake near Rome, and by the late 1600s, inventors were seeking efficient ways to resupply the diving bell with fresh air from the surface. Denis Papin used the technology he developed for another contraption – the steam engine – to pump air into the bell, allowing divers to remain submerged still longer. Gradually the bell's hull shrank to the size of a helmet, and by the 1800s marine explorers wore the forerunner of today's diving suit, the cumbersome helmet attached to a rubber or leather body covering. Still, the helmet required an air hose, that vital umbilical that restricted the depth and time a diver could survive underwater.

Sun, sand, and crystal-clear waters lure divers to the tropics, where even snorkelers can observe an abundance of marine life at shallow reefs and shipwrecks.

Previous pages: A cleaner shrimp removes parasites from a Hawaiian moray eel.

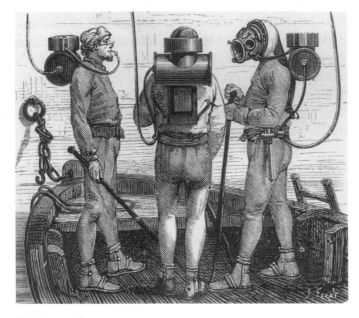

Aquanauts (left) in the mid-1800s used a breathing device connected to an air pump on the surface.

Scuba equipment (below) includes a regulator and gauges that show depth, remaining air, and direction.

A juvenile giant Pacific octopus (right) encounters a diver in the Pacific Northwest.

Homecoming

From there it was a technological leap to the Aqua-Lung, developed by Frenchmen Emile Gagnan and Jacques-Yves Cousteau in 1943. The Aqua-Lung's base was a tank of compressed air, but the real breakthrough was a regulator that delivered air to the diver on demand. The grandparent of today's Self-Contained Underwater Breathing Apparatus, or SCUBA, was born. For the first time, humans had, in a sense, discovered their gills and could move freely through the marine world.

Wondrous images began appearing from beneath the sea. In 1950, *Life* magazine published grainy black-and-white photographs of an onrushing shark hunched in classic attack posture; the images are every bit as compelling as the tack-sharp color pictures in magazines today. A curious public crowded around the television to watch divers finning over a field of coral or studying barnacle-encrusted amphorae from an ancient Mediterranean wreck. No one had to explain the primal images; the shark was clearly a predator, and the coral reefs were fertile beyond imagining.

Each year more than a million divers around the world earn a certification card and slip beneath the waves into the foreign but somehow familiar universe under the sea. "[R]ather than feeling alien in this exotic world, I was filled with the opposite sensation," wrote journalist Osha Gray Davidson of his experience on Australia's Great Barrier Reef. "It was as if all those years on land had been a sojourn in a foreign territory and now, on the reef, I had arrived back home."

But if the sea is our ancestral home, we need to become better caretakers. More than half of the world's population lives within 50 miles of an ocean. Yet today, run-off from agriculture and construction suffocates coral reefs; fisheries have been plundered to the verge of extinction; shipping traffic damages coastal areas; tankers bleed petroleum into the sea. Fortunately, more than 1,200 marine sanctuaries and parks have been established internationally since 1970, but there is still much work to be done.

Whether you are a diver or merely a beachgoer, you form a part of what environmentalist and filmmaker Jean-Michel Cousteau calls the "constituency of the sea, those who give voice to the ocean's needs." We preserve what we know. And the more we know of the sea, the deeper are its claims on our loyalty, our devotion, and our concern.

Good diving and welcome home.

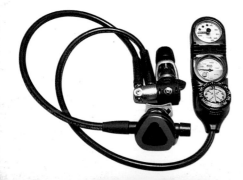

CHAPTER 2

Getting Started

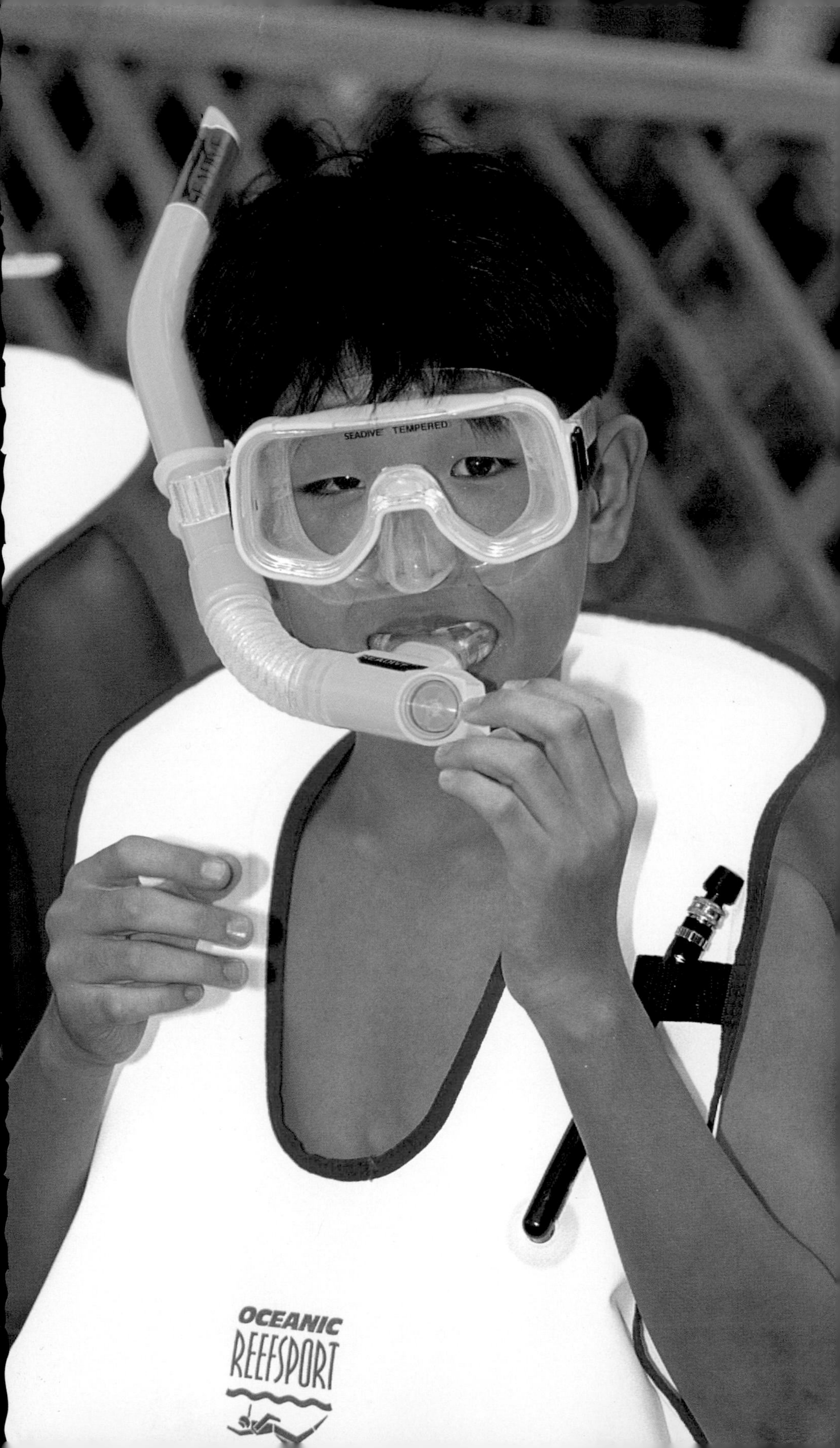

Remember learning to ride a bike? With the training wheels stripped off, you wobbled along the driveway, teetering from side to side. Older siblings offered knowing advice, and maybe mom or dad jogged along to steady you. But with a few weeks of practice, you were sailing down the street and heading into a promising new world of freedom.   ◆   Learning to scuba dive is a similar process. At first, the gear may feel strange and unwieldy. And the idea of breathing underwater may seem as unnatural as traveling on two wheels once did. But the payoff is even more exhilarating: watery worlds await your exploration.   ◆   The first step in becoming a scuba diver is to enroll in a training program offered by one of several private agencies such as PADI, NAUI, or the YMCA (see the Resource Directory for a complete list). After completing the course, you'll receive a certification, or "C-card" – your key to the world of diving. Most dive shops won't sell scuba gear to uncertified divers, and

Your C-card opens a new frontier of shipwrecks, coral gardens, and fish beyond naming in a weightless world beneath the surface.

nearly every charter boat and dive resort in the world requires divers to flash their C-cards before doing business.   ◆   Training programs cover both theory and practice and involve classroom learning as well as pool sessions.   ◆   During classroom hours, you get a basic understanding of scuba equipment and how it works, and learn the protocols of safe diving. The instructor may give a brief history of the sport and will usually share practical tips on buying, using, and caring for your gear. You'll hear about finding your way underwater using a compass, kicking with fins, and entering and exiting the water.

A young snorkeler, equipped with a mask, snorkel, and inflatable vest, learns skills that will help him make a transition to scuba diving.

Pool sessions (left and below) provide a safe "classroom" where students can practice new skills such as clearing a mask and regulator and establishing neutral buoyancy.

In addition to these practical skills, you'll be taught some physical equations and medical facts that describe how your body reacts to submersion and to breathing compressed air. For example, a tank of air that holds an hour's supply of air on the surface lasts only 15 minutes at a depth of 100 feet. The instructor will also explain the importance of exhaling compressed air as you ascend. Don't worry – there aren't any complex calculations, and you don't have to be a medical expert to pass the course. In fact, simple arithmetic and the ability to read charts are the only skills required.

After the classroom comes five to ten hours of pool time. Under the supervision of your instructor, you practice breathing through a snorkel, clearing water from your mask, and swimming with fins. Then comes the magic moment when you don your gear and submerge for the first time. There you are, sitting at the bottom of a pool, wide-eyed like the rest of your classmates. Your respiration sounds amplified and strange, and you're conscious of the remarkable fact that you're breathing in water. Inhale and there's a long *pshsht*; exhale and an explosion of bubbles rises next to your face. After a while, it begins to feel natural.

Over the course of the pool sessions, you practice setting up your gear, entering and exiting the water with your gear on, clearing water from the regulator, and sharing air with your dive partner.

Once you've successfully completed both classroom and pool work, you're off to the "open-water" or "checkout" dives, which are made in a lake, a river, or the ocean. Supervised by an instructor, you demonstrate and practice the basic skills you've learned. There you are, 20, 30, 40 feet below the

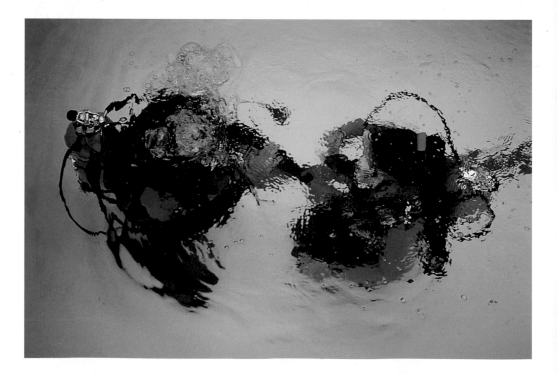

Dive briefings (above) provide information on water conditions, depth, marine creatures to watch for, and those to avoid.

A back roll (below) is one method of entering the water from a boat with low sides.

Building Experience Slowly

Don't assume that once you're a certified diver, you'll be ready to plunge in anywhere, anytime. Even seasoned divers may have difficulty adding new elements to their repertoire. Nor should you let more experienced friends talk you into making dives you aren't prepared for; they may have the skills to deal with adverse conditions, or they may simply underestimate the difficulties.

Never settle for gear, new or rented, that doesn't fit well. Many divers make their first dives in ill-fitting rental suits and as a result find themselves cold and miserable. Check rental equipment carefully, not just for proper fit but for smooth operation. Rental regulators deserve special attention; hook them up to a tank and test-breathe before leaving the rental shop.

Even if you've followed the rules, there are times when things go wrong. In such situations, there's no substitute for communication *before* you dive. Always make a backup plan if you and your buddy get separated or need to call off the dive for any reason. And be sure to review anything new, whether rented equipment or an unfamiliar style of diving.

Experienced divers have a favorite saying. Build experience slowly. This means adding new challenges gradually and only when conditions are favorable.

surface, excited and breathing loudly. Although your teacher is with you, the training wheels are off; this is the real thing. You're dependent on your gear and the skills you've developed. The instructor may lead the class on a tour of the marine neighborhood, pointing out a few life-forms. The marvel of underwater breathing is supplanted by the wonder of visiting another world. This is what you came for: You're living in an aquatic dream.

At the end of your checkout dives and after you've successfully completed a written exam, the instructor gives you a temporary C-card – the real thing follows within a few days or weeks.

Finding the Right Instructor

Now that you have an idea of the training process, let's back up a little: How do you find an instructor and choose a dive certification agency? Since you're embarking on an unfamiliar, equipment-

intensive activity, and it's the instructor who provides the coaching you need to master it, choosing the right teacher is crucial. Before working with any dive instructor, spend some time talking. Find out whether his or her teaching style and philosophy suit your needs. For example, if you're fairly athletic and have a background in water sports, you may appreciate a teacher who allows you to progress rapidly with little intervention. If you're not so comfortable in the water, you may have more success – and more fun – with someone who spends extra time developing your basic skills.

Keep in mind that instructors with extensive and varied diving experience may be able to share more informa-

tion with you. Many agencies, however, allow divers to become instructors after as few as 50 dives. This shouldn't automatically disqualify a potential instructor, though, especially if you respond well to his or her teaching style.

Just remember to screen instructors for both competency and compatibility.

There are at least six major certification agencies and a number of regional and specialty organizations. Besides providing basic training, these agencies teach advanced diving skills and offer certification ratings that range from beginner diver to instructor and beyond. Some of the larger agencies have even branched out into publishing dive guides, producing television shows, and promoting the dive travel business. While some divers prefer one agency over another, they all adhere to a similar standard of quality.

Instances of inadequate or unsafe training practices are extremely rare.

There is one more idea to consider: the resort course. This abbreviated option doesn't lead to certification, but it does give an excellent and cost-effective taste of the sport. In this course – named for the tropical hotels that usually offer it – you get a short lecture and a supervised in-water rehearsal (usually in a pool) of basic scuba skills. From there, you progress to a shallow, sheltered dive site, where you dive under the

Resort courses like this one (above) in the U.S. Virgin Islands, offer novices a taste of scuba diving in a shallow, predictable setting under the watchful eye of an instructor.

"Snorkelers welcome" (below) is the policy on many dive boats in the Florida Keys, where the reefs are shallow enough for snorkeling.

Snorkeling

Snorkeling offers much of the pleasure of scuba diving with few of the complications. It's inexpensive, requires little equipment, and is easy to learn. Most people, including children, can do it fairly well the first time out, although it may take some practice to become truly accomplished. Among the skills you'll need to master are clearing water from your mask and snorkel, kicking efficiently with fins, and equalizing water pressure against your inner ear when you dive beneath the surface.

Some dive instructors encourage students to learn to snorkel prior to their first scuba class. Although snorkeling is not a prerequisite for diving, it can hone water skills that facilitate the transition to scuba. If you're planning to learn diving as well as snorkeling, purchase equipment suited to both activities. Divers typically use slightly larger fins than snorkelers do. If you wear scuba fins for snorkeling, employ a slower, easier kick pattern to offset the added thrust and resistance of the larger fins.

Snorkeling that involves dives beneath the surface is sometimes called "free diving." Advanced free divers reach remarkable depths and may remain submerged for more than a minute. Deep diving is risky, and snorkelers shouldn't try it. And as with scuba diving, never snorkel alone.

Many coral species (right) reach to within a few feet of the surface. Some grow up to six inches a year.

close supervision of a divemaster or instructor. A resort course may help you make a decision about whether you want to invest in a full certification program.

At Home or Away

Although the content of most training programs is similar, the timing and location can differ. Options include once-a-week training modules, multi-weekend courses, or intense weeklong certification programs that you complete before or during a vacation. You can train at a local dive shop, in the warm waters of a tropical lagoon, or at some combination of the two.

The most popular option is to complete both classroom and pool portions of the program at a local dive shop, then make your open-water dives at a nearby location. The class may take several weeks or be completed in two intensive weekends.

After finishing classroom and pool training with a local instructor, some students travel to a warm-water destination for their open-water dives. At resorts that participate in "referral programs," in-house instructors take the student through the checkout dives and complete the paperwork for the C-card.

Another training option, one that many busy or landlocked divers choose, is to complete the entire certification process in a weeklong program while you're on vacation. You may have time only for your checkout dives, but you'll get to try out the total warm-water plunge – a truly sublime experience. Either way, you'll familiarize yourself with this style of diving, which is by far the most popular. The disadvantage is that you won't necessarily know the diving techniques that may be useful at home – but this isn't a big concern if you plan to dive only in warm water.

One more factor may influence your choice of instructor and training program: cost. While a scuba class advertised at a very low price may seem like a bargain, be sure to look a bit further. The price tag may not include equipment rentals, textbooks, certification fees, and other hidden costs.

Rather than reacting solely to price, focus on the quality of the training experience as well as on your personal compatibility with the instructor. Your certification class sets the tone for your future enjoyment of the sport. Divers who enjoy the training process are more likely to continue diving and collect many years of memorable underwater experiences.

CHAPTER 3

Beyond the Basics

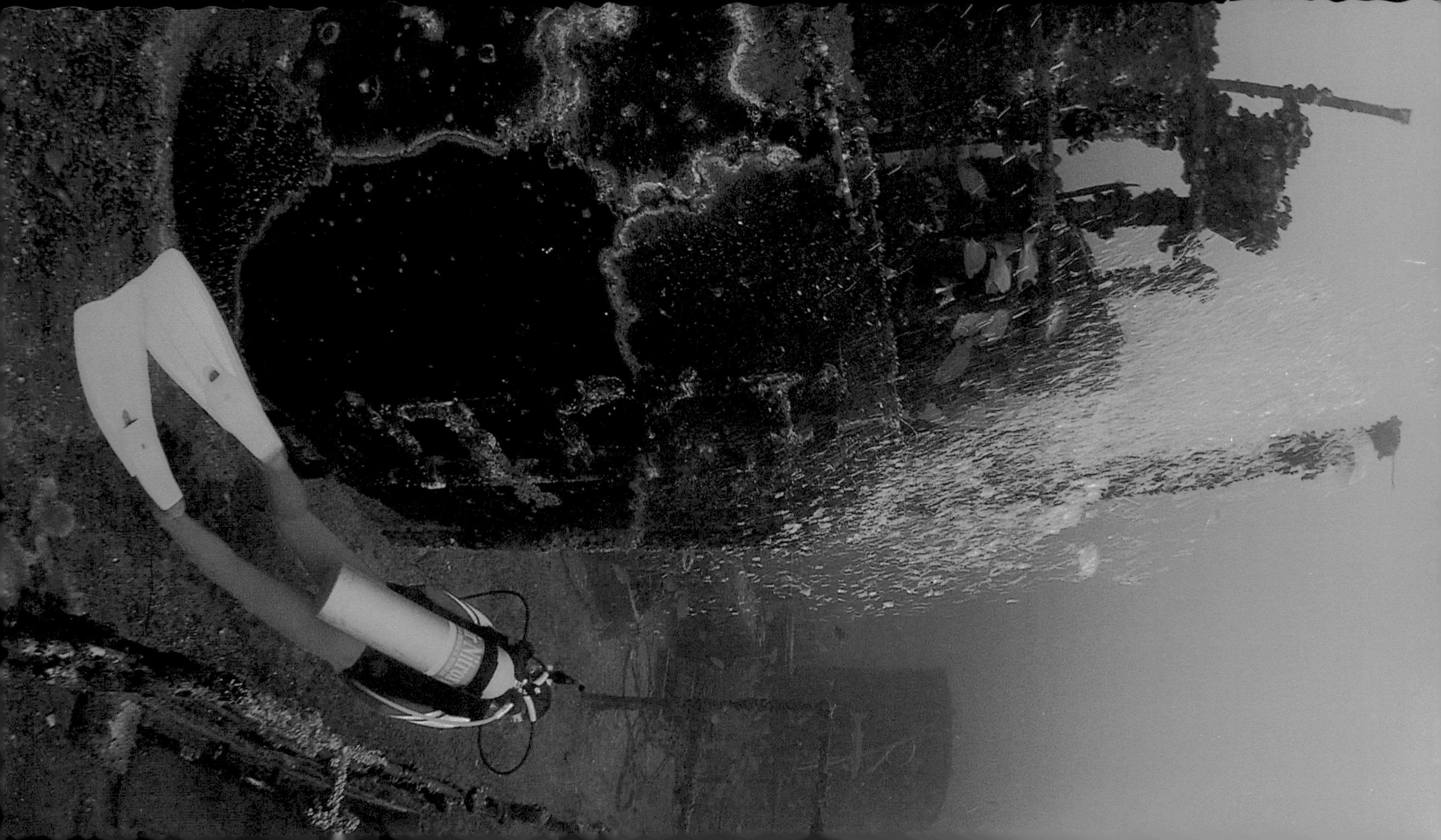

Would you like to drift dive with pygmy dolphins in the Amazon River? Wonder what it would be like to fin through Antarctica's frigid waters in a dry suit or maybe investigate historic shipwrecks? If so, specialized diving courses can help you prepare for these adventures. ◆ Once you've completed your basic scuba certification, you're eligible for more advanced courses that teach you about equipment, proper procedure, and the potentially dangerous aspects of the marine environment – all elements that you need to address in order to explore diving's challenging and less traveled byways safely. ◆ In some cases, specialty courses may be used to meet the requirements for an advanced diving certification. Indeed, completing an advanced certification class alone is an excellent supplement to the basic scuba class in which you may have spent only three or four days in open water – hardly enough time to feel truly confident in the new

Getting certified is just the beginning. With advanced training, you can explore caves and shipwrecks and pursue other forms of specialized diving.

equipment and foreign environment. With an advanced certification, you can also pursue more challenging specialties, such as night, drift, wreck, cavern, and cave diving, and the use of nitrox, discussed later. There are many more classes, including deep diving, ice diving, and search and rescue diving – all of these are open to scuba divers with advanced certification. For information, contact the various certifying agencies listed in the Resource Directory at the back of this book.

A diver using nitrox explores the *Duane*, a Coast Guard cutter in 90 feet of water off Key Largo, Florida.

Night Diving

Until you've plunged into your favorite dive site after dark, you're missing half the picture. The nightlife of marine species rivals anything you'll find on land. Luckily, night diving has only a few special requirements. Learning to use a reliable underwater light system is the first step. Most divers carry a 15- to 30-watt primary light along with one or two backup lights that tend to be more compact and less powerful. In general, a dive light that has a medium-wide beam with a bright center is best. Wider beams tend to create a haze by lighting up the particles suspended in water.

In a night-diving specialty course, you learn how to maintain underwater light

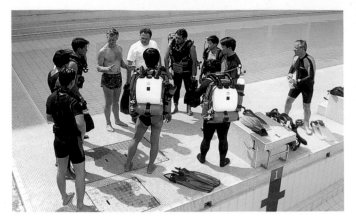

systems and place marker and strobe lights for navigation and orientation. In addition, the instructor teaches you how to evaluate night-diving conditions. It's crucial to be extra cautious at night; you'll be wise to avoid sites with high surf and strong currents and areas with poor visibility, where there is a potential for entanglement. Since there are risks that go along with div-

ing after dark, it's important to be familiar with the dive site. Try to scout a site during the day before attempting a night dive.

Drift Diving

Many spectacular diving locations around the world have currents. Take Florida's Gulf Coast, Cozumel in Mexico, and the Pacific Northwest, for example. In all these areas,

currents caused by tidal changes, the Earth's rotational pull, and prevailing winds affect diving conditions. Rather than swimming "upstream," which is exhausting as well as potentially dangerous, drift divers learn to use the current to cruise effortlessly through the marine environment.

Drift-diving specialty courses teach you how to select appropriate sites and plan entry and exit points for the dive. You'll also learn to modify dives when conditions change, and how to use floats and surface signaling devices. The two most important factors in planning a drift dive are visibility and current strength. Drift dives should be attempted only in areas where divers can see far enough ahead to notice potential hazards and then have sufficient time to react.

Given the many different drift-diving environments, safety concerns and logistical support may vary for each location. If you are drift diving an area for the first time, always go with a dive operator from the area or a knowledgeable local diver.

Wrecks, Caverns, Caves

Shipwrecks, like the ruins of ancient land dwellings, tell stories about how people lived and, in many cases, died. Whether you prefer exploring a sunken 19th-century schooner or simply admiring the abundant coral growth

Submarine caves (left) should be approached with caution; special training is essential before entering.

Superior Producer (right), a freighter that sank off Curaçao in 1978, lies in 110 feet of water; get advanced open-water certification before venturing this deep.

Students (opposite, top) learn to use rebreather units, which eliminate bubbles that scare away marine life.

that blankets a Boeing 727 submerged intentionally as an artificial reef only a decade ago, wrecks are prime diving locations. In addition to their historic value, they often host diverse populations of marine plants and animals.

As a general rule, divers don't remove anything from shipwrecks, many of which are protected historical monuments. In a wreck-diving course, you learn the laws governing shipwrecks and artifact recovery, and how to maneuver safely around wreck sites. Because of the potential instability of most wrecks, only properly trained, expert divers should penetrate a wreck.

To many divers, slipping beneath a wall of water inside a cave sounds like the stuff of nightmares. But with proper training, awe balances fear as you glide past delicate rock formations and explore the mysterious aquatic life sheltered from the outside world. Cave diving is a rare opportunity to swim, as environmental writer Bill Belleville has described it, "through the living veins of the earth."

These specialty courses have several levels ranging from an introduction to cavern diving, in which you remain within sight of the

cave's entrance, to cave specialty classes, in which you learn how to plan advanced dives in intricate caves and survey and draw maps of cave topography. Basic classes cover the fundamentals of planning a cave dive, special equipment and navigation, and finning techniques that allow you to swim without stirring up silt and reducing visibility. In addition, you'll gain insight into the geological origins of tunnel formation and learn about some of the animals that live in this unusual environment. Proper training is a must because of the inherent dangers involved in cave and cavern diving, and each dive needs to be carefully planned and executed.

Suiting Up

Divers who explore the richly productive cold water of higher latitudes such as the Pacific Northwest enjoy some of the most spectacular marine life on earth. But staying warm can be a

Get the Picture?

Taking high-quality pictures underwater poses many challenges, the most obvious of which is the attenuation of light. As sunlight hits the water's surface, a portion is reflected back into the air. Of the light that penetrates, some is absorbed by the water as heat, while the remainder is quickly scattered by suspended particles.

Shutterbugs (left) need to be stealthy swimmers to snap a picture of these half-buried stingrays, which may bolt if disturbed.

To complicate matters, light bends when it travels from one medium to another – for example, from sea water through the glass in your mask or camera lens – in a process called refraction. Refraction fools scuba divers into thinking objects are about 25 percent closer than they really are.

But the pleasures of underwater photography outweigh these frustrations. An underwater photography course can teach you how to master simple techniques for composing quality pictures using available light. You also learn when and how to use a strobe light, and how to get good pictures while working within the limits of your camera. If you don't have an underwater camera, many instructors will allow you to try out the different cameras they have on hand.

If you want to purchase a camera before taking a class or your next trip, there are several kinds appropriate for the beginner or casual user. SeaLife makes a quality easy-to-use camera with automatic film advance, fixed focus from four feet to infinity, and a protective rubberized housing. The $300 price tag includes one close-up lens and a waterproof travel case.

For a little more creative control, check out the mid-range model from Sea and Sea, priced at about $400. With adjustable aperture setting and depth of field, built-in light meter, and many accessories, this is an excellent camera for learning how to compose underwater shots.

If you think underwater photography may become more than a hobby, consider Nikon's offering in this line, the Nikonos. With more interchangeable parts than any other underwater camera, the Nikonos, priced at around $800, has been the preeminent underwater camera system since its inception in 1959.

challenge when temperatures hover in the 40s in the waters of Puget Sound, Washington State, or in the 50s in spots like Monterey, California. Dry suits allow divers to enter these areas without risking hypothermia.

Most modern dry suits are made of a treated nylon shell or compressed neoprene and incorporate a unique waterproof zipper originally designed for space suits. In contrast to wet suits, which trap an insulating layer of water, dry suits trap air. That, plus thermal clothing worn under the suit, retains warmth. Many divers find today's dry suits so comfortable that they prefer them to wet suits, even when diving in more temperate waters.

There is a trade-off for all this underwater comfort. Because of the added buoyancy of a dry suit, you need to wear more weight than you would with a wet suit. In a dry-suit course, you learn how to distribute this additional weight evenly and how to control buoyancy by regulating the dry suit's airspace when changing depths. Furthermore, many classes offer a try-before-you-buy option, so you can sample different suits before purchasing one.

Nitrox

Since the first days of commercially available scuba equipment in 1952, divers have experimented with ways to increase the length of time they can spend underwater. The outside limit has always been set by the possibility of getting decompression sickness (DCS), also known as "the bends." DCS occurs when excess nitrogen, absorbed by the body while breathing compressed air underwater, is released too quickly during the ascent, forming painful and possibly damaging bubbles in the diver's body. The longer divers stay at depth, the more nitrogen they absorb. In order to avoid DCS, researchers have calculated the maximum time divers can stay underwater at a given depth and still ascend *directly* to the surface. This is known as the "no-decompression limit" or "maximum dive time." If divers remain in the water at depth for longer than this time, they must make one or more "decompression stops" on the way to the surface in order to release the excess nitrogen slowly in exhalations, which reduce the chance of bubbles forming.

In the last few years, sport divers have begun to take advantage of new technology, developed for commercial and scientific uses, that allows divers to extend underwater time through the use of a breathing mixture called nitrox. Traditionally, the air in a scuba tank is 21 percent oxygen and 79 percent nitrogen, the same as the

atmosphere above water. Nitrox has an increased oxygen and decreased nitrogen content – a combination that allows divers to extend significantly the amount of time they spend submerged. Nitrox advocates claim other benefits as well, including less post-dive fatigue and a more alert feeling while they're in the water.

Nitrox, or "enriched air," as it's sometimes called, does have limitations; you still need training to avoid some potential hazards. In a class, you'll learn how to use special nitrox dive tables and how to measure the oxygen content of a tank using an oxygen analyzer.

As generations of divers have discovered, the watery regions of our planet are filled with secrets that insight, keen observation, and advanced training may unlock. Specialty courses give you the training to experience the oceans as an explorer.

An underwater scooter (above) propels a diver through the sea. Some dive operators offer them for rent.

Troy Spring (left), near Florida's Suwannee River, is the site of a sunken Civil War-era steamboat.

CHAPTER 4

By its nature, scuba diving is an equipment-intensive sport. Anything longer than a breath-holding peek underwater requires a self-contained air supply, a mechanical breathing system, and a number of additional adaptive technologies. In an attempt to become more like marine mammals – seals, for example – we strap fins on our feet, blanket ourselves in insulating suits, and don air-filled jackets that allow us to hover weightlessly in the water. Fortunately, using this equipment is not difficult, and buying it need not be either, provided you maintain a pragmatic approach to choosing your gear.   ◆   Before you buy, you'll want to develop a solid understanding of the gear by doing some research and seeking the advice of dive professionals and experienced friends. Most divers consider the basic equipment trio of mask, snorkel, and fins **Quality equipment and** to be highly personal items, much like shoes **a proper fit ensure a safe,** or eyeglasses. And like shoes and **comfortable, and rewarding** glasses, if you choose them with an under- **scuba experience.** standing of what's important – and what's not – they'll meet your needs for a long time to come.   ◆   No matter what the style or cost, a mask has one task: to provide an air space in front of your eyes that allows you to see underwater. What's important here is fit. This usually has less to do with price than with shape, though more expensive masks often use a softer grade of silicon, which makes for a more comfortable fit. Many snorkelers and divers prefer flatter, low-volume masks because these have less air space to clear when the mask floods. Several specialty companies can fit corrective lenses into masks. If you're planning on spending a lot of time underwater, this feature is worth the cost.

Dry suits are worn over thermal undergarments and protect divers in water temperatures down to 28°F.

than small, limber fins, but they also require more effort. Snorkelers, who have less bulk to push through the water than scuba divers do, often prefer small, stream-lined fins. Shoe-style or closed-heel fins provide the greatest kicking efficiency, but they are difficult to wear with neoprene boots and thus are better suited for warm-water use. The most versatile fin is the open-heel style worn with separate neoprene boots. You can wear the boots with or without a wet suit. Without the fins, the boots protect your feet on rocky shores or slippery boat decks. When choosing an open-heel fin, opt for models with comfortable, contoured foot pockets.

Heart of the Scuba System

Three components form the heart of the modern scuba system: the regulator, tank, and buoyancy compensator. Assembled into a working trio, these devices allow you to breathe underwater, adjust your buoyancy, and carry the tank and other accessories.

Although regulators per-form the amazing task of enabling you to breathe underwater, they are actu-ally simple, highly reliable mechanical devices. Con-temporary regulators consist of two pieces, the first and

A snorkel is a tube you can breathe through – and it can cost as much as $100. If you're serious about snorkeling, you may be able to justify a $50-plus snorkel, but most divers find everything they need in a $25 model. There are snorkels that have a flexible lower section, which reduces jaw fatigue, and a purge valve, which makes it

easier to clear water from your snorkel.

Fins not only propel us through the water; they turn us from clumsy land animals to adapted aquatic creatures. The right set of fins provides enough thrust to move you and your gear and enhances your underwater position and balance. When choosing a fin, pay attention to the three factors that really matter: size, stiffness, and construc-tion of the foot pocket. Large, stiff fins provide more push second stages, joined by an air hose. The first stage, which attaches to the scuba tank, reduces and regulates the flow of high-pressure air stored in the tank. The second stage, which includes the mouthpiece, delivers air each time the diver inhales. Nowadays, all regulators are safe. There are, however, a few performance features to consider.

Most low-priced regulators fulfill the needs of the average diver at depths of less than 100 feet, where most dives take place. Higher-priced regulators deliver more air with less effort, which becomes increasingly important at greater depths. Many mid- and high-priced regulators include an "air balance" feature. This allows delivery of a steady air flow as air pressure in the tank diminishes. Most novice divers are satisfied with a mid-priced regulator, many of which were top-of-the-line just a few years ago. And remember, it's always a good idea to try several models, renting before you buy.

Although the regulator may seem to be the most critical component of the scuba system, the buoyancy compensator, or BC, is just as vital to a diver's safety and comfort. The BC, as its name implies, adjusts for the small changes in a diver's buoyancy that occur during all dives.

Your choice: Use a printed dive table (above) or a dive computer (right) to determine how deep and long your dives should be.

It also secures the tank and distributes its weight comfortably on the diver's back. While it can float a diver on the surface, a BC is not a life jacket, nor does it replace advanced swimming skills.

Different BCs have varying "lift capacities" – that is, the ability to "lift" a diver and all his or her gear. In tropical waters, where equipment and wet suits are minimal, many divers prefer compact BCs with 15 to 20 pounds of lift.

Divers carrying heavy underwater cameras or specialized gear need additional lift capacity. Cold-water divers require more lift capacity – sometimes as much as 50 pounds – to offset buoyancy changes inherent in wet suits and dry suits. Specialty BC systems used by wreck and cave divers may run to 100 pounds of lift.

Buoyancy compensators come in three primary styles – jacket, adjustable, and

Calculating Risk

For decades, divers have depended on printed tables, originally developed by the U.S. Navy, to calculate safe depths and time limits for each dive. The U.S. Navy Dive Tables – the product of calculating the amount of compressed nitrogen absorbed into a diver's bloodstream at various depths and after specified times – have helped divers minimize the risk of decompression sickness, also known as "the bends."

Today, there's another option: divers can carry dive computers. Ranging in price from a few hundred dollars to more than a thousand, computers automatically track nitrogen saturation and indicate the amount of dive time remaining, the correct ascent rate, the necessary surface intervals, and the duration of subsequent dives. Initially, some experts opposed dive computers, arguing that printed tables provided a greater margin of error; the tables assumed that the entire dive took place at the greatest depth, with the greatest degree of nitrogen absorption. Proponents point out that the devices report on the actual dive rather than a theoretical dive plan, and they eliminate the possibility of miscalculation.

Scuba enthusiasts have logged millions of dives using computers, and accident rates are now slightly lower. Depending on the depth and duration of the dive, a computer may allow the diver to remain submerged longer. And it always offers convenient, at-a-glance information on nitrogen saturation and dive time.

Most instructors agree that a working knowledge of dive tables is crucial to safety. They recommend that new divers use tables, then move to computers once they're familiar with the calculation process.

Open-heel fins (above) are easy to adjust and allow room for neoprene booties, which provide warmth and prevent chafing.

modular. The jacket style resembles a sleeveless shirt, with air filling all parts of the shirt equally. While this style may enhance underwater swimming stability, when inflated it tends to squeeze the diver, especially if it fits snugly when deflated.

The adjustable BC replaces the front shoulder fabric of the jacket style with straps and quick-release buckles. Air is concentrated around the diver's midsection and back, and a padded cummerbund helps spread the weight of the tank. Easier to slip into than the jacket style, this BC can be worn with a bathing suit or thick wet suit. It's a good choice if you dive in a variety of environments.

The modular BC features a backpack-style harness fitted with an interchangeable air cell that slips between the tank and harness. Wreck, cave, and deep divers often favor modular BCs, which are also designed to keep a diver in a horizontal, streamlined position. New divers interested in these activities may find modular BCs worth the slightly higher cost.

A growing number of BCs have integrated weight systems, which incorporate the weights into pockets on the BC otherwise worn on a separate belt. There are also BCs designed specifically for women. No matter which style of BC you choose, it must fit comfortably and provide adequate lift and a streamlined underwater profile.

Unless you dive from shore or your own boat, you probably don't need to own a scuba tank. Most domestic dive shops rent full tanks for only slightly more than the cost of filling a personal tank, and many dive resorts around the world supply tanks as part of a dive charter.

Exposure Suits and Accessories

Beyond the basics and the scuba system, divers may use a variety of additional items. To be comfortable during and after a dive, divers need adequate thermal protection in the form of an exposure suit. Even in tropical regions, a suit may be useful. "Skin suits," or "dive skins," as they're sometimes called, are made of thin Lycra-like fabrics. Appropriate for warm water, skin suits offer protection from sun and abrasive corals and provide a small amount of heat retention.

The next level of warmth, neoprene wet suits, are designed to hold a thin layer of warm water inside the suit. Your body warms this trapped water, which becomes addi-

Shallow dives (left) in tropical water don't require a wet suit, but monitoring depth and air is always necessary.

tional insulation. Depending on the style and thickness of a wet suit, you can wear it in 40°F to 85°F water. Dry suits, the warmest alternative, seal snugly at the wrist and neck to keep the diver's body dry. Worn with insulating undergarments, dry suits provide thermal protection in water between 28°F and 60°F. More costly than wet suits, dry suits also require additional training to wear; some divers dislike them in warm water.

Most divers require some amount of ballast weight to offset the flotation of exposure suits and other gear. The least expensive option is to buy cast lead weights and thread them onto a nylon-webbing belt. For a bit more money, many divers opt for the comfort and convenience of "soft" weight systems – lead-shot-filled pouches that slip into pockets on the belt.

Like so many adventure sports, the scuba industry has generated a vast array of accessories. Some, such as weight belts, are essential, while some are suited only to specific activities. Resist the temptation to buy unfamiliar gadgets early in your diving career. Instead, save your money for the necessities – mask, snorkel, fins, buoyancy compensator, and regulator. If you live in a colder climate, put an exposure suit high on your shopping list: as with BCs, rental suits seldom provide the same comfort as your own. And if you dive only on annual vacations, consider renting the equipment beyond mask, fins, and snorkel from a reputable dive shop; put the cost of the other gear toward the overall trip.

An "octopus" (top) is an extra second-stage regulator. It serves as a backup air source for you or your dive buddy.

Buoyancy control devices (above) help you stay "neutral," neither rising nor falling, in the water.

CHAPTER 5

Marine Life and Conservation

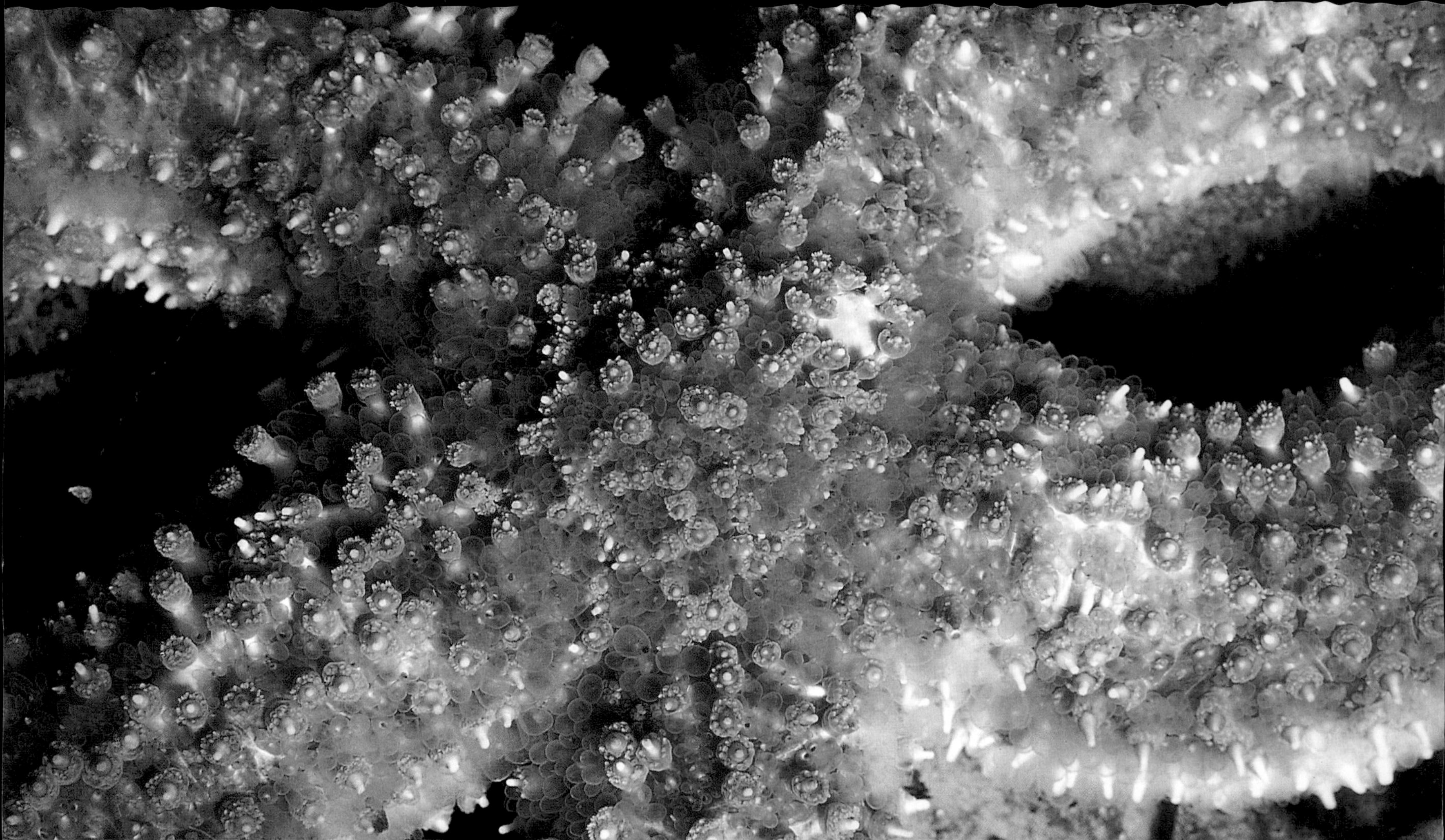

You've passed your checkout dives and your C-card is in hand. Now you can fill your scuba tank, pull on your gear, and submerge. But before choosing your next destination, take time to research what can be seen underwater, and where. This crash course in major marine habitats should help you decide on a location and how to do your part to ensure that these precious places remain unspoiled. ◆ Marine life is far more diverse than life on land. At present, scientists have described nearly 200,000 species of marine plants and animals, and new ones are discovered all the time. Most inhabit the sea. About a tenth of all plants – namely brown, red, green, and other kinds of algae – are found in salt water; the 3,000 species of ocean chordates (animals with backbones) roughly equal those on land and in fresh water combined. But it's the invertebrates that really rule the sea: 130,000 species of everything from corals to chitons to sea cucumbers, comprising nearly a tenth of all known life on Earth.

Divers encounter a dazzling array of plant and animal life beneath the waves.

◆ Few divers have trouble imagining themselves descending through clear, azure water to a sun-dappled reef, vivid in color and vibrant with life. Although tropical rain forests, the closest terrestrial counterpart to coral reefs for biological diversity, harbor many more species, tropical reefs are nonetheless one of the richest repositories of life on the planet. ◆ Though often mistaken for plants, reef-building corals are animals resembling and related to sea anemones. Corals include four distinct groups of animals: stony corals, hydrocorals, octocorals, and black corals. Only stony corals construct reefs, but

Sea stars can grow a new arm if one is lost. Some species can grow an entirely new sea star from a severed arm. There are more than 2,000 species worldwide.

most corals live in colonies and possess some form of rigid outer skeleton. Not all corals are tropical; some thrive in deep or cold water, even close to the poles. But corals occur at their most lavish in the warm, clear, shallow water straddling the equator.

It's amazing to think that such massive structures as Australia's Great Barrier Reef and the barrier reef off the coast of Belize are the handiwork of a tiny, stationary animal, the coral polyp, which resides in a cup-shaped pore in a reef by day and emerges at night. The tentacled polyp takes in calcium and carbon dioxide from surrounding seawater to make its external castle of calcium carbonate.

Reefs could not be built, however, without the single-celled algal tenants living within the gut of each polyp. Known as zooxanthellae, the algae nourish the coral and enable the reef to grow. Individual coral structures can look like giant brains, mushrooms, lettuce leaves, and deer antlers, but together they create an intricate maze of shapes and textures that characterizes a coral reef.

Coral Communities

Delicate-looking sea fans, or gorgonians, a kind of soft octocoral, add color to a reef, as do abundant basket- and barrel-shaped sponges, some large enough to swallow a diver. Schools of fish – angelfish, butterflyfish, surgeonfish, and wrasses, to name just a few – sporting stripes, spots, and swirls dazzle a diver's eyes. Sharp-beaked parrotfish in hues of green and red peck at the reef and leave a trail of coral sand streaming behind them. Divers who descend on a reef at night might encounter a sleeping parrotfish suspended in a cocoon of mucus spun from its mouth. A coral reef seems like a dizzying riot of life. But most members of a reef community cannot even be seen. Known as crypto-fauna, these sponges, worms, mollusks, and tiny crustaceans hide from view in the cracks, crevices, or holes that they bore into the

White-spotted tealia anemones (left) capture prey with stinging capsules called nematocysts on their tentacles.

Leave Only Bubbles

Some of the most rewarding dives you can make are in shallow water, among the denizens of a reef of colorful, tropical corals. About a quarter of marine species inhabit or visit coral reefs, but reefs worldwide are in trouble, getting mined, polluted, poisoned, stressed, and diseased at an alarming rate. Hard corals look enduring, even indestructible, but they are easily damaged and may take decades to regrow a single branch. Here are ways that divers can help preserve coral reefs.

Topside, tie up the boat to a mooring buoy instead of dropping anchor on a living reef. In the water, maintain neutral buoyancy – never sink onto fragile coral heads. Don't drag gauges and spare regulators across the reef or bump coral branches with a tank. Avoid kicking up sand or silt with fins, which can suffocate coral polyps.

If you leave your gloves behind, you'll be less inclined to touch the coral, an act which removes the protective mucus covering on the polyps. Instead, bring your camera so you can take pictures of corals, not pieces of them. Finally, don't feed or catch coral reef fish.

Back home, make an effort to increase your awareness of coral conservation and educate other divers and boaters about coral. Support coral reef and coastal protection. Sign up for projects that monitor reef health for research or conservation groups.

A diver (above) demonstrates neutral buoyancy, an essential skill that prevents divers from touching fragile marine life.

Octopuses (below) are found in almost all of the world's oceans.

reef itself, safe from fish and other predators.

The richest reefs are in the Indo-Pacific, particularly in Indonesia and the Philippines. About 450 species of coral exist there, more than six times as many as in the Caribbean. Pacific reefs are also among the most endangered, damaged by fishermen using dynamite and cyanide to capture their quarry. Coral reefs everywhere have been mined, poisoned, bombed, polluted, suffocated, and sickened to the point that three-quarters of all reefs could be harmed irreparably in a few decades. Recent occurrences of coral bleaching, in which the coral polyps expel algae

from their tissues after a sudden shift in temperature, salinity, or sunlight, reveal that reefs are under tremendous environmental stress.

Boat anchors also injure coral reefs. Some popular dive sites now have mooring buoys at the surface, so boats can avoid dropping anchor right on a reef. Such buoys have helped spare slow-growing coral from damage in the Cayman Islands, the Turks and Caicos, and many other Caribbean islands. The Florida Keys National Marine Sanctuary has successfully deployed a flotilla of buoys for its heavy boat traffic, and in British Virgin Islands National Marine Park, mooring

buoys protect the historic wreck of the *Rhone* from overzealous anchor-droppers.

Rocky Reefs

Just as corals provide plenty of hiding places for marine life, rocks and boulders piled on the bottom close to shore create reefs in temperate waters, full of nooks, cracks, and holes for fish and

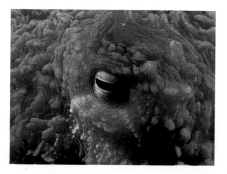

invertebrates. Any available surface gets covered with a colorful array of sponges, anemones, and algae, so rocky reefs make for promising, productive dive sites.

The more rugged and jumbled the submerged terrain, the better the prospects for finding fish, eels, crabs, sea stars, nudibranchs or sea slugs, and other animals.

Along the California coast, rocky reefs serve as an anchorage for towering stands of kelp that form dense beds or forests. Lots of creatures congregate in kelp forests, such as those in the Monterey Bay National Marine Sanctuary, and what looks like just a carpet of seaweed from the surface belies a rich and densely layered community of organisms below – much like a forest of trees on land – spanning from the surface canopy to the sand and rocks at the bottom.

Southern California kelp forests and reefs are home to the bright orange garibaldi, a damselfish that looks like an overfed goldfish. The male garibaldi chooses a rocky site for a nest, grooming it of all seaweed except for certain red algae. He swims in circles and calls to attract a female, which, if sufficiently seduced,

Natural Hazards

Since the days of sea serpents, oceans have had a bum rap as spawning grounds for dangerous beasts. Most marine animals mean no harm, but many can bite or sting. Some wield needlelike teeth or razor-sharp surfaces; others pack powerful venom that can hurt or kill unwary divers. Be sure to learn the natural risks of a particular dive destination. In the meantime, take note of these ocean dwellers.

Let's start with sharks. Fewer than a tenth of all shark species pose any threat to humans. Avoiding times when or places where sharks tend to hunt reduces the risk of attack. Submerged divers may be safer than surfers or swimmers at the surface, but if you see a large shark and can get to a boat or shore quickly, do it.

Stingrays, relatives of sharks, possess a venomous spine that sticks out from their tail. Most stingray wounds occur on the foot or ankle after the victim steps on a stingray hidden in the sand. So enter the water from shore with a "stingray shuffle," a sideways sliding of the fins that shoos away any buried rays nearby. The torpedo or Pacific electric ray lacks a spine, but its 80-volt defense should deter West Coast divers from trying to handle it.

In Hawaii or the West Indies, beware of black sea urchins sporting foot-long spines. The brittle spines easily pierce fins or gloves and can snap off under the skin, causing pain and swelling. Watch where you place your fingers, hands, and feet.

Keep skin away from abrasive coral skeletons and from the living polyps that contain stinging cells. Also avoid fire coral, a tropical hydroid that inflicts a burning rash when you rub against it.

The Indo-Pacific warrants special mention for its preponderance of poisonous species. Two of the world's most venomous fish, stonefish and lionfish, occur there, as do beautiful and deadly sea snakes of several varieties. Australian waters harbor the deadly sea wasp, a tiny, boxlike jelly with fishing-line-thin toxic tentacles, as well as the lovely but lethal blue-ringed octopus.

You will meet and observe these and other dangerous animals without any trouble. But should you have an unfortunate encounter with any of them, seek immediate medical help.

Portuguese men-of-war (left) have 2,000 stinging cells per inch on tentacles that may be a hundred feet long.

A magnificent urchin (below) can inflict painful wounds with spines up to four and a half inches long.

will deposit her eggs and leave the male to fertilize and protect them.

Seamounts and Paddies

Like rocky reefs piled into pinnacles, seamounts offer a dramatic location for a dive. Often situated in deep water, seamounts may rise high enough to be within the depth limits of recreational diving. Off La Paz in the Sea of Cortez, for example, the famous El Bajo site features a series of granite peaks that come to within 60 feet of the surface. Divers at El Bajo swim among giant, jet-black manta rays and have the even rarer chance to descend into a school of 12-foot-long scalloped hammerhead sharks. Why the usually solitary sharks school here and why they seem to act less aggres-sively in large groups remain something of a mystery.

Seamounts often attract creatures that dwell deep or inhabit the open sea. Not a place for novices, the pelagic zone surrounding remote spots like Cocos Island, 300 miles off the coast of Costa Rica, harbors all kinds of drifters and nomads, from the tiniest plankton to the largest whales. Most animals move at the whim of wind and currents; unlike reefs or rocky bottoms, there's no place to attach and stay put. Purple jellyfish streaming six-foot stinging tentacles and pulsating moon jellies hover in a dimensionless blue void. Odd-looking ocean sunfish – one of the largest of all bony fish, with two flapping, triangular fins attached to a giant oval head – inhabit

A pygmy rock crab (top) faces down a red Irish lord, a member of the bottom-dwelling sculpin family of the Pacific Northwest.

A banded jawfish male (above) off the Florida coast uses its large mouth to incubate eggs.

Humpback whales (above) bear their 14-foot-long calves in tropical waters. The juveniles remain with their mothers for up to a year.

this realm, as do blue sharks chasing schools of anchovy or squid.

Torn from their moorings close to shore and set adrift, tangled mats and balls of kelp, called paddies, make for open-ocean oases that attract a variety of fish. Miles from the southern California coast and the abundant kelp beds of the Channel Islands where they originated, kelp paddies shelter young rockfish, which live in deep water as adults. Mackerel may arrive in search of a meal, and the mackerel in turn lure larger predators like yellowtail tuna, marlin, sharks, and even pilot whales.

Mammals of the Sea

Baleen whales are the biggest creatures in the ocean, but divers rarely encounter them. Two exceptions among them are the humpback whales that winter near the Hawaiian island of Maui and the Atlantic humpbacks that winter on the Silver

California sea cucumbers (left) grow up to 16 inches long and squirt intruders with a jet of water from their back ends.

and Mouchoir banks in the Turks and Caicos. Lucky divers may see newborn calves swimming beside their mothers and feel the rumbling, resonating vibrations from the whales' high-pitched calls. Each year, the whale song picks up where it left off the previous winter and advances with a new series of stanzas.

More commonly seen marine mammals are seals and sea lions. Divers may observe sea otters in Monterey Bay and manatees in Florida, although both remain very rare and are protected by the Endangered Species Act. Also remember that from sea otters to blue whales, all ocean mammals have the federal government behind them in the form of the Marine Mammal Protection

Act. This law prohibits any harm or harassment of marine mammals on land or at sea, and anyone even approaching a marine mammal closer than 50 feet can be fined. Curious sea lions may investigate a diver – and almost certainly will if the diver has been spearing fish – and perform a few acrobatics before quickly vanishing, but don't pursue them. Besides, they have the home-field advantage and will be gone with a few flaps of their flippers.

By learning a little about the biology and behavior of marine life, you are less likely to disturb or damage anything. Start by finding a good field guide to the fish and other sea life in the area where you'll be diving. Waterproof identification cards with color illustrations can help you name the fish while underwater, but they won't tell you much else. Look for a guide that combines thorough, informative descriptions with clear color drawings or photographs. The best guides provide details about specific habitats and the strategies sea life uses to survive there.

Whether you're a photographer, a researcher, or just a neutrally buoyant observer in the underwater realm, by being better informed you'll find each dive more enjoyable and illuminating. Once you're out of the water, you'll have richer anecdotes to record in your logbook.

Doing Your Part

You don't need prior experience or even a C-card to get involved in marine conservation. Snorkelers can hold bags during reef cleanups, collect crustaceans for research in shallow coral rubble, or, with just an hour or so of training, assist in a fish survey.

If you want to dive, Earthwatch Institute (617-926-8200) has expeditions in which volunteers map coral reefs, count and identify marine creatures, and assess the impact of divers and fishermen on the ecosystem. Or you can help archaeologists explore a 19th-century shipwreck in Bermuda. Participants are usually trained on site and provided with equipment. Prices range from about $1,500 to $2,500 for a one-week expedition.

Some nonprofit organizations, such as the Coral Reef Alliance, or CORAL (510-848-0110), help volunteers find environmental organizations that need assistance with basic research and conservation. Photographers, writers, and graphic designers can help develop brochures for diving spots. If you like working with tools, join a crew attaching mooring buoys that prevent anchor damage to coral reefs. Math enthusiasts can organize data or map research sites. CORAL also encourages divers to complete informal observation reports of dive sites and posts those reports on its Internet site, so divers can track damage to specific reefs.

Florida-based Reef Environmental Education Foundation (305-451-0312) co-sponsors the Great American Fish Count in July. Brief seminars beforehand teach divers basic identification skills for the West Coast, Gulf of Mexico, Florida, and the Caribbean.

In September, the Center for Marine Conservation (202-429-5609) mounts its International Coastal Cleanup. Thousands of divers and other volunteers collect and catalog tons of debris discarded in and near rivers, lakes, and oceans. It won't be the most scenic dive in your logbook, but it may be among the most useful. – *Mary K. Miller and Blake Edgar*

Reef cleanups (top) and fish and coral counts (below) generate valuable information and improve the marine environment.

Welcome to the brave new world beyond your scuba class, filled with the liquid destinations that make up more than two-thirds of our planet. Glance at a map and consider the reefs, islands, lakes, coves, and channels that await your exploration. But where to go first? Whom to dive with? What are the most important resources you need to make these decisions? If you're overwhelmed, relax. There are plenty of strategies to ensure that you're in the right place at the right time. ◆ To begin with, one of your best options may be sticking with the group with which you trained. Many dive shops offer local diving outings and group travel abroad. Since the shop's instructors – who often act as the tour leaders – are familiar with your skill level, they can help you choose a destination. While traveling, they're close by to answer equipment questions and monitor your initial dives. Depending on the region, shops may organize day trips to nearby dive sites. Local waters – where you can jump in a few weekends in a row – are an excellent way to build your dive profile

Travel options can be confusing, but with a little research, you'll find dive sites that suit your budget, skills, and interests.

and feel increasingly comfortable with scuba gear. When you choose a shop, consider it a big plus if its staff organizes a variety of trips. This points to a dedicated following for the store and a source of potential dive buddies for you. ◆ As divers progress, some of them hop from one destination to another in search of very specific experiences. *Night dive*, check. *Manta rays*, check. *Giant sponges*, check. Others are simply looking for a way to spend a few wonderful days on vacation and see a destination from a different angle. Somewhere on that scale – from vacationing to dive to diving

Caribbean islands such as Grand Cayman offer warm water with great visibility, interesting marine life, and a selection of resorts and dive operators.

while on vacation – you'll find your own balance.

How Much to Spend?

Budget is usually a big factor in selecting a destination. Different destinations require different investments, usually not predicated on the diving alone. The cost of an average scuba day-trip seems to follow an international average of about $60 to $90 for what is known as a "two-tank dive." This generally covers a boat ride to the dive site, two tanks of air, some snacks, and the support of staff on board and dive guides underwater. Prices usually vary only for special services such as especially fast boats, rare animal encounters, small private groups, or a catered lunch on a deserted island.

Where budget really becomes an issue is beyond the diving, starting with the flight and hotel or live-aboard and ending with meals and souvenirs. For some destinations, the plane ticket is the big item, with accommodation prices reflecting a very competitive market.

Remember, too, you may need to pay extra luggage fees for your dive gear if you travel to a particularly remote area.

An excellent way to maximize your dive experience without exhausting your wallet is with shore diving. Resorts that are right on a beach have direct access to the reefs. Since tank fills are usually inexpensive, you can spend the hours between boat dives venturing off the beach on shallower quests – or even just snorkeling.

What's the Diving Like?

The next factors to consider are the level and types of diving available at a destination. Most Caribbean and Pacific destinations have a wide range of possibilities, from protected, shallow dives

Water sports such as windsurfing (above), sailing, and kayaking add to the attraction of many destinations.

Live-aboards (below) offer maximum dive time, often motoring to remote sites at night while passengers sleep.

Live-Aboard Diving

"Live-aboards" are essentially floating hotels outfitted especially for scuba enthusiasts. Whether motor vessel or sailing yacht, they are usually dive-intensive – up to five dives a day, several days in a row – and tend to attract experienced divers or beginners who want to fill their dive logs quickly. Many live-aboards are equipped with video- and film-processing capabilities, and they often specialize in encounters with elusive marine creatures such as giant mantas, humpback whales, hammerheads, and whale sharks.

Quarters may be tight, so be prepared to trade privacy for new friendships and a bit of the magic of summer camp. While some vessels offer such luxurious touches as air-conditioning, VCRs, and private bathrooms, the most important features are those that ensure a safe journey. These include onboard radio systems and oxygen, a crew with solid first-aid training, and a proven track record. The type and age of a ship can also affect the safety quotient: Look for new or newly refitted vessels. And speak with as many former passengers as possible to see if the ship's standards, style, and itinerary suit your needs.

Coral gardens (right) lie at the base of a mountain peak fringed with palm trees on St. Lucia in the West Indies.

at the novice end to full-scale adventure for the experts.

Wall Diving. The edges of reef formations or steep off-shore cliffs, where the bottom descends into hundreds – or thousands – of feet of water, are referred to as "walls." Divers can see a lot on walls, which house loads of flora and fauna on one awe-inspiring plane. However, since they do plunge into very deep water, keep a wary eye on your depth gauge and watch for currents. Other formations you might see in dive-site descriptions include pinnacles, seamounts, swim-throughs, caverns, and overhangs.

Drift Diving. Lush dive spots often grow that way because of currents that deliver a rich diet of nutrients to the local reefs. In a current-swept area, you get propelled through some tremendous marine-scapes without having to kick. Instead, the challenge is to stay with your group, get a close view of the animals on the reef, and not drift off to parts unknown. Beginners should start with shallow drift dives in spots where the current is predictable and not too fast. Choose a dive operator with a good safety record, and let the divemaster know your experience level; make sure he or she is prepared to keep an eye on you.

Night Diving. At sunset, a reef's inhabitants change.

After dark, divers encounter a completely different set of marine life feeding, mating, and prowling, all witnessed with the help of dive lights. Generally, night dives are conducted in shallower areas, so you can focus on the animals and not worry about your dive buddy every few seconds. Find out from the experts at your destination what kind of night dives

are offered; a good array often points to particularly good diving.

Wreck Diving. The human contribution to reef life, wrecks come in the form of sunken freighters, luxury liners, airplanes, buses, and more. Some have been sunk deliberately with the explicit plan of creating a reef where none existed, but the majority of wrecks found their resting places after a tragic prelude. Unless you have plenty of scuba experience and specialized wreck certification, stay on the outside of all wrecks.

Marine Highlights. Probably the chief reason many divers choose a specific destination is to meet some of nature's VIPs. Whether you head for Cocos Island off Costa Rica for the schooling hammerheads or Fiji for the famous soft coral, it's the marine life that sets the agenda. This is particularly true when tracking a migratory species such as western Australia's whale sharks, or something that is immensely rare. Make sure you find out how common sightings are and what time of year

Juvenile treefish (left), found in Southern California and Baja, lose their high-contrast coloration as they mature.

is best before you commit your dollars. And be flexible: Nature seldom wears a digital timepiece.

Once you've set your budget and know the kinds of underwater highlights available within it, you're ready to pinpoint the best time of year for your trip. Diving in many locations is seasonal. There are months when the water is warmest, the seas calmest, the visibility clearest. Novice divers should seek out locations with the best of all three. There's nothing like honing your buoyancy and navigational skills in an oceanic bathtub. However, warm, clear water may not attract certain species; for example, giant mantas and whale sharks feed on plankton, which reduces visibility. Just like the rest of life, it's all about timing and choices.

Finally, remember you can dive only so much. Check into the topside features of a destination to see what's available for the nondiver in your family and for your own nondiving hours. Obviously a destination like the Red Sea, coupled with a tour of Egypt, offers a different experience topside than, say, a small Caribbean island. This should certainly have an impact on your plans.

Trunk Bay (left), on St. John in the U.S. Virgin Islands, has a marked snorkeling trail.

The Diver's Alert Network

Scuba divers relish exotic destinations, funky critters, deep historical secrets, technical gadgetry, and a good time. It's an ideal recipe for getting yourself into some pretty interesting situations, which, unfortunately, can sometimes become dangerous.

The Diver's Alert Network, or DAN (919-684-2948), offers a safety net. Founded in 1980, the Durham, North Carolina, organization provides information and emergency medical services to divers worldwide. DAN's hotline (919-684-4326) is a public service, available to all recreational scuba divers whether they're DAN members or not.

Membership is affordable (about $40 a year for individuals) and includes a variety of critical services, including TravelAssist, which provides emergency medical air evacuation to members and their immediate families when traveling at least 50 miles from home. Most members also enroll in the optional dive accident insurance program, which covers a wide range of incidents from death and injury to lost equipment.

Given the occasionally precarious nature of scuba diving, it's a small price to pay for a little extra peace of mind.

Who's the Best Operator?

Now that the where, what, and when are becoming clearer, it's time to focus on who: the people who can make or break your dive experience. Surveys have shown that it's not the weather or missing the special animals that blesses – or ruins – a dive experience most often; it's all in the hands of the operator. In particular, if a tour leader or divemaster doesn't convey enthusiasm and local knowledge, or lacks sensitivity and training in safety measures, he or she has a far greater impact on a day of diving.

This is the toughest aspect of guaranteeing a good dive experience. Safer, larger operations often are run so clinically well that some of the spirit of the dive adventure may get lost. Equally often, what appears charming – a rickety, one-person show – may come at a dangerous price.

So evaluate the dive operations at your destination with a critical eye and consider some of these questions:

How long has the operation been running? Longevity is a big deal in this industry. Does the operation advertise? Sounds crazy, but if it can pay for marketing, you can expect a certain level of development.

How are the boats and rental gear? Look for newer and well-maintained equipment. Are the boats and staff ready for an emergency? Ask about emergency policies, onboard radio and oxygen, strategy for evacuation, and the staff's safety training. An operator should be able to verbalize a backup plan with ease.

How many divers are on an average dive? Big vessels packed with divers are often referred to as "cattle boats." Peering at tiny reef creatures with dozens of fins bumping into you can be problematic. However, some of the larger boats split groups into various skill levels and head off in different directions. It may be a process of trying several fits to find the right operation for you. In addition, inquire about the staff-to-passenger

The chilly waters of British Columbia (left) require a dry suit and knowledge of tides and currents.

ratio. Ideally, there will be enough divemasters to keep the experience safe and point out the sights. The average falls at about one for every six divers. The very best operations have plenty of friendly, experienced staff on board to present informed pre-dive briefings, make your water entry and exit comfortable, help with gear, and serve up snacks.

Does the operation offer instruction? If it has organized classes, you're likely to find a greater sensitivity to newer divers. Also find out whether the operation can provide "high-end" services. Experienced divers generally look for operators who offer extras such as nitrox (a different mix of nitrogen and oxygen) and underwater camera instruction and rentals. Chances are, if the dive operation has invested in services like this, it is committed to a life in diving.

Where to Stay?

Accommodations for divers can be found in the full range, from top-notch luxury to camping on the beach.

Many dive operators are based in a resort or manage their own hotels. In a "dive-dedicated" or "dive-friendly" resort, besides close proximity to the diving, you're likely to find simple rooms without lots of carpeting or fancy furniture – wet, sandy people are hard on rugs. Expect good food and lots of it; all that activity makes for a mean appetite. Many resorts offer dockside lockers to stow gear, so you don't need to lug it to the room. Near the lockers, look for rinse tanks and drying areas to clean the saltwater out of your equipment. These days, many dive-dedicated resorts offer special programs for children during the typical

Whale sharks (left), the world's largest fish, are gentle, pelagic creatures seen in tropical waters. They grow up to 55 feet long.

Blood stars (right) live on the Pacific Coast from Alaska to Baja California. They carry their eggs until the young are born.

dive hours of 8 A.M. to 1 P.M.

A lovely thing about diving is meeting other divers. A good dive resort offers you the chance to encounter some of the most interesting people around. And you already have a natural launch point for the conversation – where have they been diving lately?

One more very important caveat: Before you leave whatever piece of paradise you finally settle on, remember the "dive-fly rule." After diving, you've still got nitrogen in your body that needs to be released slowly. It takes a while before you'll be ready to go up in an airplane after diving. The waiting period is usually 12 to 24 hours, depending on the depth and duration of your last dives. In any case, take it easy that last day and night, and start savoring your farewell dive as a beautiful memory to carry home.

Divers Paradise, the slogan on Bonaire's license plate (opposite, bottom), underscores the islanders' dedication to protecting the marine environment.

Wreck enthusiasts can plan vacations around a special vessel like the *Cartanza Senior* (right) in the U.S. Virgin Islands.

Package Deal

Think all of these are still too many factors to juggle? Let the experts get your act together. Finding the right destination with the right diving, the right dive operators, and the right accommodations is an art form. And there's an entire industry of people called "dive travel specialists" or "dive travel wholesalers." Generally, these travel agents have a passion for diving and combine their expertise and dive experience to advise customers. They offer entire

packages from airfare to rental gear, right on the phone or through the Internet, and they can tailor a trip to your level of diving or special marine interests. Many have decades of experience in destinations around the globe, even the most exotic. So watch for package deals in the areas that interest you, or call and schedule your dream vacation. Then get ready to kick back and dive in.

Diving Destinations

♦

Coral reefs, kelp forests, and shipwrecks reveal
their secrets to scuba divers and snorkelers
throughout North America, Hawaii, and the
Caribbean. Swim with dolphins and sharks, explore
submarine canyons, and be dazzled by tropical fish
at some of the world's most intriguing dive sites.

Florida Keys

t begins to dawn on you as you swoop down off the Florida Turnpike. You're actually heading off the U.S. mainland, leaving behind the hustle and hassle of Miami 90 minutes to the north and traveling to dive among tropical islands … in your car. The 18-mile causeway leading to **Key Largo** spans Everglades-like scrub and hammock, allowing just enough time to readjust your attitude, scan the power poles for osprey nests, and let the salt start to ease into your veins. ◆ A million divers and snorkelers find their Keys each year. Some prefer the bait-and-tackle ambiance of the **Middle Keys**, and others are drawn to the touristy kitsch at the end of the road in **Key West**, while everyone has the reefs of the **Upper Keys** on his or her "to dive" lists. Since each island offers a unique combination of temperament, topside attractions, and diving, try each one

Marine sanctuaries protect a rainbow world of corals and fish just a few miles off the Florida coast.

until you find a Key that fits. All share clear, warm water, with visibility ranging from 30 to over 100 feet. In the summer and fall, water temperature is in the 80s, dropping to the 70s in the winter. The **Florida Keys** are America's islands in the stream with a home-grown great barrier reef – the third-largest reef system in the world after Australia and Belize. ◆ Many of Florida's endangered and threatened species dwell in the Keys. And all the 100 species of hard and soft coral, more than 350 species of fish, and the countless invertebrates that depend on this ecosystem live on the edge, at constant risk from pollution, ship groundings, and other human-made and natural hazards. In recognition of the reef's biodiversity and its precarious nature, in 1960 Florida created one of the world's first underwater marine parks, the **John Pennekamp Coral**

Elkhorn coral, a stony or hard coral abundant in the Florida Keys, aligns its branches with the direction of the prevailing surge.

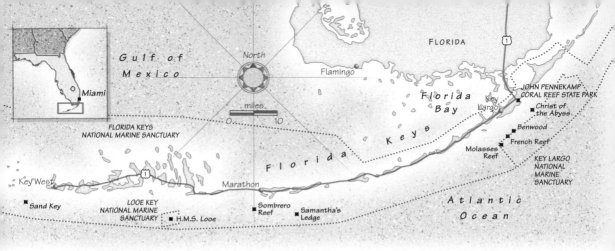

Reef State Park, off Key Largo. Thirty years later, with the designation of the 2,800-square-nautical-mile **Florida Keys National Marine Sanctuary**, protection has been extended to all the waters surrounding the Keys and the reefs beneath them.

Underwater Aquariums

Key Largo is Dive Central USA, with dive shops as common as casinos on the Vegas strip. Why all the action? The reefs here sit between a rock and a good place. The large limestone mass that makes up Key Largo prevents Florida Bay water – with a high nutrient level that would ordinarily limit underwater visibility and coral growth – from

flowing out onto the reef. Offshore, the Gulf Stream, that near-mythical current, brings the warm, clear water that allows the massive reefs of the Upper Keys to thrive even though they're near the northern limit for reef-building corals.

As your dive boat leaves Key Largo, watch for the solid green of the mangrove forest that lines the coast. The Keys have very few natural beaches; instead, there are the mangroves, standing on stiltlike roots in a saltwater environment that would kill other trees. Vital to the Keys' environment, mangroves stabilize the shoreline and provide a nursery for the many species of marine life that spend their juvenile lives hidden in the tree roots.

Passing over the clear shallow water, you enter vast beds of turtle grass, important feeding areas for the reef fish. Soon you're over white sand dotted with isolated coral heads. Farther offshore, these heads are more numerous, forming "patch reefs." At three miles, the first real reef line occurs. It's shallow – usually no more than 25 feet at its deepest – and made up of mound and branching corals attended by schools of smaller fish like grunts and snapper. Most dive boats cruise over the first reef, heading for the main reef about five miles offshore. Bright turquoise water inshore of the reef denotes the sandy bottom, while offshore the water is cobalt where the bottom drops into the abyss. In between lie the massive bank reefs of the Upper Keys, the superstar dives of America's reef system, with more than 188 separate sites marked by mooring buoys.

At **French Reef**, a wonderland of coral caves and crevices filled with marine life, snorkelers can explore from the surface while divers descend to the deep drop at 90 feet. The best swim-through caverns are in 25 to 40 feet of water. **Hourglass Cave** and **Christmas Tree Cave**, two of the most interesting features on the reef, are mountains of star coral studded with red and orange sponges and decorated with the multihued plumes of Christmas tree and featherduster worms. Dense schools of glassy sweepers, which fill the hollowed sections beneath the coral mounds, warble audibly when divers poke their heads inside. Bring an underwater light to explore the nooks and crannies.

The sweet old celebrity of the Keys, **Molasses Reef** is the most visited piece of underwater property in the nation. And it deserves to be. Long-faced trumpetfish, pugnacious pint-sized damselfish, puppy-dog groupers, and curious barracuda – Molasses is simply the world's largest aquarium, and you're free to sink yourself in as a bubbling ornament, albeit with a healthy, hands-off respect for the local inhabitants. Molasses sees the blue water of the Gulf Stream more often than other Keys reefs, which keeps the water

clearer and gives the corals the best living conditions. Snorkelers enjoy the view from the surface; divers find the lushest growth from 15 to 50 feet.

Key Largo Dry Rocks is home to *Christ of the Abyss*, the nine-foot-tall, 4,000-pound statue of Jesus standing with outstretched arms in 25 feet of water. Placed on the reef in 1965, the statue has become one of the primary attractions of the Florida Keys National Marine Sanctuary. The natural site around the statue is itself inspirational with large brain coral and ever-multiplying fishes.

The 285-foot freighter ***Benwood*** was a

Flamingo tongues (opposite, top), one of about 35,000 species of snails, are about an inch long.

Boulder brain coral (opposite, bottom) forms colonies up to seven feet across.

A snorkeler (right) snaps a picture of Alligator Reef off Islamorada, where a Navy vessel sank in 1825. The bottom is only eight feet deep in some areas.

casualty of World War II. Running without lights to avoid the German U-boats of 1942, she was rammed by another allied ship also running dark. *Benwood* staggered inshore and hit the coral north of French Reef, where she still sits today, her flattened stern in 25 feet and her bow rising dramatically intact from 50 feet of water. There is not much natural reef close to the wreck, so the coral and sponge-encrusted steel of her remains have become the major fish factory of the area.

Conch Key to Looe Key

In the bridge country of the Middle and Lower Keys, you're driving over water as often as land. When many of the Overseas Highway's bridges were replaced in the 1980s, sections of the older spans were left for fishing, strolling, and sunset gazing. Although there are fewer dive operators here than in Key Largo, you'll still find everything you need and more than 100 underwater sites to visit.

Sombrero Reef is the most popular dive site above the Seven-Mile Bridge. On glassy-calm summer weekends, boats crowd around the tower marking this massive reef in a marine rendition of the Mexican hat dance. Don't let the topside hustle bother you, though, because the real fiesta is down below. High-profile spurs of coral spread out from the shallows. Shrimp and lobster crowd under the reef ledges, while pink and purple sea fans wave from the top. A highlight of this reef, **The Arch** sports a coral rainbow eight feet high that flows with fish in every color of the spectrum.

At **Samantha's Ledge** (also known as **Shark Ledge**), the lush collection of soft corals and prolific fish life is enhanced by almost guaranteed sightings of nurse sharks. These placid sharks often sleep inside the coral caverns. The brown, beady-eyed nurse sharks, which love to feed on lobster, can grow to over 10 feet long, although the sharks you'll see at Samantha's are only four to six feet

Sleep with the Fishes

Looking for an out-of-the-way place to stay? In Key Largo, there's a B&B where the initials stand for Bed and Bubbles. Jules' Undersea Lodge is one of only three underwater habitats in the world, and it's the only one open to the public.

Originally known as La Chalupa Research Lab, the habitat was home to scientists researching offshore Puerto Rico in the 1970s. Since the mid-1980s, however, the habitat has been a "dive-on inn" at the bottom of Emerald Lagoon. Up to six guests enter the 30-foot-deep lagoon on scuba and swim to the "moon pool" – the amphibious transition point between the lagoon and the underside of the lodge where you shed your tanks and climb into the habitat.

There are televisions and VCRs in the guest rooms and common area, but the best show at any time is the real-world documentary going on outside. Check out the watery happenings from a 42-inch dome in each room, and if that window on the underwater world is not enough, jump back through the moon pool and take advantage of the diving available 24 hours a day. There are more than 160 varieties of marine life in the one-acre lagoon, which opens to the ocean.

When you've worked up an appetite swimming the grounds, a scuba-diving cook serves your meals. After a goodnight dive, you fall asleep to the rhythmic gurgling of bubbles escaping the moon pool.

long. Even without the harmless excitement of observing sharks, Samantha's is a colorful, shallow dive where you swim over coral hills overgrown with soft corals that wave and sway with the sea. You'll always find schoolmasters and blue-striped grunts sheltering among the corals awaiting sunset when they move out to the grass beds to feed.

In 1744, the captain of the H.M.S. *Looe* ran his ship onto a perfect little reef in the middle Keys. The *Looe* christened the reef with its name, and "down the loo" was, in all probability, where the captain's naval career went after the grounding. **Looe Key** is a pocket Pennekamp – the best features of Key Largo's reefs, shrunk a bit, and as carefully constructed as a scale model. This textbook spur-and-groove formation has long, well-defined fingers or "spurs" of coral separated by sandy "grooves," which transport sediment away from the reef. From east to west, the reef gains depth, and from shallow to deep, it's crowded with life. The snorkeling here is the best in the Keys. Cocky lobster and loads of friendly fish jam the **Looe Key National Marine Sanctuary**, enjoying the strict no-take protection. Indeed, it's the same protection enjoyed by the creatures at all the most popular reef areas in the Keys sanctuary. As you swim up and down between the coral spurs, it's like perusing the aisles of an overstocked fish market. Hamlets, damsels, tangs, jacks, chubs, gobies, blennies, wrasse, squirrelfish, goatfish, porkfish, hogfish, angelfish, lizardfish, scorpionfish, triggerfish – all the colorful Keys tropicals you've ever heard of are here.

End of the Road

In 1513, when the Spanish explorer Ponce de Leon sailed out in search of the fountain of youth, he found **Key West** instead. The explorer named the island "Cayo Hueso," which means "Island of Bones," so named for the skeletal remains the Spanish unearthed from Indian burial mounds on the island. After Ponce came the pirates, including Blackbeard and Captain Kidd, who ruled the waves from the 1600s until the U.S. Navy arrived in 1822 and kicked them out. The Navy stayed on in Key West, and some believe a few pirates did, too. Local boats have carried rum, drugs, Cubans, and shrimp – whatever the market would bear. The town even declared its independence from the United States in 1982, becoming capital of the "Conch Republic" in protest against customs and border patrol roadblocks. The Conchs declared war on the United States, then immediately surrendered and asked for foreign aid. Today, the Conch flag stands as the symbol of a free-spirited, Hemingway- and Jimmy Buffet-imitator-infested town with wonderful Victorian bed-and-breakfasts, rusty beach bikes, and just enough people walking around talking to themselves to keep life interesting. It's the perfect setting to find at the end of the road, and the two dozen dive sites around the island are as wild and colorful as the terrestrial nightlife.

The diminutive **Sand Key** lies six miles off Key West. Not much more than a sandbar, the island still provides a protective lee and sheltered dive sites. Dive-boat captains

Charismatic Manatees

Manatees are marine mammals of the order Sirenia, named for the mythological sea nymphs who lured ships to their doom. Early sailors apparently mistook the manatee and its cousins for mermaids. Who knows how many bottles of rum it would take to mistake these corpulent – 10 feet long and 1,000-plus pounds – walrus-faced creatures for a beautiful woman? However, there is no mistaking an encounter with a manatee as one of the most remarkable and utterly charming experiences available to anyone who can don a mask.

During warm months, West Indian manatees, the only Sirenian species found in the United States, spread out through Florida's coastal ocean, bays, and inland waterways. As soon as they sense the water temperature dropping below 70°F, they gather at their traditional and some not-so-traditional winter retreats. On the east coast of the state, manatees congregate around the outflows of power plants where water used to cool the turbines is released at a higher temperature. On the west coast, the manatees swim inland to gather at a number of natural springs where water bubbling up from the Florida Aquifer remains a constant 72°F. It is at these springs that you have an opportunity to swim among these gentle giants.

Crystal River, west of Ocala, Florida, is the most popular spot. Since the sound of scuba gear scares them away, you'll use only a snorkel. Although 72°F may be toasty for a thick-skinned siren, wear a wet suit because you won't want to leave the water once you meet them.

Florida's manatees are endangered, with only about 2,400 left in the wild. Their main enemies are the boats that speed along the state's waterways; it's a rare adult manatee that doesn't bear propeller scars across its back. It is illegal to disturb the manatees in any way, so all encounters are initiated by the manatees. If you're lucky, you'll get to see a mother and calf. Take special care not to separate the two, but if you watch quietly you may see the calf nursing underwater.

Manatees (below) sometimes approach snorkelers for a closer view or to nibble on their hair.

M.V. *Benwood* (opposite, top), a 285-foot freighter lying on French Reef, was sunk during World War II.

Silversides (opposite, bottom) flow around a diver, demonstrating behavior that makes it difficult for predators to single out an individual.

try to sneak as far to the seaward side of Sand Key as the waves allow to reach the best sites, such as **Grand Canyon**. Here huge mountains of star coral are undercut on all sides and blanketed with schooling fish. A stand of elkhorn coral gives way to a sloping reef covered with boulder-size coral heads. A swim-through canyon slices through the reef and leads to a drop-off where you can see larger fish like barracuda and pompano patrolling the blue.

Joe's Tugboat represents a cool bit of Key West Conchmanship. As the story goes, a local Joe allegedly kidnapped this 85-foot river tug that was lying at a dock waiting to be turned into scrap. On a dark night, he and a few accomplices cut the ship loose, towed it out to a nice spot, dropped it on an even keel in 65 feet of water, and went on the lam. Key West divers remain ever grateful. Filled with snapper and grunts, covered with barracuda, home to a few Godzilla-sized

members of the grouper family, and often awash in clear Gulf Stream water, the intact *Joe's Tug* provides a wonderful back-drop for pictures.

As you witness the daily sunset celebration on the Key West water-front, you realize how lucky you are to have found your Keys. You've driven to the southernmost point in the continental United States and sampled some of the best diving in this part of the world. But with literally hundreds of dive sites to see, you have only one choice – turn the car around and dive your way back north.

TRAVEL TIPS

DETAILS

When to Go

Ironically, summer, the hurricane season, is the best time to visit. Seas then are *usually* warm and calm, although hurricanes and tropical storms can pass through at any time. Wind may hamper winter trips. Temperatures average 80°F in January, in the low 90s in summer. Water temperatures rise from a winter low of 72°F to the mid-80s in late summer.

How to Get There

Major airlines serve Key West, the southernmost city in the continental United States. Many visitors drive south from Miami on the Overseas Highway.

Getting Around

Taxis are rare outside of Key West. Car rentals are available at Key West International Airport. The one-lane Overseas Highway is prone to backups.

INFORMATION

Florida Keys National Marine Sanctuary

216 Ann Street, Key West, FL 33040; tel: 305-292-0311 (main office) or 305-852-7717 (Key Largo) or 305-743-2437 (Marathon).

Islamorada Chamber of Commerce

P.O. Box 915, Islamorada, FL 33036; tel: 800-322-5397 or 305-664-4503.

John Pennekamp Coral Reef State Park

P.O. Box 487, Key Largo, FL 33037; tel: 305-451-1202.

Key Largo Chamber of Commerce

106000 Overseas Highway, Key Largo, FL 33037; tel: 800-822-1088.

Key West Chamber of Commerce

402 Wall Street, P.O. Box 984, Key West, FL 33040; tel: 800-527-8539 or 305-294-5988.

Lower Keys Chamber of Commerce

P.O Box 430511, Big Pine Key, FL 33043; tel: 800-872-3722 or 305-872-2411.

Marathon Chamber of Commerce and Visitors Center (Middle Keys)

12222 Overseas Highway, Marathon, FL 33050; tel: 800-352-5397 or 305-743-5417.

Southwest Florida Artificial Reef Association

1112 13th Street North, Naples, FL 34102; tel: 941-352-3328.

Visit Florida USA

P.O. Box 1100, Tallahassee, FL 32302-1100; tel: 888-735-2872.

CAMPING

There are campgrounds and RV parks on almost all of the Keys. Some are affiliated with national and state parks, others are private. Contact chambers of commerce for information.

LODGING

PRICE GUIDE – double occupancy

$ = up to $49 $$ = $50–$99
$$$ = $100–$149 $$$$ = $150+

Caribbean House

226 Petronia Street, Key West, FL 33040; tel: 800-543-4518 or 305-296-1600.

Set in the Bahama Village section of Key West, two blocks from the main street, this inn is popular with budget-minded travelers. There are 10 no-frills rooms, each with a private entrance, bath, air conditioner, and refrigerator. Continental breakfast is included. $–$$

Conch Key Cottages

62250 Overseas Highway, Walkers Island, FL 33050; tel: 800-330-1577 or 305-289-1377.

Twelve kitchen-equipped studios and one-bedroom apartments occupy five acres of landscaped beachfront on a private island. Hire the resort's boat at the private marina for a dive or snorkel charter, or drive to a nearby dive operator. $$–$$$$

Islander

P.O. Box 766, Islamorada, FL 33036; tel: 305-664-2031.

The laid-back Islander has 114 standard rooms on sandy grounds well off the highway. Guests swim in fresh- and saltwater pools, fish, play volleyball and basketball, and snorkel nearby. John Pennekamp Coral Reef State Park is 20 miles to the north. $$–$$$

Jules' Undersea Lodge

51 Shoreland Drive, Key Largo, FL 33037; tel: 305-451-2353.

Guests here can't dive into bed until they've dived to the lodge. Once a scientific research facility, the underwater habitation was turned into a lodge in the 1980s. Two snug guest rooms offer aquatic views through 42-inch windows. Guests share a bathroom. Equipment rentals and diving lessons are available. $$$$

Pier House Resort and Caribbean Spa

One Duval Street, Key West, FL 33040; tel: 800-327-8340 or 305-296-4600.

On a private, white-sand beach, steps away from Old Town Key West, the grounds of this four-star resort cover a city block. Each of the 142 guest rooms offers luxurious accommodations. Live entertainment, four restaurants, and spa facilities are available. $$$$

DIVE OPERATORS

Bone Island Dive Center

700 Front Street, Key West, FL 33040; tel: 305-294-2249.

The center, which has a private dock in Old Town Key West, carries 10 passengers aboard its 35-foot dive boat. Equipment is rented to clients only. Resort courses, nitrox instruction, and training to the divemaster level are available.

Conch Republic Divers

90800 Overseas Highway, No. 9, Tavernier, FL 33070; tel: 800-274-3483 or 305-852-1655.

This operation specializes in Upper Keys diving, including wrecks, reefs, and drift dives from a big, comfortable boat. Dive and hotel packages are available. Equipment rental and private or semiprivate PADI instruction are offered.

Dive Key West

3128 North Roosevelt Boulevard, Key West, FL 33040; tel: 800-426-0707 or 305-296-3823.

The largest professional dive center in Key West, with more than 27 years of experience, runs two-tank trips twice daily, plus night dives. Services include equipment sales, rental, and repair; a curbside air-fill station; and training for PADI, NAUI, NASDS, SSI, and YMCA certification.

It's A Dive Watersports

103800 Overseas Highway, Key Largo, FL 33037; tel: 800-809-9881 or 305-453-9881.

On the grounds of the Marriott Key Largo Bay Beach Resort, this full-service center conducts trips aboard a 45-foot motorized catamaran. Equipment sales and rentals, glass-bottom boat trips, boat and bike rentals, and training for certification are available.

Excursions

Biscayne National Park

9700 S.W. 328th Street, Homestead, FL 33033-5634; tel: 305-230-7275.

Manatees, elsewhere endangered by development and speedboats, share the water with snorkelers and boaters at this marine park, a 45-minute drive from Miami International Airport. Biscayne Bay is warmed by the Gulf Stream and visited by relatively few divers – conditions necessary for the preservation of some of North America's healthiest coral. In addition to coral reefs, divers here explore seagrass beds and mangrove creeks.

Dry Tortugas National Park

P.O. Box 6208, Key West, FL 33041; tel: 305-242-7700.

This aquarium without walls suits both snorkeling children and advanced divers – provided they're amenable to the primitive setting. The park is reached by a 45-minute seaplane flight or a two- to four-hour boat ride from Key West. Clear, warm water washes over the coral reefs and seagrass beds from May to September. Night snorkeling around Fort Jefferson offers a different kind of Florida night life: glimpses of octopuses, basket stars, and resting fish. The park prints a self-guided tour of the *Windjammer*, a three-masted sailing ship that sank in 1901. There are no accommodations in the park; camping is permitted.

Florida's East Coast

Visit Florida USA, P.O. Box 1100, Tallahassee, FL 32302-1100; tel: 888-735-2872.

Artificial reefs off Florida's Atlantic coast are adorned with a bounty of sea life. Advanced divers off West Palm Beach, for example, can investigate an ocean liner in 90 feet of water and the *Princess Anne*, a 350-car ferry, at a depth of 100 feet. There are 50 such reefs between Ft. Lauderdale and Miami alone.

Bahamas

CHAPTER 8

From the air, the archipelago of the **Bahamas** seems as ephemeral as cloud vapor – on the verge of dissolving and reforming again inside a vast turquoise swash of water. The first of these 700 islands and 2,500 small cays appears just 50 miles off the South Florida peninsula in an island chain that stretches all the way down to Great Inagua, not so very far from the tip of southeastern Cuba. ◆ Look closer and you'll see that this entire island-nation sits atop two vast limestone plateaus, sand-covered "banks" that rise from the abyssal sea floor, a mile or more below. Look closer still and you'll find islands edged with mangroves and white sand beaches, coconut palm, and willowy casuarina, all cooled by prevailing trade winds. ◆ Underwater you'll find a spectacular diversity that surprises even veteran divers, with both shallow and deep reefs, plunging walls, shipwrecks, symmetrical blue holes, and lots of megafauna – from dolphins to sharks. ◆ When Columbus first sighted

A classic menu of shipwrecks, coral reefs, sharks, and dolphins lures divers to these sun-drenched islands.

these islands in 1492, he wrote in his journal, "very green and fertile and the air very balmy." In the 1700s, British Loyalists, angry with the way the American Revolution turned out, sailed here from the United States with their slaves in attempts – most of which failed – to set up cotton and sugar plantations. Today, the Bahamian natives are descendants of both, united by their stormy history and their archaic English-island patois. Survivors have learned to cope with the sea, becoming skilled shipbuilders and fishermen over the last 250 years. Now, with most of the 30-odd inhabited islands running dive operations, many have also learned to ferry visitors underwater. Hard-core divers who prefer untamed sites out of the reach of local shops

Hand-feeding sharks is done only by experts wearing protective suits, while spectators watch from a few feet away.

predators like Atlantic amberjacks and horse-eye jacks patrol the wreck, and both spotted eels and morays hide in the crannies deeper inside. Underwater segments of James Bond movies like *Thunderball* were shot in these islands – indeed, this dramatic wreck seems as if it could be one giant underwater film set.

Staged "shark dives" were also pioneered in the Bahamas, with divemasters chumming and sometimes even hand-feeding local gray and Caribbean reef sharks as divers watch from a safe spot on the bottom. Freeport and Nassau both have veteran operations, while **Long Island** to the southeast may be the granddaddy of this practice. Although disruptive to the sharks' natural feeding cycle, such dives do expose

sign on with live-aboards, which travel to remote locales like the Acklins, the Ragged Islands, and the uninhabited Cay Sal Banks.

Most visitors only know the Bahamas as **Nassau-Paradise Island** on **New Providence**, or **Freeport-Lucaya** on **Grand Bahama**, simply because these destinations have made themselves over to accommodate mainstream tourists via cruise-ship ports and fancy resorts, casinos, and international airports. Indeed, four-fifths of the population is centered here. However, travelers seeking less glitz and more solitude often find their way to the **Out Islands**, which includes all the rest of the Bahamas.

Islands in the Stream

For a sampler of underwater opportunities, begin your trip at **Freeport**, perched on the westerly tip of **Grand Bahama Island** where it is washed by the deep blue of the Gulf Stream. One of the most spectacular wrecks is found lying on its port side in 100 feet of water just offshore. Called *Theo's*, the wreck is a 230-foot freighter intentionally sunk in 1983 as an artificial reef. With large holes cut into its hull, intermediate divers can swim through the interior of the ship, past portals colonized by colorful algae and corals. Huge

divers to the grace and wild beauty of this impressive predator – and the education may help build consensus for the protection of all sharks, which are diminishing worldwide because of heavy commercial fishing.

Deserted beaches (below) such as this one on Ship Channel Cay make the Bahamas an ideal destination for divers and snorkelers who crave seclusion.

Parrotfish (left) sleep inside cocoons made of mucus bubbles that the fish secrete at night.

Make the transition from megacritter to megamyth by traveling to **Andros**, a scantily populated Out Island where an old Bahamian legend still has a monster called a Lusca hiding at the bottom of geological formations known as blue holes. Andros, largest of the Bahamian islands, perches on the westward edge of the **Tongue of the Ocean**, which has licked out a 6,000-foot-deep abyss in the **Great Bahama Bank**. The 40-by-104-mile island is scored with wild hog trails and dotted with limestone ruins of old Loyalist plantations and some dry caves named for the pirate Henry Morgan. Andros is also serrated by bonefish-rich bights and tidal flats and punctuated with at least 400 blue holes,

only a fraction of which have been explored. Offshore are 120 miles of barrier reef, the third longest in the hemisphere. If your wall-diving skills are up to it, a dive anywhere off the reef's outer edge takes you soaring over the abyssal Tongue.

While blue holes are found elsewhere in the wider Caribbean, the Bahamas – and Andros in particular – sit atop the shallow karst terrain that lends itself to them. These perfectly symmetrical formations punctuate the otherwise green shallows with chasms of cobalt blue, some plunging sharply down for hundreds of feet. In deeper holes, pelagics like sea turtles, sharks, and rays swim out in the middle. The walls inside the holes are

the uninformed, these swirling vortexes once translated into unseen mythic dangers. Lusca or not, it's wise to avoid diving in the holes during tidal changes; deeper sites and those with tunnels also require special training.

Landmark Preserve

If you travel east across the Tongue to **Great Exuma**, you'll soon discover it's one vast jigsaw comprised of 365 smaller islands. At **George Town** in the south, where the natural **Elizabeth Harbor** is protected from the sea by a blufflike beach, you'll find one of the most popular sailboat anchorages in all the Bahamas. Just across the dirt main street from the harbor, islanders sell handwoven straw hats and explosively hot "goat peppers" in outdoor markets.

To the north is the **Exuma Cays Land and Sea National Park**, a landmark preserve that predates Florida's venerated John Pennekamp Coral Reef State Park by two years. The wilderness preserve is a 176-square-mile biosphere of wild sand beaches, shallow patch reefs, and water so clear you'll think you're swimming in a marine aquarium. Fishing and even collecting shells are banned to keep this place as locked in time as it was when it was created in 1958. Sign on with a kayak tour and camp here at the edges of deserted sandy coves scalloped into the limestone cays, and snorkel isolated sea caves teeming with a spectrum of tropicals just offshore.

often covered with a patina of hard and soft corals, and sometimes indented with room-sized caverns.

But what about this fearsome Lusca? The holes of Andros are remnants of terrain that collapsed when the Bahama Banks were dry during the last Ice Age and aquifers flowed in caverns under them. Since the holes are often linked to one another via these same tunnels, the sea over them will "blow" or "suck" during tidal changes. To

Some claim that **San Salvador** on the Atlantic rim of the chain lays claim to the best visibility, because oceanic currents keep the water swept clean of island detritus. But **Cat Island** just to the northwest has the same zap-blue visibility, plus a curious topside reality bred by the insularity of the place. Mapped as "San Salvador" until 1926, the slender, 50-mile-long Cat was renamed not for a feline but for a pirate, Arthur Catt, who is rumored to have squirreled away his gold here in one of the limestone caves. Island historians claim Columbus not only made landfall here but also founded a colony on the south coast that thrived for a century.

Cat is spined with an ancient ridge of coral that peaks at **Mount Alvernia**, which at 206 feet is the highest point in all the Bahamas. From the village of **New Bight**, follow an overgrown pathway to the top of the ridge where a former architect-mason and priest, Father Jerome, once hauled blocks of limerock to create a scaled-down replica of a monastery, today called the Hermitage. You can see both sides of Cat Island from here and watch as the surf foams over the

Swimming with Dolphins

We humans have been trying to bond with dolphins for millennia, expressing our fascination with these intelligent marine mammals in art and myth. After all, dolphins had ancestors that once lived on the land and then returned to the sea – a practice akin to what we try to do with high-tech scuba gear.

If you've known dolphins only as captive, trained performers inside a marine park, seeing them underwater in their natural habitat can be a transcendent experience. Several live-aboards, including a sailing schooner and a catamaran, and a couple of land-based dive operations specialize in traveling to the remote banks around Grand Bahama Island where pods of Atlantic spotted dolphins congregate.

The good news for nondivers is that snorkeling is the best way to experience the dolphin. In fact, veteran scuba divers with hundreds of dives to their logbooks seldom see wild dolphins underwater.

Indeed, unlike "swim with the dolphin" programs where you can touch or even "ride" captive dolphins, the appearance of wild dolphins is evanescent. As you float in the window-clear waters on the shallow Bahama Banks, the animals seem to materialize from the ether, arriving with an exuberant stream of clicks and squeaks. They may stay around for a few minutes or a few hours – somersaulting underwater like playful kids, approaching you for a closer look, even swimming next to you. Then they suddenly disappear, called back to the deep sea by a voice only they can hear.

For more of an educational experience, sign on with a program that has a marine biologist aboard, where you'll have a chance to study more closely the intelligence, behavior, and physiology of our wild mammal cousins. As for the dolphins, no one is sure yet what they're studying about us.

Queen conch (opposite, left), a large tropical snail, was once common throughout the Caribbean but has suffered from overharvesting. If you wait quietly after approaching a queen conch, you may see one of its eye stalks poking out of the shell (opposite, right).

A snorkeler (below) enjoys the company of an Atlantic spotted dolphin. Divers should never pursue dolphins; the animals come and go as they please.

What Big Teeth You Have

At first glance, the barracuda is nothing if not daunting. There's that hydrodynamic body, those rows of needle-sharp teeth, and a mouth that seems to be panting endlessly with gastronomic anticipation. To make matters worse, this silvery apparition also has the uncanny habit of following you about on the reef, glaring ceaselessly with its patented Charles Manson stare. But its bark, so to speak, is worse than its bite.

This is the great barracuda (*Sphyraena barracuda*), and while its range is nearly circumtropical, it seems no more at home than in the shallow waters of the Bahamas. Indeed, if you dive near a boat that has been anchored in place for a few weeks, you are guaranteed to come face to face with a resident barracuda that has claimed the space under the boat for itself. As curious as they are territorial, barracuda approach divers far more often than divers would like – and they do so inquisitively, eyeing you as if you were their next meal of mullet.

Biologists, who write off the barracuda's menacing air-chomping habit to respiration, say there have been no documented reports of attacks by barracuda on divers. So once you come to grips with this fish's seemingly stalking habits, it's easier to relax and enjoy the spectacle, watching an animal that maxes out at over six feet in length as it watches you.

It's not a very good idea to tempt the fates by wearing shiny jewelry, though – especially the silvery kind resembling the "spoon" lures fishermen use to catch barracuda. Otherwise, the barracuda's biggest threat to humans comes not from the outside but from within. Since it's near the top of the food chain, the barracuda often accumulates coral neurotoxins that can cause a debilitating case of ciguatera food poisoning. Prevention is simple: Don't eat barracuda, and be particularly careful in identifying the species of the catch of the day when eating at restaurants on the islands.

Great barracudas (left) range from Massachusetts to Brazil but are most common in the tropics.

Yellowline arrow crabs (right) are about two inches in diameter. They travel over the reef on long stiltlike legs and usually aren't afraid of divers.

Site of Atlantis

If you yearn for a more cosmic experience, travel up to **Bimini**, just 50 miles east of Miami, where pilgrims drawn by Edgar Cayce's reference to Atlantis have located the very tippy-top of the sunken continent. Known as the **Bimini Road**, this shallow dive site is comprised of a set of massive, pavementlike stones set in the sandy bottom. On shore is an artesian spring said to have magical powers, a place true believers go to be at one with their inner Oz. When you've had enough of this, explore some of the offshore reefs, like one known as **Little Caverns**. It's a 70-foot-deep site where platter-sized French angels seem to guard the portals of the coral caves, and giant spotlight parrotfish bob and weave like wind-up toys through thick schools of yellowtail snapper. Look out toward the Gulf Stream, just in case any marlin or tuna happen to be cruising by.

Back on land, drop by the **Compleat Angler**, the ramshackle bar and lodge in rustic **Alice Town**, where vintage photos of Hemingway and his fishing buddies still line the aged mahogany walls. Pull up a chair, order a cold Kalik ("The Beer of the Bahamas"), and crack open Papa's *Islands in the Stream*, since that is exactly where you happen to be.

reef off the wild windward shore. Colonial wrecks, many still unexplored, are hidden under the waters of Cat.

Wall diving around Cat starts in most places in 50 feet of water, where the bottom drops out to a mile and more. In the shallows, you'll find classic spur-and-groove reefs, mini-canyons bracketed by sand channels and pockmarked with coral caves. Expect to see most anything here, from schools of spadefish and rainbow runners to fairy basslets and trumpetfish as slender as the island itself.

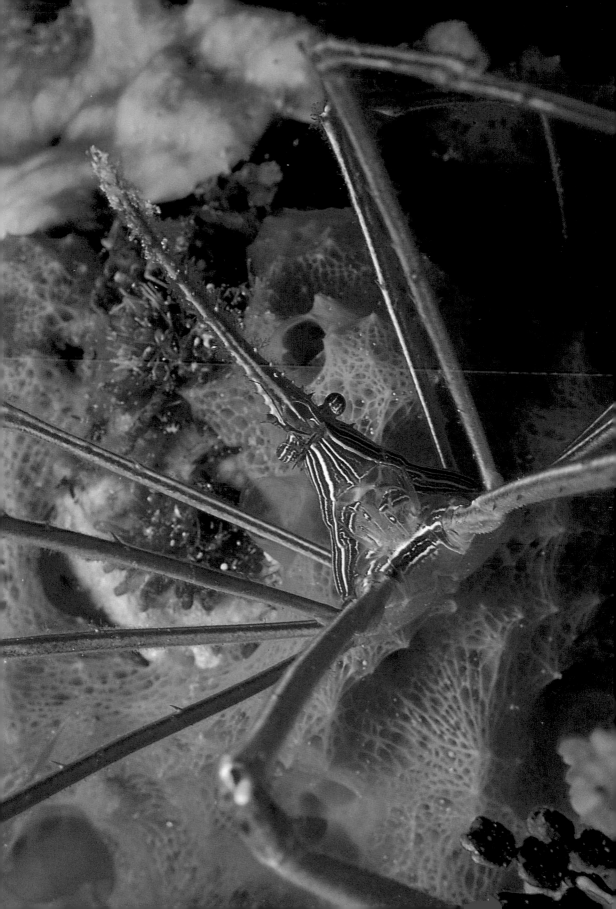

TRAVEL TIPS

DETAILS

When to Go

The peak season lasts from December to May, with temperatures in the low 70s. Temperatures are usually in the low 80s from June to November, when tropical storms are more likely. Accommodation rates drop nearly 30 percent during the off-season. The water temperature ranges from 74°F in winter to 80°F in summer.

How to Get There

Major airlines serve Nassau and Freeport International Airports. Several carriers fly from Ft. Lauderdale and Miami to the Out Islands.

Getting Around

Rental cars are available at the airports; motorists drive on the left side of the road. Taxis, available on major islands, operate at a fixed rate. Air travel between islands is provided by charter plane and the national airline, Bahamasair, 800-222-4262. Some resorts offer a charter air service for guests. Adventurous travelers may opt for rides on a mailboat or ferry, but be warned: Passengers often share vessels with lumber and livestock.

INFORMATION

Bahamas Out Islands Promotion Board

1100 Lee Wagener Boulevard, Suite 312, Ft. Lauderdale, FL 33315; tel: 800-688-4752 or 954-359-8099.

Bahamas Tourist Office and Dive Association

One Turnberry Place, 19495 Biscayne Boulevard, Suite 809, Aventura, FL 33180-2321; tel: 800-866-3483 or 305-932-0051 or 242-322-7500.

CAMPING

Camping is not permitted in the Bahamas.

LODGING

PRICE GUIDE – double occupancy
$ = up to $49 $$ = $50–$99
$$$ = $100–$149 $$$$ = $150+

Bimini Big Game Fishing Club and Hotel

P.O. Box 699, Alice Town, Bimini, Bahamas; tel: 800-737-1007 or 242-347-3391.

This self-contained resort's 49 contemporary rooms, suites, and cottages overlook a marina and courtyard. Patrons are primarily divers and fishermen. Rooms, spacious enough to store scuba gear, have two double beds and air conditioning. Cottages include a dining area and refrigerator. $$$–$$$$

Castaways Resort

Box F-42629, East Mall, Freeport, Bahamas; tel: 242-352-6682.

The four-story hotel is next to the International Bazaar, near the Bahamas Princess Casino. Two buildings, together housing 130 rooms, are linked by walkways suspended over garden courtyards. A large swimming pool, restaurant, bar, and nightclub are on the grounds. $$–$$$

Compleat Angler Hotel

P.O. Box 601, Alice Town, Bimini, Bahamas; tel: 242-347-3122.

This weathered hotel, built in the 1930s, is sided with wood taken from rum barrels used during Prohibition. Ernest Hemingway lived here from 1935 to 1937 while writing *To Have and Have Not*. The hotel, in the middle of Alice Town, has 12 guest rooms and a small Hemingway museum. Dive packages are available. $$

Fernandez Bay Village

1507 South University Drive, Suite A, Plantation, FL 33324; tel: 800-940-1905 or 242-342-3043.

Rustic and quiet, this Cat Island resort has 12 villas on a mile-long stretch of beach. Dinners are served by candlelight on a terrace overlooking Fernandez Bay. A full-service dive shop is on the premises. $$$$

Island Outpost Bahamas/Compass Point

P.O. Box CB-13842, West Bay Street, Gambier, Nassau, Bahamas; tel: 800-688-7678 or 242-327-4500.

Built on two private acres of Love Beach, these 18 multicolored cottages have homey rooms, kitchens, and private decks. A shoreside restaurant and swimming pool are on the premises. $$$–$$$$

Small Hope Bay Lodge

P.O. Box 21667, Ft. Lauderdale, FL 33335-1667; tel: 800-223-6961 or 242-368-2013.

The lodge, on North Andros, has 20 beachfront cottages, hand-built of coral rock and Andros pine. Cottage interiors have ceiling fans and locally crafted furniture. Rooms have no phones, televisions, keys, or air conditioning. Family-run since 1960, the laid-back retreat welcomes divers. $$$$

DIVE OPERATORS

Andros Undersea Adventures

P.O. Box 21766, Fort Lauderdale, FL 33335-1766; tel: 800-327-8150 or 242-368-2795.

This operation, which runs a fast, 38-foot dive boat, lies outside the tourist area. Packages with Lighthouse Yacht Club are available. Services include equipment rental, guided dives, and training for open water and advanced certification.

Bimini Undersea

P.O. Box 693515, Miami, FL 33269; tel: 800-348-4644 or 305-653-5572 or 242-347-3089.

This full-service diving and watersports facility partners with Bimini resorts to offer vacation packages. The operator specializes in wild-dolphin excursions. Services include equipment rental, guided and night dives, and training for referral and open water certification.

Stuart Cove's Dive South Ocean

P.O. Box CB-11697, Nassau, Bahamas; tel: 888-357-4275 or 242-362-4171.

The operator specializes in extreme adventure dives and underwater film production. Some of the outfit's dive sites have appeared in James Bond films. Services include equipment rental and a full-service photo center. Training ranges from basic to technical. Shark dives are available.

Underwater Explorers Society (UNEXSO)

P.O. Box 22878, Ft. Lauderdale, FL 33335; tel: 800-992-3483 or 954-351-9889 or 242-373-1244.

Established in 1965, this large operation in Freeport, Grand Bahama, is known for its "Diving Adventure" program, which includes dolphin dives and shark-feeding programs. Services include equipment sales, rental, and repair, and guided dives. Training includes resort courses and referrals, open water and advanced certification, and many specialty classes.

Valentine's Dive Center

3928 Shelbyville Road, Louisville, KY 40207; tel: 800-383-6480 or 242-333-2309.

Based at Valentine's Resort on Harbour Island, the dive shop runs two custom boats to wreck, reef, and blue-hole sites. Equipment sales and rental, and guided dives are available. Training includes introductory, referral, open water, and advanced certification.

Excursions

Cay Sal Bank

Nekton Diving Cruises, 520 S.E. 32nd Street, Fort Lauderdale, FL 33316; tel: 800-899-6753 or 954-463-9324.

Draw a triangle between Key West, central Cuba, and Andros Island; within these shallow waters lies Cay Sal Banks, the most remote area of the Bahamas. A series of broken reefs, a few of which peek through the surface, offers a 60-by-30-mile expanse of wild and pristine diving. Divers, propelled by the Gulf Stream, drift past blue holes, shallow reefs, steep walls, and abundant fish. The week-long, live-aboard trip is best made between April and October.

Great Inagua

Walk-Inn Guesthouse, Matthew Town, Inagua, Bahamas; tel: 242-339-1612.

"Bring your own mask, fins, and snorkel" is the key to the Great Inagua experience; there's no scuba support on the island. Reputed to hide the treasure of an exiled, 19th-century Haitian ruler, the Bahamas' southernmost island is known today for a different sort of treasure: two national parks, one dedicated to an enormous colony of flamingos, the other devoted to sea-turtle research. This is the Bahamian outback, with very little tourism and only a handful of accommodations, but the reefs are fascinating.

The Abacos

Bahamas Out Island Promotion Board, 1100 Lee Wagener Boulevard, Suite 312, Fort Lauderdale, FL 33315; tel: 800-688-4752 or 954-359-8099.

The Abacos encompass the Loyalist Cays, named after British sympathizers who took refuge here in the 1770s during the American Revolution. This collection of small islands at the northern end of the Bahamas offers excellent diving and an infrastructure (on most islands) to make it easy. On Great Abaco, travelers can try snorkeling with wild dolphins in Pelican Cays Land and Sea Park.

Turks and Caicos

CHAPTER 9

Missing altogether from many maps and lost in the necklace of the Bahamian island chain on others, the **Turks and Caicos Islands** are overshadowed as a dive destination by the Bahamas to the north and the Caymans to the west beyond Cuba. The relative obscurity, along with an aggressive ecosystem protection plan, gives real credence to overused words like *unspoiled* and *pristine*, which can be easily applied to the diving here in this, one of the last sandy bits of the crumbled British empire. ◆ The 49 islands of the Turks and Caicos lie on the same limestone plateau as the Bahamas. Only nine of the islands are inhabited; the rest are a mix of solidified sandbars and rocks covered with scrub-and-mangrove forests. The "and" of the name connects two distinct island groups, the larger Caicos Islands to the west and the tiny Turks to the east, separated by the 7,000-foot-deep Turks Island Passage. ◆ What really

Share the sea with turtles, rays, and humpback whales in the unspoiled reaches of this remote archipelago.

makes these remote islands 575 miles southeast of Miami a highlight reel of Caribbean diving are the local inhabitants: sea turtles paddling along reef tops, eagle rays gliding in the blue beside steep coral walls, migrating humpback whales filling the entire water column with their soulful songs, and even a neighborly dolphin. ◆ The center of tourism is **Providenciales,** better known as "Provo." Residents pronounce the island's nickname *pravo*, while everyone else rhymes it with *mojo*. There are 300 miles of beach in this chain, and the 12 miles of powdery white sand lining Provo's **Grace Bay** have been named one of the world's top beaches. The ocean lapping at the shore is so clear that it reflects blue when lighted by

A lone graysby perches on a sponge. These small groupers have a fascinating reproductive adaptation: They start life as females, then change to males.

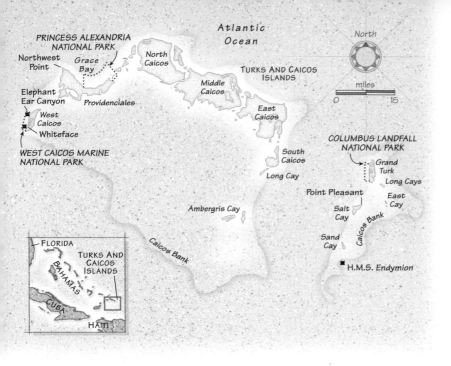

PRINCESS ALEXANDRIA
NATIONAL PARK

Northwest
Point

Grace
Bay

North
Caicos

North

TURKS AND CAICOS
ISLANDS

Middle
Caicos

miles

Elephant
Ear Canyon

Providenciales

0   15

West
Caicos

East
Caicos

Whiteface

COLUMBUS LANDFALL
NATIONAL PARK

WEST CAICOS MARINE
NATIONAL PARK

South
Caicos

Grand
Turk

Long Cay

Long Cays

Point Pleasant

East
Cay

FLORIDA

Ambergris Cay

Salt
Cay

Caicos Bank

TURKS AND
CAICOS
ISLANDS

Caicos Bank

Sand
Cay

BAHAMAS

CUBA

H.M.S. Endymion

HAITI

around a Caribbean island. Turks and Caicos dive operators also discourage divers from feeding fish to prevent the swarms of yellowtails and sergeant majors that infest other destinations as a diver-nibbling hassle. The ban also allows divers to see fish exhibiting more natural behavior. The one exception is a grouper who local divers have named Scratch.

Scratch is cagey, a marine entrepreneur that has learned to use night divers as meal tickets. This chubby, puppy-faced fish snuggles up to divers and follows them throughout the dive, using their dive lights like spotlights at a seafood buffet. When Scratch sees something tasty in a diver's light, he rushes forward and gulps down the prey. After the initial shock, divers learn to shield small fish from this night snacker.

No mention of Grace Bay's resident animals is complete without Provo's mascot, JoJo. This male Atlantic bottlenose dolphin prefers, for some unfathomable reason, the company of humans to his own kind. Pamphlets and posters around the island tell his story and list the rules of protocol for anyone encountering him in the water. The rules protect the dolphin as well as the swimmers and divers. Many visitors and residents have had fascinating and enjoyable

only a pale moon. A short walk away from the resorts that line the bay is prime stargazing territory.

Provo's Protected Waters

Grace Bay dive sites begin with large, high-profile spurs of coral separated by sandy grooves. The broad lines of reef converge at 30 feet to form a solid wall that drops abruptly to 80 feet. Caribbean reef sharks patrol at a distance off the wall, while scores of grouper hold the high ground. Green and hawksbill turtle sightings are common on daytime dives, while night divers find huge schools of bar jacks surrounding the dive boats.

Grace Bay lies within the protective arm of **Princess Alexandria National Park** – just one of more than 30 nature reserves on the islands – where fishing and collecting are prohibited. The protection has allowed "food fish" such as grouper and lobster to inhabit the reefs in numbers not normally seen

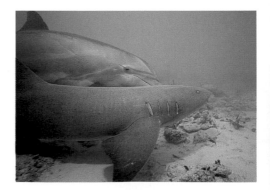

Cleaner shrimp (opposite, top) like this banded coral shrimp eat parasites and dead skin off much larger animals.

Provo's mascot (opposite, bottom), JoJo, a bottlenose dolphin, picks on something his own size – a nurse shark.

A dive guide (right) points out unusual sights like this rope sponge to a group of visiting divers.

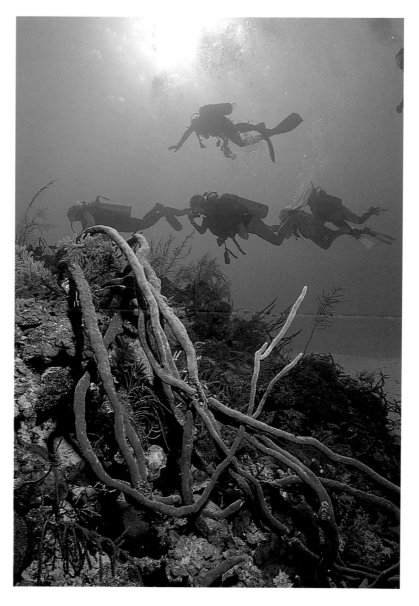

encounters with JoJo, a rare opportunity to see a wild bottlenose up close. The operative word for JoJo, however, is *wild*, and local divemasters remind you not to touch him, especially around the eyes and blowhole, not to let him lead you away from the beach, and to make sure you hang on to your bathing suit.

Vivid Sponge Life

Provo's dive operators travel to sites outside Grace Bay as often as possible in the diver's eternal quest for the best visibility. Grace Bay is subject to tidal changes that kick up sand and lower water clarity over the dive sites on outgoing tides.

Northwest Point, also designated a marine park, is the most dramatic section of Provo's fringing reef. Vertical walls start at 50 feet, and large schools of horse-eye jacks swirl into silvery tornadoes along the edges. Eagle rays are common, and sponge growth here is spectacular.

West Caicos Marine National Park encompasses two miles of reef and coral wall along this uninhabited island, six miles southwest of Provo. It is the main haunt of the live-aboard boats that ply these waters, and Provo's land-based operators make the trip to West Caicos as often as possible. In consistently clear water – over 100 feet of visibility is the norm – gaudy sponge life festoons the sheer walls. The possibility of seeing flights of rays, large reef hammerhead sharks, and mantas makes West Caicos the most electrifying diving in the Turks and Caicos.

The walls start relatively deep, 50 to 70 feet, but the inshore portion of the drop-off provides plenty to see on the shallow end of your dives. Look in the shallows for flying gurnards – globe-eyed, blue-speckled

Cayman, it's the bright-lights, big-city relative to **Grand Turk**. The cozy little island of Grand Turk, just over six miles long, is the capital of the Turks and Caicos, but on any busy Saturday night along Front Street, probably as many donkeys as people stroll along the narrow road. People come to Grand Turk to dive; the donkeys presumably come for the peace and quiet.

Submerge off Grand Turk for archetypal wall diving; the conditions are perfect. The drop-off is within swimming distance of the beach, and the reef along the wall grows to within 20 feet of the surface. Diving is off the western, lee shore of the island, and calm water, coupled with the short runs, allows operators to use small, fast boats.

The 22 buoyed sites along the wall, all within **Columbus Landfall National Park**, offer swim-through tunnels, cascading sand chutes, imposing coral pinnacles, dizzying vertical drops, and undercuts where the wall actually goes beyond vertical and fades back beneath the reef. Multi-level and computer divers appreciate the shallow depths where the wall begins. You can remain close to the reef action nearly all the way up to the safety stop at the end of the dive. The reef landward of the wall has intricate hard coral formations and provides shelter for large numbers of fish. In fact, the entire west coast of the island has been designated as a national park since 1991.

Walking around **Salt Cay** is like traveling back in time over 100 years – just watch where you step. This triangular island, two miles on a side, supports a wandering menagerie of donkeys, cows, and chickens that outnumbers the human population of just more than a hundred. Donkeys tired of the bustle on Grand Turk probably wish they could hop the five-minute flight to Salt Cay to unwind. Settled in the 1600s by ambitious salt traders looking for a quick fortune in "white gold," the island is still dotted with the abandoned windmills that pumped water in and out of the salt ponds for which the island is named.

Offshore, the wall running along the western side of Salt Cay varies from a slope

fish with frilled pectoral fins that flare into butterfly wings, the better to fly away from inquisitive divers; see, too, a single room-sized sponge that lends its name to a wall site called **Elephant Ear Canyon**. At **Whiteface**, on the West Caicos wall, watch for an undercut of 60 to 160 feet where black coral and sponges drip from the ceiling like wax from a multicolored candle. The additional attraction of a mysterious anchor encrusted with bright sponges, plus squadrons of eagle rays and regular shark sightings, make this one of the best wall dives in the world.

Taking in the Turks

Whereas Provo is undeveloped compared with Nassau in the Bahamas or Grand

to a true precipice. Huge, deep-water gorgonians grow all along the wall, fanning out perpendicular to the slight current that carries their planktonic food. Just inshore of the drop-off, remarkably robust hard corals veil the shallow reef. Stands of aptly named pillar coral erupt from the reef like children's drip castles on a summer beach. **Point Pleasant** is a shallow, 20-foot dive accessible only at high tide. The reef reaches the surface and is honeycombed below with small caves and caverns. A school of glassy sweepers decorates one cave, glittering like panned gold when you shine a dive light inside. A longer boat trip brings you to the shallow wreck site of the **H.M.S. *Endymion***, a British warship that went down in 1790, with anchors, cannons, and ballast stones visible among a bright coral garden.

Salt Cay lies very close to the migration route of

the North Atlantic's humpback whale population. Sightings are common from January through March, when the whales arrive for mating and breeding. Underwater sightings are not guaranteed, but each season lucky divers can usually jump in and snorkel as the whales swim by.

On any dive in the Turks and Caicos, listen for the plaintive wails and moans of the humpbacks during their marine nursery season. The keening fills the water and echoes off the walls, creating an ethereal soundtrack for your underwater visit to this often overlooked wonderland.

Sponges (opposite) grow in a variety of shapes and sizes and shelter thousands of smaller organisms.

Sea fans (below), a type of gorgonian, are colonial animals found at depths of up to 1,200 feet.

Diving the Wall

For many scuba enthusiasts, wall diving is the ultimate underwater experience. You swim along a living reef as clouds of brightly colored fish hover among the corals. Suddenly, the bottom drops away, and there's only blue. You've flown off the edge of the world. As you hang weightless above the abyss, the sun overhead seems an aquamarine splash melting into the darker blues. You are floating over the edge of a continental shelf or deep canyon that may be thousands of feet deep.

Divers are attracted to walls for this otherworldly experience and for the chance to see marine life that does not normally approach shallow reefs. Mantas, sharks, marlin, sailfish, and tuna all live over the edge. Invertebrate life on the wall is equally spectacular, with giant barrel sponges, elephant ear sponges, and large "bushes" of black coral common in many tropical areas.

Along with these attractions come increased challenges. To safely dive walls, remember this checklist:

● Monitor your depth gauge or dive computer frequently. There will be no bottom reference by which to judge depth.

● Maintain neutral buoyancy to prevent yourself from sinking below your planned depth.

● Check your pressure gauge frequently. The increased depth means a faster rate of air consumption.

● Monitor your alertness. Increased depth increases the chance of nitrogen narcosis. Move to a shallower level if you experience symptoms such as foggy thinking, tunnel vision, nausea, dizziness, apprehensiveness, or euphoria.

● Plan your dive to be on the deepest part of the wall first, then ascend throughout the balance of your dive. This minimizes the risk of decompression problems.

TRAVEL TIPS

DETAILS

When to Go

Prime diving conditions are available from May to September, a period of calm waters and optimum visibility. Water temperatures range from 75°F in winter to 85°F in summer. In the absence of run-off (there is little rainfall on the islands), offshore conditions remain crystalline throughout most of the year; March to April, spawning season for sponges, is the exception. Daytime air temperatures reach the 90s in summer and seldom drop below 70°F in winter.

Getting There

Commercial airlines fly between Miami and Providenciales several times a week, and between Fort Lauderdale and Grand Turk three times a week. Local airlines link Provo, Grand Turk, Salt Cay, and South Caicos.

Getting Around

For a week's stay on Provo, consider renting a car. Visitors usually don't need a car on the other islands, where scooters and golf carts are the standard mode of transportation.

INFORMATION

Turks and Caicos National Marine Parks

Department of Parks, Heritage, and Environment, Grand Turk, Turks and Caicos, BWI; tel: 649-946-2801 or 649-946-2855.

Turks and Caicos Tourist Office

11645 Biscayne Boulevard, Suite 302, North Miami, FL 33181; tel: 800-241-0824 or 305-891-4117.

Turks and Caicos Resort Association

P.O. Box 251, Providenciales, Turks and Caicos, BWI; tel: 649-946-5128.

Where, When, How: Turks and Caicos Magazine

Ad Vantage Ltd., P.O. Box 192, Providenciales, Turks and Caicos, BWI; tel: 649-946-4815.

CAMPING

Ocean Outback, 649-941-5810 or 649-941-0824, offers packages for camping on otherwise deserted islands. The operator provides food, equipment, and transportation.

LODGING

PRICE GUIDE – double occupancy

$ = up to $49 $$ = $50–$99
$$$ = $100–$149 $$$$ = $150+

Caribbean Paradise Inn

P.O. Box 673, Grace Bay, Providenciales, Turks and Caicos, BWI; tel: 649-946-5020.

This new bed-and-breakfast is 200 yards from Grace Bay. The inn's 16 rooms have air-conditioning, ceiling fans, a refrigerator, television, phone, and large veranda or balcony. The resort offers direct beach access. Dive closets and rinse tanks are on the premises; fishing, golf, restaurants, and shopping are within walking distance. $$$–$$$$

Castaways Beach House

c/o Viking Resort, 680 East Lake Road, Penn Yan, NY 14527; tel: 800-645-1179 or 315-536-7061 or 649-946-6921.

Open mid-November to mid-April, this oceanfront resort on Salt Cay has six one-bedroom apartments with kitchens and a large private deck facing the sea. Outside the tourist areas, Castaways is more of a retreat than a glitzy resort. Salt Cay Divers is available for guests. $$

Eagles Rest Villas

240 Pebble Beach Boulevard, Suite 712, Naples, FL 34113; tel: 800-645-1179 or 941-793-7157.

These duplexes on Middle Caicos, the least developed island, offer comfort with a Caribbean atmosphere. Seven units are available, including beachfront villas and fully equipped condos with up to three bedrooms. Eagles Rest also rents dive equipment and boats. $$$–$$$$

Ocean Club Resort

153 East Chestnut Hill Road, Newark, DE 19713; tel: 800-457-8787 or 649-946-5880.

These 100 luxury suites adjoin a strip of sandy beach on Provo's Grace Bay. All have kitchens, air conditioning, phone, and television. A first-rate scuba shop shares the premises, and dive enthusiasts can either hop on the boat at the dock or wade in from the beach. $$$$

Seagate

P.O. Box 505, Penns Road, Providenciales, Turks and Caicos, BWI; tel: 800-645-1179 or 649-946-4706.

This Mediterranean-style villa houses six units. The one-, two-, and three-bedroom condominiums are equipped with a kitchen, ceiling fans, and air-conditioning. The manager arranges car rentals, diving, and other activities. $$$$

DIVE OPERATORS

Blue Water Divers

P.O. Box 124, Grand Turk, Turks and Caicos, BWI; tel: 649-946-2432.

This three-boat operation offers instruction for small groups and gives special attention to novice divers. Services include guided dives, dive and photo equipment sales and rental, and PADI certification up to the divemaster level.

Cecil Ingam's Sea Eye Diving

P.O. Box 67, Grand Turk, Turks and Caicos, BWI; tel: 800-645-1179 or 649-946-1407.

This full-service shop offers daily trips to the Grand Turk Wall. Services include dive and photo equipment sales and rental, complete PADI and NAUI instruction, and numerous specialty courses.

Dive Provo

5601 Powerline Road, Suite 206, Ft. Lauderdale, FL 33309; tel: 800-234-7768 or 954-351-9771 or 649-946-5029.

This PADI dive center on Grace Bay in Provo offers equipment sales and rental, and training for referral, resort, open-water, and advanced certification. Other activities include biking, parasailing, golfing, fishing, kayaking, and windsurfing.

Flamingo Divers

P.O. Box 322, Providenciales, Turks and Caicos, BWI; tel: 800-204-9282 or 649-946-4193.

Daily trips include boat, guide, two tanks, weights, snacks, and hotel transfer. Discounts are available for multi-dive and accommodation packages. The operator is based at Erebus Inn. Services include equipment rental, guided dives, and PADI certification to the divemaster level.

Oasis Divers

P.O. Box 137, Grand Turk, Turks and Caicos, BWI; tel: 800-892-3995 or 649-946-1128.

The operator has more than a decade of experience on the walls of Grand Turk and caters to small groups aboard 28-foot boats. Services include equipment, camera, and video rental, hotel pickup, PADI certification, and specialty training.

Excursions

Little Water Cay

Turks and Caicos Tourist Office, 11645 Biscayne Boulevard, Suite 302, North Miami, FL 33181; tel: 800-241-0824 or 305-891-4117.

Little Water Cay is ruled by the endangered Turks and Caicos rock iguana. Located near Provo, the island is part of 33 protected areas in the country's national park system. Visitors pay a fee to go ashore and wander among the iguanas on raised boardwalks. Snorkeling around the cay is good, and a combination trip to see the prehistoric-looking creatures and browse the shallows is a worthy venture. Sand Dollar Cruises, 649-946-5238, offers daily trips.

Molasses Reef

Turks and Caicos National Museum, P.O. Box 188, Grand Turk, Turks and Caicos, BWI; tel: 649-946-2160.

The inspiration for the Turks and Caicos Islands National Museum was a 10-year archaeological investigation of the Molasses Reef, the wreck site of an early-16th-century Spanish ship. Archaeologists speculate that the wreck, the oldest European ship ever found in the new world, may be that of *La Pinta*, one of Christopher Columbus's ships. Coral breaks the surface at the site, where, in addition to wrecks, the deep-water side of the reef makes for a memorable dive. Sharks, spotted eagle rays, and Nassau groupers appear frequently.

Iguana Cay

Turks and Caicos Internet Reservations Center, 240 Pebble Beach Boulevard, Suite 712, Naples, FL 34113; tel: 800-645-1179 or 941-793-7157.

Dubbed a "lovers' drop-off" by tour operators, Iguana Cay is reached by a 15-minute boat ride from Providenciales. Clients are furnished with an umbrella, a picnic lunch, mask, fins, snorkel, and iguana food. About 60 of the reptiles, eager for a handout, wander the sandy islet. Before the boat returns four to six hours later, visitors have plenty of time to explore offshore wonders, including colorful reefs within a few fin kicks.

U.S.
Virgin Islands

CHAPTER **10**

The flat blue water behind the dive boat bubbles and foams, and soon a pair of heads emerge, broad grins visible behind their regulators. Two by two, divers climb onto the boat and gather – still dripping wet, still wearing their tanks – to compare notes on what they saw.   ◆   The post-dive huddle is a common phenomenon in most Caribbean destinations, but here in the **U.S. Virgin Islands** (U.S.V.I.) there's a subtle difference. Instead of the jaded, too-cool-to-be-impressed banter of "experienced" divers, these vacationers happily revel in the smallest details of a common parrotfish (or a turtle, ray, tarpon, or moray eel). They aren't out to impress anyone. They're just enjoying themselves.   ◆   That's one of the benefits of diving this trio of islands erroneously dubbed a "beginner's destination." Thanks to shallow ocean banks that limit many dive sites to a maximum depth of 80 feet, the U.S.V.I. are an extremely beginner-friendly destination, but experienced

Renowned for shallow, novice-friendly diving, these islands offer a sampler of Caribbean marine life and culture.

divers will find deep wall-diving, too. Another reason vets turn up their noses: diving's shopworn cliché – gin-clear, 100-foot visibility – doesn't apply. Because of an abundance of plankton in the water, visibility averages 60 feet with occasional peaks of 100. These tiny organisms form the base of the aquatic food chain, and while they do reduce visibility, they also fuel a dynamic ecosystem of diverse and colorful marine life. So leave the experts to their snobbery. Who wouldn't want to dive islands where colorful parrotfish outnumber divers, sea turtles and southern stingrays are frequent dive companions, and green moray eels are so common that divers have gotten blasé about their presence?

Cruz Bay is the commercial heart of St. John, with several blocks of businesses, restaurants, and shops, and ferries from nearby islands.

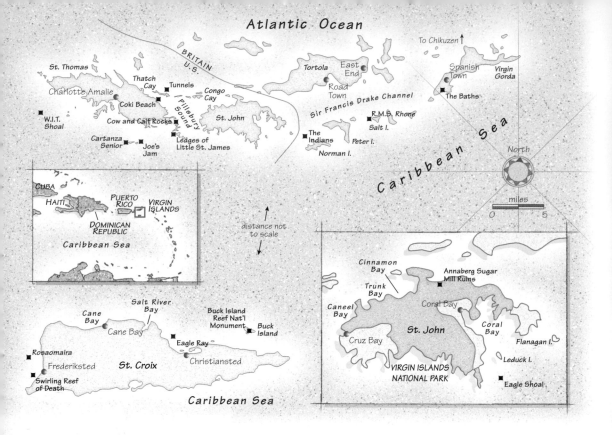

The flag flying over the islands of St. Thomas, St. John, and St. Croix is the Stars and Stripes, but the warm trade wind snapping it to attention is as West Indian as peas and rice. In fact, everywhere you look in the U.S. Virgin Islands, you see a mix of Caribbean ambiance and American convenience.

Situated 1,730 miles southeast of Miami, the islands are straight from a Technicolor idea of paradise: green peaks fringed by palm-lined beaches and lapped by aquamarine bays. If you've never traveled the Caribbean before, this is a great place to start. A U.S. territory since 1917, the islands offer easy flight connections and no hassles with immigration, currency, or language, but they still serve up a full, flavorful dose of Caribbean culture – and diving.

Each of the three U.S. islands offers a decidedly different combination of div-ing and topside diversions. The choice is yours.

Wrecks and Reefs

One of the most visited islands in the Caribbean, **St. Thomas** is a popular cruise-ship port of call, duty-free shopping capital, and international jet-set destination. A thriving seaport since the 1600s, the capital city of **Charlotte Amalie** is also packed with historic sites.

More than 40 recognized dive sites ring St. Thomas, and since most dives are only 15 to 45 minutes away by boat, a morning of diving at two locations usually has you back in time for lunch and after-noon sightseeing.

The most popular dive sites lie along the southern shore of the island, or in the north end of **Pillsbury Sound**. It's not necessary to go below 60 feet on some of the prettiest reefs, like **Tunnels of Thatch Cay** and **Ledges of Little St. James**. One of the finest examples is **Cow and Calf Rocks**, named for the twin boulders that break the surface. Below the surface, they are connected by a subway system of tunnels decorated in the paint-splatter pattern of colorful encrusting sponges. As you fin your way past schools of the small, pot-bellied baitfish known as glassy sweepers, you end up inside the famous "champagne cork," a tunnel in which surge action sends you shooting out the side of the reef like a human cannonball.

On other moderate depth sites like **Joe's Jam**, coral ridges slope down to 70 feet. There are popular wreck dives like the freighter **W.I.T. *Shoal***, and the *Cartanza Senior*, a broken barge located in the protected shallows off **Little Buck Island**. Shore diving for all skill levels is available at **Coki Beach**, a popular spot for resort courses and certification classes.

Dive, Snorkel, Hike

Located just three miles across Pillsbury Sound from the east end of St. Thomas, **St. John** manages to exist worlds away from its larger neighbor. With 51 splendid beaches and bays, and a national park covering two-thirds of the island, St. John is the nature lover's alternative to bustling St. Thomas. It even has a woodsy fragrance that travel writer Bucky McMahon described as "a mixture of cinnamon, wild soursop, bay rum, and a mimosa-like tree known locally as mother's kiss – the peculiar scent of the West Indies, like something tasty baking in dry heat."

Pack a snorkel and a good pair of shoes, because the national park on St. John has some great hiking trails and some of the most picturesque beaches you'll find anywhere, including **Caneel**, **Cinnamon**, and **Trunk Bays**. You can also soak up the local culture by touring the ruins of the 18th-century **Annaberg Sugar Plantation** or by "liming" (local slang for relaxing) in "downtown" Cruz Bay.

As for the scuba sites, you can see it all on a typical St. John dive like **Congo Cay**. Here, in water no deeper than 80 feet, you'll find hunting parties of the big, steely tarpon herding massive waves of baitfish. Grizzled hawksbill turtles lumber by inches away, indifferent to the divers who have come to

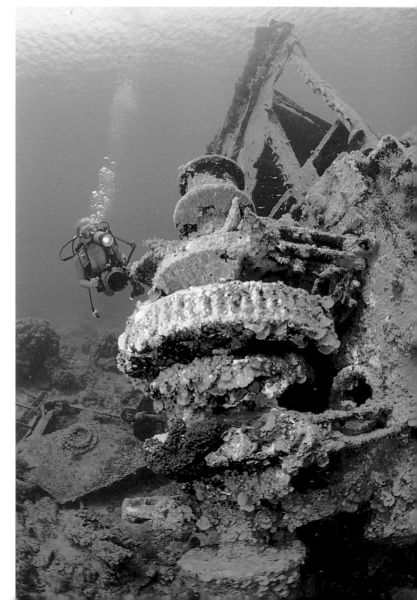

A trumpetfish (left) hovers head-down near the seafloor, waiting to suck unwary prey into its snout.

Cartanza Senior (right), a cargo ship lying at a depth of about 40 feet, is an excellent wreck for novice divers to explore.

Frederiksted Pier by Night

The local kids must have seen divers do this before, but maybe there isn't much else to do on a Friday night in Frederiksted on St. Croix. So they watched and laughed as the divers wiggled into wet suits and slipped on masks.

Providing humor was a small price to pay for the cheap thrills that evening, a night dive on Frederiksted Pier. With a maximum depth of 40 feet, the concrete pilings of the large boat dock offer almost limitless bottom time and an incredible array of animals, from schools of grunts to seahorses and crabs.

In the beam of a dive light, orange cup corals dance like flames as they extend their tentacles to feed. Normally shy moray eels swim from piling to piling, and lobsters scuttle across the sand. Playing an aquatic game of hide-and-seek, you just swim from piling to piling to see what's clinging to each one. At the east end of the pier, a granite foundation makes a rocky shelter for invertebrates such as juvenile spotted and spiny lobsters, arrow crabs, octopuses, and banded coral shrimp.

The original wooden pier was damaged by Hurricane Hugo in 1989, torn down, and replaced by the current version, giving divers a chance to see how the ocean goes about colonizing a new structure. Only pieces of the old pier remain, but the new pilings have attracted their own mix of intriguing marine life.

Local dive shops lead dives to the pier, or you can do it yourself – just be sure there aren't any large ships scheduled to dock when you go.

Secretive creatures, octopuses (above) are fond of a good hiding place – even a tin can.

Longsnout seahorses (below) often hook their tails onto a coral branch to secure their six-inch bodies in the current.

Elkhorn coral (right) forms colonies that spread up to 12 feet in diameter. Like other hard corals, it requires water temperatures between 70° and 85°F.

explore this rock island converted by the ocean into a living mural of hard corals, sponges, and delicate, lacy sea fans. You start the dive by settling down in the sand flats to commune with the leathery-backed southern stingrays buried in the sand, and you end it in a waving field of sea rods and sea fans that sway to the ocean's rhythms. From **Coral Bay**, located on the far east end of St. John, the list of dive sites includes **Eagle Shoal**, a large reef plateau with a hollow center that is accessed by numerous tunnels safe for beginners as long as they stay in ambient light. **Flanagan**, a deeper reef exposed to open ocean

conditions, features a mini-wall from 35 to 80 feet, and for beginners, the fringing reefs of **Leduck Island** are spur-and-groove reefs with an abundance of tiny tropical reef fish.

Dive, Dive, Dive

At 84 square miles, **St. Croix** is the largest of the U.S. Virgin Islands. It also stands out from her sister islands for the steeply sloping wall that runs along the north shore.

Larger than St. Thomas but almost as laid-back as St. John, the island is undergoing a tourist renaissance. In 1999, new construction included a hotel and casino complex and a boardwalk linking hotels, restaurants, and dive shops along the waterfront of Christiansted Harbor.

The two largest towns on the island, **Christiansted** and **Frederiksted**, both provide access to St. Croix's wealth of diving options. Off Christiansted, the wall begins sloping away about a quarter-mile from shore, dropping to hundreds of feet, but there are plenty of sites suited to intermediate and beginning divers as well. **Blue Hole** is a shallow coral garden of sea fans and brain and star corals marked by a 40-foot-diameter sand bowl at its center. Just outside the bay, **Eagle Ray** is a sloping series of sand gullies running between coral ledges. With depths of 30 to 80 feet, this beginner-friendly dive suits advanced divers too, thanks to the frequent sightings of eagle rays and sea turtles.

Even some of the deeper wall dives start shallow enough to make beginners feel comfortable. At **Cane Bay Drop-off**, just 40 feet of depth puts you on a coral garden of sea whips and brain corals dominated by schools of creole wrasse, black durgon, and blue chromis, and you can dive it from the beach. Accessible by boat, the drop-off at **Salt River Canyon West** offers a sheer vertical

plunge sprouting pipe organs of purple tube sponges, as well as deepwater gorgonians and black coral saplings.

From Frederiksted on the west shore of the island, you can dive a dense sloping patch reef that erupts from the sandy bottom. At the misnamed **Swirling Reef of Death**, for example, hordes of diverse tropical fish populate a calm, shallow site. Divers of all skill levels also enjoy the armada of wreck dives found off Frederiksted. The flagship wreck is the lady in red – the intact freighter *Rosaomaira*. You'll know her by the clingy red-and-orange dress of encrusting sponges.

So maybe you won't find the U.S. Virgin Islands on the hot list of dive destinations compiled by the been-there, done-that crowd. You won't find the dive boat full of self-styled experts, either. Instead, you'll meet a group of relaxed, happy-to-be-here divers who haven't forgotten how to enjoy the simple pleasures of a day under water.

TRAVEL TIPS

DETAILS

When to Go

Prime diving conditions exist in summer, when seas are calm and clear and hotel rates drop as much as 40 percent. Nearly constant trade winds sweep the islands and moderate the warm climate. The average year-round temperature is 78°F, but temperatures can reach the high 80s in summer. Expect average underwater visibility of 60 feet, with occasional peaks of 100 feet. Water temperatures stay in the low 80s year-round. Like many Caribbean islands, the U.S. Virgins are packed with travelers during winter months and holidays.

How to Get There

Commercial airlines offer service between several U.S. mainland cities and San Juan, Puerto Rico, then on to St. Thomas and St. Croix. St. John is reached by a short ferry ride from St. Thomas.

Getting Around

Cabs are readily available at airports, hotels, and ferry docks. Cars may be rented at the airports on St. Thomas and St. Croix and at Cruz Bay on St. John. Note: Motorists drive on the left side of the road.

INFORMATION

U.S. Virgin Islands Department of Tourism

P.O. Box 6400, St. Thomas, USVI 00804; tel: 800-372-8784 or 340-774-8784.

CAMPING

There are two camping areas on St. John. Cinnamon Bay Campground, 800-539-9798 or 340-776-6330, lies inside a national park, a short walk from the beach. Its 112 sites include primitive spots, tent-covered platforms, and cottages. Make reservations well in advance. The privately owned Maho Bay Campground, 800-392-9004 or 340-776-6240, has 114 tent cottages outfitted with kitchen supplies, a dining area, and deck. A restaurant is on the property.

LODGING

PRICE GUIDE – double occupancy

$ = up to $49 $$ = $50–$99

$$$ = $100–$149 $$$$ = $150+

Colony Cove

3221 Estate Golden Rock, St. Croix, USVI 00820; tel: 800-828-0746 or 340-773-1965.

Four buildings comprise this beachfront resort, which has 60 two-bedroom, two-bath condos. Each unit includes a full kitchen, washer and dryer, television, VCR, and balcony. Bedrooms are air-conditioned, and guests have full use of the swimming pool and tennis courts. Dive packages are available. $$$–$$$$

Hotel Caravelle

44A Queen Cross Street, St. Croix, USVI 00820; tel: 800-223-6510 or 340-773-0687.

On the water's edge in historic Christiansted, this European-style hotel integrates modern amenities and old-world charm. The hotel's 44 rooms offer a private bath, air-conditioning, television, phone, and refrigerator. Hotel Caravelle partners with St. Croix Ultimate Bluewater Adventures to arrange sailing, fishing, and diving excursions from the hotel dock. Beaches, tennis courts, and two golf courses are nearby. $$$

Estate Concordia Studios

20-27 Estate Concordia, Cruz Bay, St. John, USVI 00830; tel: 800-392-9004 or 340-693-5855.

Surrounded by a national park, Concordia's 10 condominium units are situated above a salt pond, set back from the beach. Most accommodations consist of a large open room and kitchen; a few units offer loft-style bedrooms. A pool and laundry room are on the premises. $$–$$$$

Galleon House

Government Hill, P.O. Box 6577, Charlotte Amalie, St. Thomas, USVI 00804; tel: 800-524-2052 or 340-774-6952.

Galleon House is located on Main Street, one block from the island's central shopping area and a short walk from St. Thomas Harbor. Fourteen guest rooms with air-conditioning are spread out among several hillside buildings. A small swimming pool is on the grounds. The price includes a continental breakfast. $$–$$$

Sapphire Beach Resort and Marina

P.O. Box 8088, St. Thomas, USVI 00801; tel: 800-524-2090 or 340-775-6100.

Families are welcome at this relaxed resort. Children under 18 stay free in their parents' rooms, and there's a kids' club for ages 4 to 12. A quarter-acre pool, watersports facility, and dive shop are on the premises. All 171 suites and villas have balconies with ocean views, kitchens, and spacious quarters. The resort borders two crescent-shaped beaches and encompasses a 67-slip marina. $$$–$$$$

DIVE OPERATORS

Admiralty Dive Center

P.O. Box 307065, St. Thomas, USVI 00803; tel: 888-900-3483 or 340-777-9802.

Admiralty partners with three St. Thomas hotels to provide discount accommodation packages. The center's two 25-foot dive boats accommodate six divers each. Services include equipment sales and rental, and full PADI and NAUI certification.

Chris Sawyer Diving Center

6300 Estate Frydenhoj, Suite #29, St. Thomas, USVI 00802-1411; tel: 800-882-2965 or 340-775-7320.

In operation since 1982, the center leads excursions to popular and lesser-known sites in both the British and U.S. Virgin Islands. Twelve divers ride aboard a 40-foot boat. Equipment is included in the dive price. Training includes open-water, advanced, and referral certification. $$

Low Key Watersports

P.O. Box 716, St. John, USVI 00831; tel: 800-835-7718 or 340-693-8999.

Diving St. John and the surrounding cays, this PADI five-star instructor development center runs two boats, a 42- and 36-footer, and caters to small groups. Services include equipment sales and rental and guided dives. PADI resort and referral training is available as well as certification to the instructor level. $$

St. Croix Ultimate Bluewater Adventures, Inc.

14 Caravelle Arcade, Christiansted, St. Croix, USVI 00820; tel: 877-789-7282 or 340-773-5994.

The operator's fast boats reach most of the island's dive sites within 20 minutes. Reservations for snorkeling trips, hotels, condos, and rental cars are available. Equipment is included in the dive price. Dive charters, PADI certification through divemaster, and resort courses are available. $$

Excursions

St. Kitts-Nevis

Department of Tourism, 414 East 75th Street, New York, NY 10021; tel: 800-582-6208 or 212-535-1234.

The islands of St. Kitts and Nevis are linked not only by ferry but by common history as British colonies and, since 1967, a federation that made the neighbors a self-governing state. Divers off Nevis observe turtles and squirrelfish in the coral grottoes of the Caves. For a classic Caribbean shallow dive, try St. Kitts' Booby Shoals, with depths of 30 feet. Bring hiking shoes to explore Brimstone Hill Fortress on St. Kitts; the restored 18th-century outpost was termed "the Gibraltar of the West Indies."

St. Martin/St. Maarten

St. Martin Tourism Board, tel: 312-751-7800, or St. Maarten Tourism Board, tel: 800-786-2278.

This island has two names, resulting from an odd political confederation. At 37 square miles, it's the smallest landmass shared by two countries (France and the Netherlands) and one of the most visited islands in the Caribbean. Snorkeling is the simplest way to explore the underwater nature reserve on the northeast shore. The wreck of a 133-foot-long British war frigate lies in 15 to 45 feet of water about a mile off the island's southern coast.

Eagle Shoals, St. John

Low Key Watersports, P.O. Box 716, St. John, USVI 00831; tel: 800-835-7718 or 340-693-8999.

Compared to crowded St. Thomas, St. John is visited by only a handful of tourists, who arrive by ferry in Cruz Bay. Few travelers cross the island to the village of Coral Bay, the jumping-off point for dive trips to Eagle Shoals, a coral labyrinth of swim-throughs, ledges, and tunnels that connects to a central cavern. The site is best suited to intermediate divers. Dive operators usually limit shoals trips to summer, when the weather is calm.

British Virgin Islands

Like ghosts dancing around an ethereal ballroom, sun-bleached sailboats flutter across the antifreeze-blue waters of the **British Virgin Islands** (B.V.I.). So many boats, in fact, that the sound of canvas whipping the wind and lines clanging on aluminum masts is at times almost deafening. Divers, however, prefer the silent world beneath all that tacking and jibing, where they quietly savor an altogether different kind of nautical experience. Shipwrecks – scores of them – litter the shallow coral gardens of the B.V.I. ◆ The Virgin Islands form the bony elbow in a long, gangly arm of islands that embraces the Caribbean Sea and shield it from the roiling, swelling North Atlantic. Like brothers separated at birth, the U.S. and British Virgin Islands seem a world apart, even if divided by only a mile of ocean. Sailing into the British side, you can immediately feel a difference. The population thins, the pace slows, and the atmosphere becomes a bit more reserved. The high-rise resorts

The atmosphere is mellow and the diving first-rate in this quiet corner of the Caribbean.

and cruise-ship armadas of the U.S. Virgins morph into whitewashed sailboats and romantic inns no taller than the palm trees. ◆ That's just the way the locals want to keep it. Islanders held a vote a few years ago on whether or not to install traffic lights in the capital, **Road Town**. Today, cars putter around the island, never having to stop at a single red light. And you won't find a hotel chain or franchise burger joint – they've been outlawed. What you will discover are restaurants with character, and charming inns and resorts that are more intimate than corporate. ◆ So if you're wondering whether the B.V.I. are for you, take this simple test. If you're looking for heart-pounding nightlife or

Enormous granite boulders form a sunlit grotto at the Baths, a popular diving and snorkeling spot near Virgin Gorda's southernmost point.

Azure vase sponges
(left) seldom grow taller
than 18 inches.

The R.M.S. *Rhone*
(below), at depths of
20 to 80 feet, can be
explored by both scuba
divers and snorkelers.

Volcanic activity
formed caves and out-
crops such as those at
the Chimney (opposite)
between Tortola and
the Dogs.

American-style infrastructure, search elsewhere. If not, you may just love these
islands, where there's a conspicuous absence
of the global tourist industry that seems
to have washed ashore on other tropical
isles and the only pick-up scene is the daily
ritual of boats collecting divers and snorkelers
from resort docks.

Wreck-Divers' Wonderland

Oddly enough, thousands of people made
their first wreck dive right here on the **R.M.S.
*Rhone*** without even realizing it. Granted, it
was made vicariously through Nick Nolte
and Jacqueline Bisset on the set of the 1977
flick *The Deep*, but for many, this first dive
introduced them to the mysterious and
beautiful world of wrecks.

Today, divers come here to rekindle some
of that mystery, making the *Rhone* the B.V.I.'s
most popular dive. But the wreck is not just
some Hollywood prop. Her fabled history
predates the movie by more than a century.
In the mid-1800s, she delivered passengers
and mail on a route that took her to the far-
flung corners of the Caribbean. Part sailing
ship, part propeller-driven steamer, the 310-
foot vessel was revolutionary in design, built
at the cusp of nautical technology. But Mother
Nature has no pity for humans' futile efforts.
Attempting – unsuccessfully – to shelter her
from a hurricane in 1867, the crew of the
Rhone tucked her into a cove off **Salt Island**,

which would become her final resting place.

Over time, the ship split in two, dividing her bow and stern sections into two completely different dives and experiences, both protected by marine-park status. Her bow is more intact and lies in water about 80 feet deep, while her stern is strewn in pieces from 20 to about 60 feet below the surface. In 13 decades on the seafloor, the *Rhone* has grown a dazzling Technicolor coat of sponges and corals and attracted a dizzying array of tropical reef fish, including yellow-speckled French angelfish, pastel-hued parrotfish, and schooling snapper, jacks, and grunts.

The fish, coral, and other creatures you'll encounter on the *Rhone* and throughout the B.V.I.'s reefs are standard Caribbean fare. Larger, more tasty fish species like grouper may be more common on restaurant menus, but there's no shortage of smaller tropicals. Hawksbill and green turtles are a dime a dozen, and you're quite likely to see a spotted eagle ray or two, and plenty of moray eels. If you're lucky, you may snag a rare glimpse of humpback whales, especially from December through April, when the leviathans come here to calve. Look for them frolicking in the **Sir Francis Drake Channel**.

Home of Sharks and Barracudas

While the *Rhone* may be the most dived of the B.V.I.'s – and perhaps the entire Caribbean's – myriad wrecks, the remote *Chikuzen* is its best-kept secret. Two decades ago, the engine of the 246-foot Korean refrigerated ship died, but fishermen continued to take advantage of her cold storage and anchored her off St. Martin. After her days of service were over, she was banished to the open seas and set ablaze, to be sunk in deep water. But she drifted and drifted. As she neared the B.V.I., nervous locals dispatched a tugboat to steer her clear of shore. She finally sank on her port side in 75 feet of water nearly 10 miles north of **Virgin Gorda**. On a calm day, it's a perfect site for beginning and intermediate divers. The maximum depth is 75 feet, but there's plenty to see without venturing to the very bottom.

Although the *Chikuzen* is much younger

than the *Rhone*, it is no less fascinating, and a trip to the *Chikuzen* pays off with rare sightings of really big fish, including sharks, jacks, and shoals of barracuda. If you're the first in the water, you stand a good chance of seeing a handful of reef sharks that call the wreck home and are easily spooked by the noisy dive-boat engine and divers splashing down into the water. Sure to stick around, however, are thick masses of tomtates, snappers, jacks, and spadefish crowding the hull, which is slowly gathering a furry coat of corals and sponges and will someday be as colorful as the *Rhone*. A school of barracuda forms a silvery curtain on the wreck, draped on top of each other from the surface to the seafloor.

Wrecks like the *Rhone* and *Chikuzen* may elicit gung-ho machismo and a little derring-do, but before you set off in search of Davey Jones's locker, be sure your diving skills are shipshape. Never enter an overhead environment such as the inside of a ship or cave unless you're properly trained in wreck penetration. Upon descending, orient yourself on the wreck before leaving the anchor line, so you know where to return to make your ascent. Keep your gear streamlined by clipping your hoses, lights, and consoles close to your body. Carry a dive knife in a spot you can easily reach, in case you get tangled on a line or net, both of which tend to snag on these marine obstacles.

No Artificial Colors or Flavors

If you're looking for a break from diving the artificial reefs, try some of the B.V.I.'s natural ones. **The Indians**, between Norman and Peter Islands, are so named for four rocky pinnacles that protrude from the water like a feathered headdress. Below the waves, a garden of staghorn and elkhorn corals are tended by throngs of lively tropical fish. Above water and below, **The Baths** of **Virgin Gorda** are a unique, otherworldly experience. Thrust up from the earth's molten core in rivers of magma, the giant granite boulders look like a big pile of stony Legos. The jumble of rocks creates sunken

High-speed catamarans (left) make quick, comfortable trips to sites around the islands and serve as stable dive platforms.

Sailing (opposite, top) leaves you free to explore on your own or join a dive operator's scuba group.

A brittle star (right) moves swiftly across a sponge. Its flexible, spiny arms can span up to eight inches from tip to tip.

Wherever the Wind Blows You

If you feel torn between the sedate, slow-motion world of sailing and the butterflies-in-your-stomach, adrenaline rush of scuba diving, you can have the best of both worlds. The British Virgin Islands is the home of rendezvous diving, where the dive shop comes to you, wherever you are.

Sailing here is like a walk in the park. The charter companies give practically anyone with a captain's license the keys to a sailboat; the boat's length is relative to the thickness of your wallet. The calm, protected water of the Sir Francis Drake Channel is a great place to take a weeklong spin, and routes among islands can be navigated visually, as the islands are never out of sight.

As captain of your own live-aboard dive yacht, you'll find that with one call on the marine radio, a local dive shop brings you tanks and any piece of gear you need, from mask to flippers. Just be sure to have your certification card ready. On a bareboat (you drive) or crewed (you're just along for the ride) sailboat charter, you set the dive itinerary and choose your favorite sites. Really enjoy a particular reef? Dive it again; you're the boss.

For those who prefer an organized tour, dive shops also pick you up off your sailboat and take you out for a guided one- or two-tank dive. Afterward, the boat drops you back on your yacht, no matter where it sailed off to. Now that's service.

antechambers filled with glassy sweepers and lighted eerily by sun beaming through cracks and crevices, painted with rainbow-hued encrusting sponges and orange cup corals.

The shallow continental shelf that rings the islands dictates maximum depths of around 80 feet and has given the islands a reputation for being more of a beginner dive destination. But the short boat rides of 15 to 30 minutes to dive sites and shallow depths that allow marathon bottom times appeal to even the most jaded divers. While it's possible to squeeze in three or four dives a day, this is a place where even die-hard divers aren't afraid to take it easy.

While most people get their thrills on two-tank morning dives (and sightsee or relax the rest of the day), some nitrogen-starved

divers opt for additional afternoon and night dives. Most B.V.I. dive operators offer hands-on service, which means the first time you haul your scuba gear to the dive boat is also the last for the duration of your stay. There's no mandatory depth limit, either, since your gauges never read more than two digits. The longer you're in the water, the colder you'll get, so wear a little thicker wet suit if you get chilled easily.

After a week on the British Virgin Islands, you will either long for or question the logic of a society with traffic lights, fast-food chains, and home-shopping networks. But rest assured, there will always be a place where you can escape the hectic pace of the modern world – and now you know exactly where it is.

TRAVEL TIPS

DETAILS

When to Go

In this idyllic, year-round climate, temperatures range from 75° to 85°F. Rain is infrequent, except in early autumn, when downpours usually last only 15 minutes. Prevailing trade winds keep the humidity to a minimum.

How to Get There

Major airlines offer transfers to the British Virgin Islands through San Juan, Puerto Rico, or St. Thomas, U.S. Virgin Islands. There are no direct flights from the United States.

Getting Around

Depending on the island, taxi service may be readily available (for example, on Tortola) or rare (on the smaller out islands). Reserve a rental car well in advance, especially during the winter season. Remember: Motorists drive on the left side of the road. Travel between islands is by plane, water taxi, or ferry.

INFORMATION

British Virgin Islands Tourist Board

1804 Union Street, San Francisco, CA 94123; tel: 800-835-8530 or 415-775-0344 or 212-696-0400; or P.O. Box 134, Road Town, Tortola, BVI; tel: 284-494-3134.

British Virgin Islands Hotel and Commerce Association

P.O. Box 376, Road Town, Tortola, BVI; tel: 284-494-3514.

CAMPING

Brewer's Bay Campground, 284-494-3463, on Tortola has 22 fully equipped sites, as well as some bare sites on the beach. White Bay Campground, 284-495-9312, on Jost Van Dyke has tent and screened cabin sites, as well as bare sites perched on the bluff over a bay. Anegada has three camping options: Anegada Beach Campground, 284-495-9466; Mac's Place, 284-495-8020; and Neptune's Treasure, 284-495-9439.

LODGING

PRICE GUIDE – double occupancy

$ = up to $49 $$ = $50–$99

$$$ = $100–$149 $$$$ = $150+

Bitter End Yacht Club

P.O. Box 46, Virgin Gorda, BVI; tel: 800-872-2392 or 284-494-2746.

Informal yet elegant, the Club has 95 units (40 of which are air-conditioned) scattered among hillside chalets and beachfront villas. Bay views are available. Guests may also stay aboard one of the 30-foot yachts; sailing privileges, dockage, daily maid service, meals in the Yacht Club, and overnight provisions are available. A dive operator is on the premises. $$$$

Guavaberry Spring Bay Vacation Homes

P.O. Box 20, Virgin Gorda, BVI; tel: (284) 495-5227.

These one- and two-bedroom redwood cottages are set in lush undergrowth just a few minutes' walk from Spring Bay's gold, sandy beach. The 14 cottages each have a living and dining area, plus a sun deck. The Baths are to the south, and the island's main town, with restaurants and shopping near the Virgin Gorda Yacht Harbor, is a mile to the north. The managers make scuba arrangements with nearby operators. $$–$$$

Long Bay Beach Resort and Villas

c/o Island Destinations, P.O. Box 284, Larchmont, NY 10538; tel: 800-729-9599 or 914-833-3300.

Perched on a 52-acre hillside estate, this Tortola resort is 10 minutes from the island's north shore. The retreat offers 118 rooms and cottages, plus 26 two- and three-bedroom villas with a kitchen, living room, and large deck. Ocean views are available from the hillside units; cabanas rest along a mile of white-sand beach. $$–$$$$

Nanny Cay Resort and Marina

P.O. Box 281, Road Town, Tortola, BVI; tel: 800-742-4276 or 284-494-4895.

The resort, designed for water-sports fans, occupies a 25-acre islet. Three miles from Road Town and 10 miles from the airport, Nanny Cay has 42 studios with air-conditioning, a balcony or patio, kitchenette, and television. Two swimming pools, a dive shop, sailing, snorkeling trips, deep-sea fishing, tennis courts, and dining are available. $$–$$$

Prospect Reef Resort

P.O. Box 104, Road Town, Tortola, BVI; tel: 800-356-8937 or 284-494-3311.

Guests enjoy panoramic views of Sir Francis Drake Channel. The resort, comprised of 24 two-story buildings, has 131 rooms and suites. On its 15 landscaped acres are five swimming pools, a dive shop, fitness center, and Upstairs Restaurant, hailed by *Gourmet Magazine*. Sailing, snorkeling, diving, and golf are offered. $$–$$$$

DIVE OPERATORS

Baskin in the Sun

8890 Coral Way, Suite 220, Miami, FL 33165; tel: 800-650-2084.

This full-service, PADI five-star instructor development center operates a facility on Peter Island and two shops on Tortola. At Tortola's Prospect Reef location, underwater shutterbugs can check out Rainbow Visions Photo Center and Gallery next door.

Services include equipment sales and rental and guided dives; training ranges from full certification to the instructor level.

Blue Water Divers

P.O. Box 846, Road Town, Tortola, BVI; tel: 284-494-2847.

This operator is located at Nanny Cay and Hodge's Creek but will pick up divers on a

yacht. Dive packages are available through nearby resorts. Inquire about group discounts. Services include equipment sales and rental and guided dives; training includes PADI referral, introductory, and open-water certification. $$$

Dive BVI

P.O. Box 8309, Cruz Bay, St. John, USVI 00831; tel: 800-848-7078 or 284-495-5513.

This operator, the territory's largest, has PADI five-star facilities in both Virgin Gorda and Tortola. Dives are conducted from four boats; a 45-foot catamaran leads snorkel excursions twice weekly. Services include equipment rental and guided dives; training ranges from PADI certification to instructor. $$$

Underwater Safaris

P.O. Box 139, Road Town, Tortola, BVI; tel: 800-537-7032 or 284-494-3235.

Two shops with three custom dive boats offer trips to sites near Road Town, Tortola, and Cooper Island. Custom charters may also be booked. The outfit's Rendezvous Tours meets divers on a private yacht at any popular anchorage. Services include equipment rental and guided dives; training ranges from certification through assistant instructor. $$$

Excursions

The Dogs

Dive BVI, P.O. Box 8309, Cruz Bay, St. John, USVI 00831; tel: 800-848-7078 or 284-495-5513.

With a name like the Dogs, these small, uninhabited islands west of Virgin Gorda may be expected to yield bones instead of reefs. Not so. Divers in this protected area, part of a national park, discover abundant fish life swarming the marine canyons and bridges. The site is visited by dive operators from Virgin Gorda and Tortola.

Puerto Rico

Puerto Rico Tourism Company, 666 Fifth Avenue, New York, NY 10103; tel: 800-223 6530.

The diving is classic Caribbean, with a twist. Rivers pour into the sea, reducing visibility to about 70 feet, although the fresh water attracts legions of fish. Nutrient-rich estuaries attract and sustain manatees. The best diving is from March to November. Humpbacks migrate through Puerto Rican waters in fall.

Norman Island

BVI Tourist Board, P.O. Box 134, Road Town, Tortola, BVI; tel: 800-835-8530 or 284-494-3134.

Uninhabited Norman Island, located in the southwestern end of the British Virgin Islands, is the setting for Robert Louis Stevenson's *Treasure Island*. Since 1750, the privately owned isle has yielded three buried treasures, and many individuals are convinced that more loot is to be found. These days, most visitors find the treasure underwater. At the Caves, where the shallow depth (just five feet in spots) is perfect for snorkelers, visitors explore a cave lined with coral and sponges that pushes 70 feet into the hill.

Bonaire
Netherlands Antilles

CHAPTER **12**

There may be no easier way to reach a coral reef than on the island of **Bonaire**. It's a simple drill: You walk out of your hotel room, hoist on a tank, and, sidestepping the half-naked Europeans scattered on the coral-sand beach, ease under the shallow edge of the warm Caribbean Sea. From here, you fin easily away from shore, just above the stands of elkhorn coral, until the bottom begins a gradual seaward slope. Within minutes, the sandy shelf under you becomes a living tapestry of hard and soft corals, populated with scads of tropical fish and small, colorful invertebrates. ◆ Down it goes, into the sweet everlasting blue, a yellow brick road of a slope richly textured with plate corals and orange tube sponges, black feathery starfish called crinoids, lettuce sea slugs – and more fish than the average person can even identify. And here you are, in solution with it all, soaring. In case you've forgotten, it suddenly occurs to you: *This is the reason I wanted to learn to dive in the first place.* ◆ This is the reef of Bonaire, a coral system that esteemed nature writer Barry Lopez described as "among the most astonishing in the Americas," and with almost no effort at all, you are now floating weightlessly over it. No wonder the local auto license plates carry the slogan "Diver's Paradise." Indeed, while travelers to a single place usually have widely disparate reasons for their sojourning, some 75 percent of visitors who arrive on Bonaire do so for one purpose: going underwater. ◆ And no wonder. "The visual impact of Bonaire's reefs," writes Lopez, "is further intensified by the fact that they have changed very little since [Amerigo] Vespucci's ships passed overhead." The coral here is not only easy to find;

Careful conservation keeps these reefs as pristine and abundant as they were 500 years ago.

French angelfish, one of five angelfish species found in Bonaire, often swim over the reef in pairs. They are remarkably tolerant of divers.

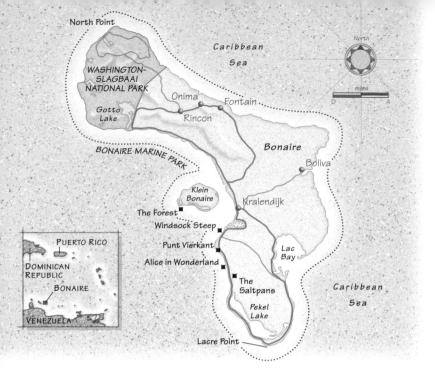

the entire system of creatures it supports is exceedingly healthy. In a world in which coral reefs are increasingly at risk, this is no small thing.

Protected and Pristine Reefs

Keenly aware of the potential and pitfalls of their easy-to-reach but fragile reef system, dive operators helped develop some of the world's most stringent marine conservation measures more than two decades ago, banning spear-fishing and coral collecting, and marking local sites with mooring buoys to stop anchor damage. By 1979, that ethic spearheaded the creation of the **Bonaire Marine Park**, which surrounds the entire 121-square-mile island,

down to depths of 200 feet. By 1992, the park got the staff it needed to keep tabs on the science and to enforce rules. Today, all divers pay an annual $10 entrance fee that allows unlimited dives in the park. The fee helps fund the park management, balancing both use and preservation, and making it one of the most successful marine preserves in the world. If a dive site is in danger of being overstressed, it's placed off limits until it recovers.

What was to be Bonaire was born over 70 million years ago some 50 miles off the northern coast of South America in a burst of volcanic eruptions. Eroded by the wind, the ebb and flow of the tides, and sea level change, the worn old volcano retreated under the sea, became covered with living coral, and then rose one more time at the end of the Ice Age. Today, its geological history can be clearly read in its topside terraces and hills, which still wear a cover of fossilized brain and star corals.

When the Spanish first sailed here 500 years ago, they found it inhabited by Caiquetio Indians, who referred to their island as *bajnaj*, for "lowland." Seventeenth-century Dutch colonists semantically massaged the Caiquetio description until today it has become *Bonaire*.

Bonaire is as arid as a desert. Outside the harbor town of **Kralendijk** and beyond, where most dive resorts occupy the inside curve of the island north of town, lie rolling clay-colored hills grooved with arroyos and studded with cactus. Indeed, topside Bonaire seems as much a part of the American Southwest as anything Caribbean. But this is part of its great biological success; with little freshwater run-off to dilute coral growth, halos of marine life entirely rim Bonaire

Color changes throughout their lives make coneys (right) difficult to identify. They can be two-tone, gold, brown, or red.

Blackbar soldierfish (opposite) lurk in caves during the day. Sometimes they swim upside down on the cave ceiling.

and the adjacent islet of **Klein** ("Little") **Bonaire** just offshore.

Almost all diving takes place off the leeward coast and from the 1,500-acre Klein Bonaire, both of which are cupped inside the tips of the boomerang-shaped larger island and sheltered from the raging easterly winds. Dive operators, centered along the crook of the lee's elbow, send boats out morning, afternoon, and evening, rotating dive sites each day.

One resort advertises itself as the home of "Diving Freedom," and that's not a bad description of how the sport is approached on this island. As a newly arrived diver, you get an orientation lecture on ecology and safety, a checkout dive, and a little plastic tag certifying you to get your tank filled and dive anywhere in the country. Where and when you go is up to you. Getting across the 600-foot-deep channel to Klein requires signing aboard a dive boat, but much of the fringing reef can be reached from shore.

First-time visitors usually welcome the guiding skills of divemasters. Even veterans appreciate a guide's help in locating cryptic and territorial creatures like the seahorse, which tends to find a favorite gorgonian and wrap its tail around the stalk. Or octopuses, which leave a garden of empty shells around their dens.

Terraces, Buttresses, and Double Reefs

With 86 marked dive sites (including 26 on Klein), it's natural that some locales are topographical clones of others. When you arrive on Bonaire, get a handy map of the island's sites at any dive shop. For now, let's go underwater and take a look at three representative sites, keeping in mind that each shares biological similarities with a number of others.

South on the coastal road from Kralendijk, you'll find the **Windsock Steep** opposite the airport runway. Like other sites accessible from shore, it is marked by a small concrete pillar with its name. Windsock is typical of the approximately 20 terrace-slope sites near the center of the island,

although it is far less commonly dived.

Enter from the beach and swim over a terrace covered with elkhorn, sponges, sea whips, and fans. Stands of staghorn coral mark the area where the terrace begins its slope into deeper water. Look seaward and you're likely to see four-foot-long barracuda, ocean triggerfish, and large tiger groupers along the reef's edge. Like other sloping shore reefs, the coral falls away into sheet corals shaped like miniature

pagodas. Here you're likely to find rock hinds, and queen and French angels – including their brightly colored juvenile versions. Peek in the cavities between the living corals for the heads of moray eels, mouths endlessly opening and closing.

For a look at the buttresses that characterize some 12 sites, hop a dive boat to **The Forest** off the southwesterly tip of Klein Bonaire. Most boats drop divers just landward of the drop-off, so you simply descend to the reef crest and fin across mountainous star corals, which give way to a wall packed with giant brain coral, patches of yellow pencil coral, and club finger coral. The wall flares out into a series of buttresses separated by distinct valleys. The site is named for the forest of black coral at 100 feet and below, delicate and spindly tentacles that are yellow and beige. The black inner stem is cut and polished by craftsmen to achieve the coveted black effect. In nature, black coral is no more aesthetically pleasing than any other coral, but because it is ordinarily limited to waters of 150 feet and deeper, its inaccessibility gives it a certain cachet, which, in countries where it's

Washington-Slagbaai National Park

The sea is not the only protected area on Bonaire. The other is a terrestrial preserve called Washington-Slagbaai National Park. If the only way you've ever experienced the Caribbean is in umbrella-drink resorts, the singularly wild grandeur of this place will pleasantly startle you – from the parrots and flamingos to the peaked limestone hills and igneous-rock bluffs. There's some pristine shore diving here, too, sites where you'll seldom see another soul except your own dive partner.

Reaching the park is an adventure in itself, accomplished by driving north from Kralendijk past an underbrush of mesquite and spiky aloe dusted red by the desert landscape, dodging feral goats and donkeys, and watching for yellow orioles flitting into pendulumlike nests dangling from tree limbs.

As you approach the northern tip of the island, you'll enter the park, pay a nominal fee, and then veer west to a spot where steep limestone cliffs bookend a picturesque cove. The main site here is Boca Slagbaai, one of the most pristine found off Bonaire. Instead of swimming straight out, enter the water from the edges of the bay. Fin out from the north and you'll glide over six cannons at depths of about 16 feet. Although they look real, they're concrete replicas, left behind after the filming of *Sharks' Treasure* in 1974. Continue swimming north and seaward until the bottom begins to drop out from under you. The slope gives way to a series of dramatic coral buttresses separated by deep valleys. Look for huge tiger groupers, torpedo-sized barracuda, and a school of giant tarpon sparkling like disco balls whenever a shaft of sunlight strikes their scales.

Enter from the south, and if you have good eyes you'll find two cannons covered with purple crustose coralline algae. These authentic guns toppled into the sea from a long-gone fort on the top of the cliff above instead of sinking with a ship. Continue beyond the cannons and watch the reef fall away into walls of mountainous star coral populated with schools of massive jacks and sleek, exotic, dark-black durgons, the Darth Vader of tropical fish.

Desert plants (left) such as cactus and aloe provide sparse cover at Washington-Slagbaai National Park.

Hilma Hooker (opposite, top), a popular Bonaire dive site, is a 235-foot smuggler's freighter that sank in 1984.

Banded butterflyfish (right) are often seen darting about the reef in pairs.

not protected, can wipe out entire colonies.

Some six dive locales have a double-reef system, and all are located on the cove below **Punt Vierkant**. **Alice in Wonderland** is the best known of these. A couple of hundred yards worth of finning from shore puts you squarely in Wonderland, but the easier way is simply to leap off a dive boat. As you sink underwater, you'll see the reef sloping down to 90 feet where it dead-ends into a flat sand channel. Explore the first reef, which is dominated by soft corals, and then head across the 100-foot-wide sand flats. Look for garden eels swaying with their heads out of their burrows, and watch as schools of goatfish poke their barbules into the sand for tiny shrimp and worms. The second reef rises up 30 feet from the 100-foot bottom, a natural tabernacle of many varieties of coral. Check out the blue water beyond for schools of large horse-eyed jacks and other pelagics.

Noticing the Details

In terms of fauna, there is a lingering belief that sites more distant from the midsection of the island contain a more diverse selection of fish. It's not true. Veteran divers report identifying just as many kinds of fish mid-island as they do on the more remote sites. What you will find off the more heavily used mid-island are voracious yellowtail snappers the size of dinner plates. Protected by law and chummed into a Pavlovian frenzy by years of hand-feeding, these fish will nibble anything that looks remotely like food, including the hair on your head.

A little advice for any site: Slow down and pay attention instead of zipping over the site as fast as your fins will take you. If you closely examine a few square yards of *any* Bonairean dive site, you will likely find animals uncommon elsewhere in the Caribbean. That includes the fingernail-sized Pederson cleaner shrimp spotted with lavender, the descriptively named corkscrew anemone, and the red-tipped fireworm, which, during certain inspirational moments, will actually rise from the bottom and swim.

Beyond ecological soundness and accessibility, the other enduring charm of Bonaire

is the sheer placid nature of its warm tropical waters. While currents swirl more ferociously at the north and south ends of the island, Klein and the middle island remain nearly always pond-calm. And because of the southerly latitude and balmy trade winds, winter chills seldom nudge the temperature too far away from the 82°F average. With little freshwater run-off, industry, or coastal development to cloud it, the water visibility frequently hits the triple digits. Wherever you submerge in this gentle Diver's Paradise, you'll find all the inhabitants still here – the jungle of hard and soft corals, the photogenic invertebrates, and the fish – doing what they did centuries ago when the Caiquetio Indians lived on a low and arid tropical island they called *bajnaj*.

TRAVEL TIPS

DETAILS

When to Go

South of the hurricane belt, Bonaire has temperatures in the 80s year-round, above and below water. The warmest days are in August and September. High season runs December through March.

How to Get There

Direct flights from North America are available on ALM, the national airline of the Netherlands Antilles, 800-327-7230. The airport is south of Kralendijk, the capital city.

Getting Around

Car rentals are available in Kralendijk and at large hotels. Taxis run on government-established rates, which are higher in the evening. Bonaire Sightseeing Tours, 011-599-7-8778, offers excursions.

INFORMATION

Bonaire Government Tourist Bureau

Kaya Libertador Simon Bolivar 12, Kralendijk, Bonaire, NA; tel: 011-599-7-8322.

Bonaire Tourist Office

Adams Unlimited, 10 Rockefeller Plaza, Suite 900, New York, NY 10020; tel: 800-266-2473 or 212-956-5912.

Bonaire Marine Park and Washington-Slaagbai National Park

Visitor Information Center at Karpata Ecological Center, P.O. Box 368, Bonaire, NA; tel: 011-599-7-8444.

CAMPING

Camping is available only at Boca Slagbaai in Washington-Slagbaai National Park for a fee of about $50 per night. A rental vehicle is necessary to reach this remote area, which has no services. For more information, contact the Bonaire Tourist Office, 800-266-2473.

LODGING

PRICE GUIDE – double occupancy

$ = up to $49	$$ = $50–$99
$$$ = $100–$149	$$$$ = $150+

Bruce Bowker's Carib Inn

P.O. Box 68, Bonaire, NA; tel: 011-599-7-8819.

This small, dive-oriented resort prides itself on repeat clients who come back for the reasonable prices, beachside location, and 24-hour availability of scuba tanks. The inn has 10 units, including a three-bedroom house, several one- and two-bedroom apartments, and standard rooms. The on-site dive shop, a PADI five-star facility, is staffed by dive instructors. $–$$

Captain Don's Habitat

c/o Maduro Dive Fantasies, 4500 Biscayne Boulevard, Suite 320, Miami, FL 33137; tel: 800-327-6709.

This informal, 93-room resort, perched on the cliffs above the Caribbean, has been operated by Captain Don Stewart since 1962. The captain helped form Bonaire's Marine Park, and about 90 percent of his guests are divers. Dive packages are available. $$–$$$$

Divi Flamingo Beach Resort and Casino

6340 Quadrangle Drive, Suite 300, Chapel Hill, NC 27514; tel: 800-367-3484 or 607-277-3484.

This classy beachfront resort north of Kralendijk has 100 seafront rooms and 40 studios. Time-share units with kitchenettes are available by the day or week. Two dive shops and two restaurants are on the premises. $$$–$$$$

Harbour Village Beach Resort

Kaya Gobernador North Debrot 72, P.O. Box 312, Bonaire, NA; tel: 800-424-0004 or 011-599-7-7500.

The island's most luxurious resort, with 64 rooms, is set on a private beach adjoining a marina. Three restaurants are on the premises. Amenities include a dive shop, pool, tennis courts, bike rentals, and water-skiing. $$$$

Sand Dollar Condominiums

Kaya Gobernador North Debrot 79, P.O. Box 262, Bonaire, NA; tel: 011-599-7-8738 or 800-288-4773.

This resort near Kralendijk offers studio apartments and one-, two-, and three-bedroom units, all with kitchens and oceanfront decks or balconies. Enroll in the resort's Fish Watching School and learn to identify at least 50 species of fish. $$$$

DIVE OPERATORS

Bon Bini Divers Bonaire

Lions Dive Resort, Kaya Gobernador North Debrot 90, Kralendijk, Bonaire, NA; tel: 011-599-7-5425.

Divers at this universal referral facility, which has two locations, complete scuba certification through any one of seven agencies, in one of five languages. Services include equipment sales, rental, and maintenance. Training includes open-water certification, and specialty courses.

Buddy Dive Resort

Kaya Gobernador Debrot 8, Kralendijk, Bonaire, NA; tel: 011-599-7-5080.

Pull up to this drive-through air-fill station, drop off your empty tanks, and grab full ones without turning off the engine. Ask for a "drive and dive" package, which includes a vehicle and unlimited air-fills.

Captain Don's Habitat

P.O. Box 88, Bonaire, NA; tel: 800-327-6709 or 011-599-7-8290.

The PADI five-star resort and photo center emphasizes "Diving Freedom." Open 24 hours a day, 365 days a year, Habitat conducts great shore diving, three daily boat dives, and night dives. Services include dive and photo equipment rental and training for all levels of certification, including specialty courses.

Dive Bonaire

T. A. Abraham Boulevard 40, Kralendijk, Bonaire, NA; tel: 011-599-7-8285.

The island's longest-running dive business is on the grounds of the Divi Flamingo Beach Resort. Shore divers have access to tanks 24 hours a day; six boats, from 36 to 42 feet, transport divers offshore; night diving is available every evening. Services include dive and photo equipment rentals, repairs, and sales. Training ranges from resort courses to divemaster, with a handful of specialty classes.

Sand Dollar Dive and Photo

Kaya Gobernador North Debrot 79, Bonaire, NA; tel: 011-599-7-5252.

Sand Dollar offers dive trips on three boats (10 to 16 divers maximum per boat) and shore diving. Services include dive and photo equipment rental and photo processing. Training ranges from PADI certification to the instructor level and is offered in six languages.

Excursions

Aruba

Aruba Tourist Bureau, 1000 Harbor Boulevard, Ground Level, Weehawken, NJ 07087; tel: 800-862-7822.

A 40-minute flight from Bonaire, whose desert landscape it resembles, the island of Aruba rises from superbly clear water. The German freighter *Antilia*, the largest wreck in the Caribbean, lies in 54 feet of water off the island's northwest shore. Follow a drop-off covered in brown, sheet, and star coral to the sunken vessel, adorned with giant tube sponges. Keep an eye out for green morays and stingrays.

Curaçao

Curaçao Tourist Board, 475 Park Avenue South, Suite 2000, New York, NY 10016; tel: 800-270-3350.

Experienced and novice divers explore dive sites almost fin to fin on the largest of the Antilles islands, a 30-minute flight from Bonaire. With a fringing reef that starts near shore, Curaçao offers shallow-water dives on the lip of the reef, combined with challenging drop-off and wall dives. The Curaçao Underwater Marine Park, on the southeast shore, is calmest in fall and winter.

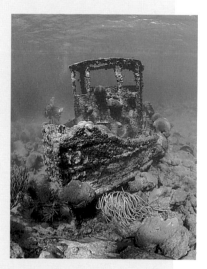

Los Roques National Park, Venezuela

Venezuela Tourism Association; tel: 415-331-0100.

For a remote adventure, take a cruise on a live-aboard through Los Roques National Park, which includes 350 small rocks and islets and miles of open water north of Venezuela. Thanks to the park's ban on fishing, divers see Nassau, black and tiger groupers, large lobsters, parrotfish, and schools of black jacks. Catch a flight to Caracas, Venezuela, from Curaçao, Bonaire, or the United States, then take an hour's flight to the main island of Los Roques to board a boat.

Grand Cayman

CHAPTER 13

The year: 1957. Chevrolets had fins, Chuck Berry had hit records, and on the island of **Grand Cayman**, a pioneer named Bob Soto had a vision of the future.   ◆   A salvage diver for the U.S. Navy in World War II, Soto thought tourists might be interested in peeking beneath the clear blue sea of his native island. With a home-built plywood boat, a surplus compressor, and a handful of early scuba regulators, he went into business selling dives to tourists on **Seven Mile Beach** – $7.50 for two tanks of air.   ◆   Back then, lounging on the long stretch of white sand that runs along Grand Cayman's leeward west shore was about all a tourist could find to do. But Soto's humble business – the first dive shop in the Caribbean – would forever change life on this island, located 490 miles south of Miami. As diving evolved from an elite macho hobby to a family-oriented vacation activity, Grand Cayman grew with it.   ◆   Stand on Seven Mile Beach today, in the capital city of **George Town**, amid the ritzy hotels and gleaming

Explore tunnels, arches, and grottoes sculpted by prolific reef-building corals in some of the Caribbean's clearest water.

condominiums, and it's hard to imagine the early days. Fleets of well-appointed boats take on divers sporting the latest in color-coordinated, high-tech gear. Where Soto once struggled to find customers, there are now almost 50 dive operators, including live-aboard dive boats, offering everything from snorkeling trips to advanced technical training. Grand Cayman, the once-quiet backwater, is now one of the most popular vacation islands in the Caribbean.   ◆   Ever since Soto talked his first customers into diving here, people have been raving about the coral underworld. With water that's considered the Caribbean's clearest (average visibility is 100 feet) and diverse

A southern stingray gets "friendly" with a diver at Stingray City. The rays have grown accustomed to humans after years of feeding.

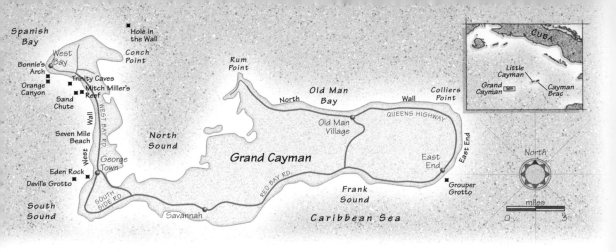

Spanish
Bay

West
Bay

Bonnie's
Arch

Orange
Canyon

Sand
Chute

Trinity Caves

Mitch Miller's
Reef

Seven Mile
Beach

Hole in
the Wall

Conch
Point

Rum
Point

North

Old Man
Bay

Colliers
Point

Wall

Little
Cayman

Grand
Cayman

Cayman
Brac

CUBA

QUEENS HIGHWAY

Old Man
Village

George
Town

North
Sound

Grand Cayman

East
End

East End

North

Eden Rock

Devil's Grotto

South
Sound

Savannah

RED BAY RD.

SOUTH
SIDE RD.

WEST BAY RD.

West
Wall

Frank
Sound

Grouper
Grotto

Caribbean Sea

miles

0   3

diving terrain found off each of its four shores, Grand Cayman is naturally well equipped for recreational diving stardom. Like her sister islands, **Cayman Brac** and **Little Cayman**, Grand Cayman is a terrestrial speck, a dry afterthought in the deepest realm of the Caribbean. Twenty-two miles long and about eight miles wide, the island rises just high enough above the sea to form a convenient place to change tanks. Just beyond the shore, the ocean floor plunges almost straight down into the 25,000-foot depths of the Cayman Trench.

In the first 130 feet of that plunge, the reef doesn't just grow big, bold, and colorful, it builds things. Over thousands of years, coral, sand, rock, and sponges have together crafted tunnels, archways, pinnacles, and amphitheaters. If Atlantis ever did exist, surely it looked a lot like the reefs of Grand Cayman.

West Wall Wonders

More than 150 recognized dive sites ring the hook-shaped island. And with four distinct shores – the West Wall, North Wall, East End, and South Sound – divers are certain to find a protected diving venue in virtually all weather conditions. But the vast majority of divers who come to Grand Cayman stick to **West Wall**, the

place where it all began.

Stand on **Seven Mile Beach** and trace the line where the water graduates from light to deep blue. That line marks the point where the shallow reef suddenly plunges into the **Cayman Trench**. It was here that Soto brought his first customers and showed them what it was like to swim out over the coral lining of this drop-off and hang weightless, like a skydiver suspended in free fall. More than 40 years later, a new generation of Cayman divers are writing their own legends every day, every dive, at sites like **Orange Canyon**, **Trinity Caves**, and the breathtaking **Bonnie's Arch**.

Bonnie's is a great site for new divers. Channels of brilliant white sand cut through the coral as they slope down the wall to a novice-friendly depth of 70 feet. Turn a corner and you find a thick coral archway spanning the entrance to a sand-floor amphitheater. The arch looks sturdy, but it's a fragile work of art, decorated in the living colors of corals, sponges, and sea fans, so remember the diver's creed: Hands off the reef. The surrounding coral is also home to massive barrel sponges that can grow to the size of hot tubs by filtering nutrients from the water. Inside these sponges (again, because of their delicate nature, peer in; don't swim in), you'll find small gobies and tiny crabs seeking shelter. The entire reef swarms with colorful angelfish, filefish, and triggerfish.

Among West Wall's rich variety of dive sites, there's **Sand Chute**, a 50-foot-wide sand channel that slips down the wall like a ski slope, and **Mitch Miller's Reef**, an extremely shallow site where pockets of coral growth erupt from the sand to provide shelter for colorful reef fish like blue tang, stoplight parrotfish, yellowtail snapper, and the comical sharpnose pufferfish. There are a handful of wreck dives as well – the broken *Oro Verde* and the intact *Doc Poulson*, to name two – but some of the most stunning visuals are found on the shallow coral grottoes at the wall's southern tip.

The reef is closer to shore here, and from several dive shops and lodges you can swim right off the dock to sites like **Devil's Grotto** and **Eden Rock**. These two sites are a connecting labyrinth of caves and tunnels that burrow inside the shallow fringing reef, located just 100 yards offshore in 50 feet of water. The tunnels are safe even for new divers, thanks to shallow depths and numerous openings. Shallow reefs like these absorb the fury of storms and are visited by thousands of divers a year. Inside these tunnels, look for hundreds of tiny silversides and glassy sweepers, running from large, steely tarpon in a never-ending game of marine cat-and-mouse. Natural skylights allow brilliant beams of dappled sunlight into the caverns, where it glints off millions of tiny scales when silverside schools pass through.

Fairy basslets (opposite, top), popular fish for home aquariums, often swim near reef overhangs or caves.

Nurse sharks (left), a bottom-feeding species frequently seen by divers at coral reefs, pose little threat unless harassed.

Tube sponges (right) vary in color depending on water chemistry and the kind of algae living inside them.

Stingray City

Armed with a sharp barb on the business end of its agile tail, the southern stingray is the last ocean creature you'd expect to give you a big hug. But here on Grand Cayman, you may even wind up with a hickey from a ray's loving embrace.

Scuba divers are surrounded by rays at Stingray City (right, top and middle). Although gentle by nature, they can inflict painful wounds with sharp, venomous spines on their tails if harassed. The largest stingrays are more than five feet across.

A yellowline arrow crab (bottom) perches on an anemone. Like other arthropods, the crab has a complex exoskeleton that it periodically sheds, or molts.

Oro Verde (opposite), a 181-foot wreck in the West Bay, became Cayman's first artificial reef when it was sunk in 1980.

The hottest underwater ticket in Cayman is Stingray City – a guaranteed encounter with more than 50 stingrays on the North Sound sand flats. Each day, boatloads of divers and snorkelers arrive at the 12-foot-deep site where, armed with chunks of bait, they can interact with one of the sea's otherwise most reticent creatures. As soon as the rays smell the bait, they flock to the divers like hyperactive puppies. Once you know how to hold the food, you can even pick out a ray and lead it through acrobatic loops. When it's reward time, simply open your hand flat and allow the ray to vacuum the morsel into its mouth.

It's a captivating experience, but the rays can get aggressive. They've learned, for example, that by wrapping their body around your head, they can usually convince you to let go of the food. If a stray finger gets caught in a stingray's mouth, you'll get a sharp – but harmless – nip. Finally, if you get the scent of bait on exposed skin, a misguided ray is sure to start sucking around that spot, leaving you with the mother of all passion marks.

Stingray City trips are offered by most dive operators.

Dives Less Traveled

On most days, weather and wind conspire to make conditions on the West Wall too good to pass up, but occasionally the winds shift and the seas of the broad **North Wall** lie down. When this happens, boats may race around to dive this side of the island, where the wall starts at 70 to 80 feet. The payoff is big drama – in the form of more pelagic species, including eagle rays, turtles, barracuda, and even an occasional Caribbean reef shark. At **Hole in the Wall**, a North Wall favorite, a coral archway, adorned with bushy black and wire corals, grows out from the wall.

Black corals are the size and shape of pine saplings. Despite being protected by law on Cayman, they are somewhat rare here, as well as in the rest of the Caribbean. "Trees" of black coral are harvested so that the "trunk" can be carved and polished into black coral jewelry. Once you've seen the real thing underwater, you'll understand why eco-conscious divers swear off buying the trinkets. Wire corals, growing up to 20 feet in length, spring from the reef like twisted pipe cleaners.

The full brunt of trade winds and ocean currents strikes the remote **East End** of Grand Cayman, where a handful of dive lodges cater to customers with a taste for quiet nights and extreme diving. Be sure you've got the advanced skills to handle diving outside the barrier reef that caps the rounded coastline, where the drop-off starts anywhere from 45 to 90 feet. There are just a few novice sites like **Grouper Grotto**, a reef that rises to within 20 feet of the surface and swarms with packs of blue chromis and yellowhead wrasse. For new divers, however, the East End is better suited for lounging on deserted beaches. Just be careful where you step; these isolated stretches of sand are the last undisturbed turtle nesting sites on the island.

The exposed **South Sound** is dived only on those rare days when the weather conditions have gone completely haywire, forcing divers off the West and North Walls. Most sites start at 50 to 70 feet and take place in the spur-and-groove coral formations on top of the wall. These formations are like Mother Nature's grocery aisles – shelves of corals and sponges stacked high with tropical reef fish, crabs, and eels and separated by flat aisles of white sand. And as if grocery shopping, you simply wander down one, turn, and wander back up the other.

With this kind of coral wealth, Grand Cayman was destined to be a popular dive island, but it hasn't stayed on top for more than 40 years simply for good bottom time. A thriving offshore banking industry and a tradition of colonial propriety have shaped modern Grand Cayman into the cleanest, safest, and most efficient island in the Caribbean. Jetliners from major U.S. cities buzz in like clockwork, and passengers are whisked away to the modern accommodations of Seven Mile Beach with the efficiency one would expect from a British Crown Colony. And if the pervasive influence of American tourist culture, the rush-hour traffic jams in George Town, and the strip malls begin to get to you, remember there's always an escape nearby. Just do what you came here for in the first place: Slip on a tank, slide beneath the water, and stroll on down to Atlantis.

TRAVEL TIPS

DETAILS

When to Go

The best time to visit is summer, when seas are usually calm and warm. Winter temperatures hold in the 70s; summer temperatures reach the high 80s. The average water temperature is 77°F in winter and 82°F in summer. Count on 100 feet of visibility, with occasional peaks of 200 feet. As on most Caribbean islands, rates go up during holidays and in winter.

How to Get There

Commercial airlines offer direct flights from the United States to Grand Cayman Airport.

Getting Around

Taxis are widely available but expensive. Rental cars, available at the airport, are necessary to explore beyond Seven Mile Beach. Purchase a temporary Cayman license ($5) from a rental car agency. Motorists drive on the left side of the road.

INFORMATION

Cayman Islands Department of Tourism

6100 Blue Lagoon Drive, Suite 105, Miami, FL 33126-2085; tel: 305-266-2300; P.O. Box 67, George Town, Grand Cayman, Cayman Islands, BWI; tel: 345-949-0623; 847-678-6446 (Illinois); 212-682-5582 (New York); 713-461-1317 (Texas); 213-738-1968 (California); 416-485-1550 (Canada).

CAMPING

Camping is not permitted on Grand Cayman.

LODGING

Caribbean Club, Ltd.

P.O. Box 30499, Seven Mile Beach, Grand Cayman, Cayman Islands, BWI; tel: 800-327-8777 or 345-945-4099.

The Club's 18 oceanfront and garden-view villas lie three miles north of George Town. One- and two-bedroom cottages have a large living area and fully equipped kitchen. All accommodations have air-conditioning, telephones, and cable TV. $$$$

Cayman Diving Lodge

PMB-191, P.O. Box 65600, Lubbock, TX 79464-5600; tel: 800-852-3483 or 345-947-7555.

In operation for more than 25 years, this lodge on the quiet East End is devoted to divers. The 10-room lodge claims to have a "land-based, live-aboard" feeling. PADI certification is available, and guests may dive three or four times a day. The dive operation is available only to guests. A two-tank dive costs about $75. $$–$$$

Silver Sands Condominiums

P.O. Box 205GT, Grand Cayman, Cayman Islands, BWI; tel: 345-949-3343.

With 42 two- and three-bedroom units, this is a good choice for families. There's ample room for dive gear in the condos or on the balconies. Guests can snorkel off the beach or make arrangements with a dive shop. A pool and laundry facility are on the grounds. $$–$$$$

Spanish Bay Reef

P.O. Box 903; George Town, Grand Cayman, Cayman Islands, BWI; tel: 800-482-3483 or 345-949-8100.

Situated in a tiny cove on Grand Cayman's northwestern tip, the resort caters mostly to divers.

Casual furnishings decorate the 48 rooms, which have air-conditioning, phone, television, and patio or balcony. Amenities include a pool, two Jacuzzis, private beach, shared jeeps, bicycles, and dining facilities. Dive packages are available. $$$$

Treasure Island Resort

P.O. Box 1817, George Town, Grand Cayman, Cayman Islands, BWI; tel: 800-228-9898 or 340-949-7777.

This renovated resort on Seven Mile Beach is one mile from George Town. The 280 air-conditioned rooms have a balcony or patio, telephone, television, in-room safe, and ceiling fan. One of the largest resorts in the Caymans, Treasure Island specializes in water sports. A full-service dive operation is on the property. Additional amenities include two pools, tennis, and gourmet and casual dining. $$–$$$

DIVE OPERATORS

Bob Soto's Diving

P.O. Box 1801, Grand Cayman, Cayman Islands, BWI; tel: 800-262-7686 or 345-949-2022.

The largest operator on the island runs four full-service dive shops. Many dive/accommodation packages are available. Services include equipment sales, rental, and repair; boat and shore diving; resort courses and open-water certification.

Cayman Aggressor IV

P.O. Box 10028, APO, Grand Cayman, Cayman Islands, BWI; tel: 800-348-2628 or 345-949-5551.

The crew of this 110-foot live-aboard with nine staterooms leads dives off Grand Cayman, Little Cayman, and Cayman Brac. The vessel is equipped with a hot tub, dive deck, and nitrox. A seven-day trip costs $1,895 and includes unlimited diving, airport transfers, meals, tanks, weights, and weightbelts.

Dive Time
P.O. Box 2106, George Town, Grand Cayman, Cayman Islands, BWI; tel: 345-947-2339.

In operation for more than 20 years, this small outfit transports up to six passengers to remote dive sites. Equipment rental, certification, and resort courses are available.

Divers Down
P.O. Box 1706, George Town, Grand Cayman, Cayman Islands, BWI; tel: 345-916-3751 or 345-945-1611.

With two eight-foot dive boats, Divers Down focuses on small groups and offers three dives daily, plus night dives. Services include dive and photo equipment rental, resort courses, and training for PADI certification.

Don Foster's Dive Cayman
P.O. Box 31486, Seven Mile Beach, Grand Cayman, Cayman Islands, BWI; tel: 800-833-4837 or 345-945-5132.

Located in George Town, this photo and water sport facility has been operating for more than 16 years, offering three dives a day on four mid-sized boats, plus Stingray City trips and night dives. Services include dive and photo equipment rental, resort courses, and training for certification.

Red Sail Sports
P.O. Box 31473, Seven Mile Beach, Grand Cayman, Cayman Islands, BWI; tel: 877-733-7245 or 345-945-5965.

A large, multifaceted operation, Red Sail has shops at several Cayman locations, offering rentals of dive equipment, waverunners, windsurfers, sailboats, and waterskis. Training is available to the divemaster level.

Excursions

Cayman Brac
6100 Blue Lagoon Drive, Suite 105, Miami, FL 33126-2085; tel: 305-266-2300.

Veteran divers often fly into Grand Cayman, then catch the first puddle-jumper to Cayman Brac, about 90 miles northeast. The Brac has the Western Hemisphere's only diveable Russian warship. The M/V *Captain Keith Tibbetts*, a 330-foot destroyer, was purchased from Cuba and sunk as an artificial reef. On land, Cayman Brac is known as "the island that time forgot." Visitors slow to a relaxed pace, explore caves, and plan their next descent at one of nearly 50 dive sites charted along the shore.

Little Cayman
6100 Blue Lagoon Drive, Suite 105, Miami, FL 33126; tel: 305-266-2300.

On the smallest of the Cayman Islands, many divers head straight for Bloody Bay Wall, which starts in 20 feet of water and drops off to thousands of feet. It's been called the best wall diving on the planet. Little Cayman is a classic getaway served by an airport with a grass runway, a handful of resorts, and one restaurant. The island has a population of about 60 – and just as many dive sites. At one spot, Eagle Ray Roundup, divers and snorkelers encounter large eagle rays, who come to snag dinner from the sandy bottom.

Dominican Republic
2355 Salzedo Street, Suite 307, Coral Gables, FL 33134; tel: 305-444-4592 or 818-358-9594.

The Caribbean's second largest nation has nearly a thousand miles of coastline. On the north shore, marine diversions range from humpback sightings on the Silver Banks to 16th-century shipwrecks. In the south, divers can fin over shallow coral reefs at dozens of locations. Snorkelers and divers can check out the 135-foot *Hickory*, one of the Caribbean's most colorful wrecks. The vessel rests in 60 feet of water, with hull and mast stretching upward; the mast ends just three feet below the surface.

Belize

CHAPTER 14

A generation ago, this tiny country just south of the Yucatan Peninsula was best known, if known at all, as a colonial backwater, the sort of place Paul Theroux had in mind when he wrote *Mosquito Coast* (in fact, the movie was filmed there). British Honduras, as it was then called, gained its independence, and a new name, in 1981. It also gained a reputation among tourists for its considerable natural and archaeological treasures – a vast swath of rain forest, scores of Mayan ruins, and, as divers soon learned, a barrier reef second in size only to Australia's. Wrapped neatly in a country just slightly larger than New Jersey, Belize was soon being marketed as a virtual paradise for divers and other eco-tourists, the kind of tropical getaway where you can swim with sea turtles on a reef bursting with marine life, then stroll through a tropical jungle before your hair dries. ◆ The barrier reef runs the entire 185-mile length of

One of the world's largest barrier reefs attracts divers to a pocket paradise on the Caribbean's western shore.

the country, starting about 10 miles offshore in the north and angling away from the coast in the south. Dive sites are found on the barrier reef itself, around islands or smaller reefs inshore of the barrier, or on offshore atolls. Most tourists base themselves at **Ambergris Caye** (pronounced "key"), the largest of the inshore islands, about 35 miles northeast of Belize City. ◆ Named for a waxy secretion that forms in the bowels of sperm whales, Ambergris was once a fishing village, but over the past two decades its residents have fully embraced tourism. Visitors hop a short flight from Belize City to Ambergris's tiny San Pedro airport. Small hotels

A diamond blenny hides from predators in the stinging tentacles of a giant anemone. The two-inch fish is immune to the anemone's toxic sting.

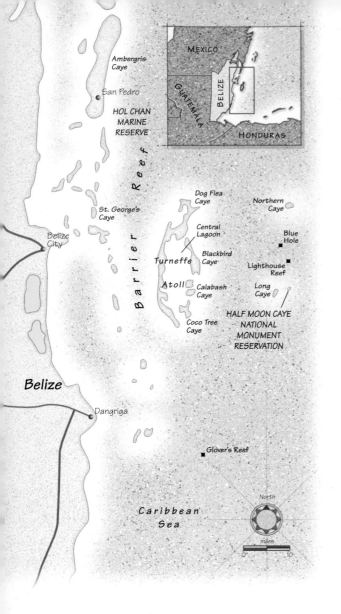

shore, the high volume of boat traffic prevents swimming to the sites from the beach. Instead, local operators pick up divers at the hotel piers and run their open mahogany boats through narrow cuts in the reef out to the dive sites.

Mooring buoys on most Ambergris sites prevent anchor damage to the fragile corals. The current makes drift diving the best method of seeing the reef, so operators use the buoys mostly as drop-off points. Just over the crest – a kind of underwater hilltop – the reef slopes down to 50 feet. You start your dive here and swim offshore along huge coral spur formations. At the seaward edge, many of the spurs end in pinnacles that tower as much as 100 feet off the sandy bottom. Between each spur, and connected by tunnels large enough for divers to swim through, are steep canyons decorated with colorful sponges and soft corals. Large schools of fish, including horse-eye jacks, spadefish, yellowtail snappers, and blue-bar jacks, congregate to feed high in the water column off the reef. In late winter and early spring, the amount of plankton increases off Ambergris Caye, which in turn increases the chance of seeing large filter-feeders like manta rays and whale sharks. Later in the spring, turtle nesting season brings huge sea turtles to the waters near the caye, and visitors often see them cruising around, waiting to come ashore on the beaches outside town where they drop their Ping-Pong ball eggs into sandy nests.

The female sea turtles return after some 20 years to the same stretch of sand where they were hatched, and Belize has several important nesting beaches where they lay their eggs. Recognizing the vulnerability of the easily caught turtles and easily poached eggs, Belize has signed the Inter-American Convention for the Protection and Conservation of Sea Turtles, thereby agreeing to protect the turtles and their habitat. Species such as the hawksbill turtle are now protected throughout the country.

Hol Chan Marine Preserve, the most popular diving and snorkeling spot on the island, has the most prolific fish life of any

crowded along the city's sand streets front the water, each with a pier stretching across the narrow beach and into the lagoon toward the barrier reef. Frigate birds – large, forked-tail seabirds usually seen flying solo far out at sea – gather in force over the Ambergris shoreline, and bird-watchers can spot flamingos, egrets, herons, and pelicans feeding in the backwaters.

The Other Great Barrier Reef

The barrier reef crests about half a mile off the Ambergris shore, and just beyond that is the island's selection of medium and deep dives. Although the dives are close to dive near Ambergris Caye, as well as the premier novice-diver sites. Hol Chan ("little channel" in Mayan) is adjacent to a small cut in the reef that gives it its name. Currents wash the five-square-mile site at each change of the tide. Water pouring across the barrier reef carries food to the hundreds of big fish that flourish within the protected area. Schools of rarely seen, three-foot-long permit, the bright tropical sun flashing off their silvery sides, tack back and forth across the narrow cut looking for baitfish. Hordes of reef fish loiter behind big coral heads, protected by the massive formations – and the park rangers. Edible species especially seem to have benefited from sanctuary status; large grouper and hogfish are common only at Hol Chan among the Ambergris reef sites. Moorings bob in 10 feet of water just behind the reef. Schools of fat snapper mob divers and snorkelers here, while very large grouper often laze directly beneath the dive boats. The current can be swift at Hol Chan during the change of tides; take care not to stray too far down current from the boat.

Queen triggerfish (left) prowl the reef in search of their favorite food, sea urchins.

Fish frenzies (below) are common in areas where divers have been feeding the fish. Remember, healthy animals find their own food.

Night dives are wonderfully eerie at Hol Chan. It seems as if every stingray in the Caribbean meets here when the sun goes down. Each bump in the sandy bottom has two big eyes sticking up. Divers finning over this otherworldly scene set off a series of explosions as the rays erupt from their silty cover. Nocturnal shutterbugs will enjoy the photo opportunities of the big stingrays and the parrotfish huddled in their sleeping cocoons spun of mucus bubbles.

Adventure among the Atolls

South of Ambergris, Belize's barrier reef begins to veer away from the mainland. Outside the main reef lie several of the unique coral formations called atolls. Common in the tropical Pacific and Indian oceans, atolls

are rare in the Caribbean. These roughly circular rings of coral rise from deep water to enclose a central lagoon. Belize has three of the four atolls in the Western Hemisphere, and each is a coral necklace bejeweled with mangrove-green islands set in bright gold beaches and laid against the velvety blue Caribbean Sea.

Turneffe Atoll, largest of the bunch, sports three dive resorts in its 205 square miles of blue water and green islands. The atoll is six miles offshore of the barrier reef and separated from it by a 1,000-foot-deep channel. Mayans used some of the 35 islands of this atoll as fishing camps, and later pirates made them a home base between raids on Spanish shipping. In modern times, the atoll has become well known for its excellent bonefishing and scientific research stations –

The Blue Hole

The single most famous dive in Belize is the Blue Hole, about eight miles north of Half Moon Caye in Lighthouse Reef Atoll. The site is an aptly named circular drop of sapphire among aquamarine shallows. The dark blue is a sign of depth: The hole is 400 feet deep, while the surrounding water's depth is from 5 to 15 feet.

There are blue holes in other countries with similar limestone geology, but Belize's Blue Hole owes its fame to Jacques-Yves Cousteau and his research vessel, the *Calypso*. Cousteau and crew came here in 1984 and blasted a pathway for the boat across the shallow ring of reef so they could explore the mysterious crater. Cousteau concluded that the entire bank of limestone around the Blue Hole was riddled with a network of caves. The hole itself is a water-filled sinkhole, a cave in which the roof collapsed and opened a cavity to the surface. Scientists estimate that the collapse happened some 12,000 years ago.

Though surrounded by lush coral reefs, the Blue Hole itself is nearly barren of life. This doesn't mean it's without interest. Deep inside the sinkhole is a cavern decorated in eerie, gothic style. As divers reach the top of the cavern at 130 feet, they enter an upside-down forest of stalactites. These limestone icicles prove that the Blue Hole was once a dry cave. The stalactites formed when rainwater slowly seeped through the limestone above, picking up a load of minerals. Once the fortified water hit the dry air of the cavern, the dissolved minerals solidified and slowly built these long fingers of stone.

Live-aboards and boats from Belize City, Ambergris Caye, and Lighthouse Reef go to the Blue Hole. Because of the depth of this dive, bottom time is very short. Divers must monitor their time and maximum depth carefully.

A bottlenose dolphin (above) swims alongside a snorkeler. Dolphins use a type of sonar, called echolocation, to pinpoint prey and other creatures.

Belize's Blue Hole (below) and the surrounding waters have been protected as a national monument since 1996.

Gray, or mangrove, snapper (opposite) school in shallow water near mangrove cayes.

and the diving. Turneffe's most noted dive is the drop-off called the **Elbow**, where swirling currents make for an electric mix of big pelagic fish like horse-eye jacks and permit.

Glover's Reef is the southernmost and most remote atoll, 70 miles south of Belize City, and receives less diver traffic along its 50-some miles of reefs. During the 1970s, a team of international scientists determined that Glover's was the most biologically rich of the Caribbean atolls. Wall diving at Glover's begins on the reef crest at 30 feet, and then the black-coral-encrusted walls drop through the blue to more than 2,000 feet.

All the atolls have incredibly diverse habitats both on land and underwater. Eagle rays, hammerheads, and sea turtles cruise above colorful worlds of fish and sponges that adorn the reef below. As testament to the quality of diving among the atolls, live-aboard boats in Belize spend almost all of their time along the fringing reefs.

Belize's easternmost dive outpost and the third of the country's atolls, **Lighthouse Reef**, specializes in clear water and spectacular

walls. The six small, mangrove-lined islands in this atoll 50 miles east of Belize City could pass for the tropical Pacific. The Audubon Society counted 98 species of birds on Half Moon Caye alone, including ospreys, mangrove warblers, and red-footed boobies. In the spring, you can walk among the nesting boobies on **Half Moon Caye National Monument**, Belize's first nature park created to protect this, the second largest breeding colony in the world. Crocodiles also breed among Lighthouse's mangrove-covered isles. The crocs are best spotted at night on guided tours of the estuaries.

While Lighthouse Reef's most renowned

dive is the **Blue Hole** (see sidebar), the ones that keep the live-aboard boats hanging around the atoll are its wall dives such as **Hanging Gardens**. The wall starts relatively shallow and by a depth of 60 feet starts curving back under the reef. The light currents feed a dazzling collection of gorgonians and sponges, including the huge orange elephant ear and strands of red rope sponge that look black in the deeper water.

Pound for pound, acre for protected acre, Belize provides more adventure for the traveling diver and eco-tourist than almost anywhere else in the world. The only problem is deciding what to see and do first.

TRAVEL TIPS

DETAILS

When to Go

January to May is relatively dry, June to September extremely wet. The average temperature is 80°F year-round, with 80 percent humidity. Avoid the rainy season, when runoff obscures the water along the coast. Water ranges from a winter low of 74°F to a summer high of 86°F.

How to Get There

Several commercial airlines serve Phillip Goldson International Airport, a 20-minute drive to Belize City. It's a two- to three-hour flight to Belize City from Houston, Los Angeles, and Miami. Smaller planes make the 20-minute flight from Belize City to San Pedro Airport on Ambergris Caye.

Getting Around

Rental cars are available but tend to be costly. Taxis operate on route rates rather than meters. Inexpensive buses run in cities on regular schedules. Charter flights provide offshore travel.

INFORMATION

Belize Tourist Board

415 Seventh Avenue, New York, NY 10001; tel: 800-624-0686; or P.O. Box 325, Belize City, Belize; tel: 011-501-231825 or 231913.

Belize Embassy

2535 Massachusetts Avenue N.W., Washington, DC 20008; tel: 202-332-9636.

CAMPING

Camping is permitted only in these designated areas: Gales Point, Caracol Natural Monument, Placencia, and San Ignacio. Special permits, required at Caracol Natural Monument, are available through the Department of Archaeology in Belmopan, 011-501-822106.

LODGING

PRICE GUIDE – double occupancy

$ = up to $49 $$ = $50–$99

$$$ = $100–$149 $$$$ = $150+

Blackbird Caye Resort

14423 S.W. 113th Terrace, Miami, FL 33186; tel: 888-271-3483 or 305-969-7947 or 011-501-232767.

This Turneffe Islands resort accommodates 30 guests. There are ten cabanas, each with a porch, hammock, bathroom, and air-conditioning. Also available are five guest rooms; a triplex for groups; and the Blackbird Bungalow, a two-bedroom suite with a bath. The dining area serves three meals daily. Dive and ferry boats depart regularly from the resort's three docks. $$$$

Journey's End

5847 San Felipe, Suite 2195, Houston, TX 77057; tel: 800-460-5665 or 713-780-1566.

Set on Ambergris Caye, this resort occupies 50 acres outside of town and operates a well-equipped dive shop. Journey's End offers 70 oceanfront, garden-view, and poolside cabanas and air-conditioned rooms. Two private homes are available for rent. An upscale restaurant, swimming pool, and tennis courts are also on the premises. $$$–$$$$

Lighthouse Reef Resort

P.O. Box 1435, Dundee, FL 33838; tel: 800-423-3114 or 941-439-6600.

The only hotel on Lighthouse Reef Atoll encompasses 11 beachfront villas and a number of suites, mini-suites, and cabanas with private porches. A private airstrip and beach are on the premises. Prices include meals, dives, and air transfers. $$$–$$$$

Ramon's Village Resort

P.O. Box 1946, Laurel, MS 39441; tel: 800-624-4215.

Sixty palm-thatched cabanas make up this diver-focused resort on Ambergris Caye. Most of the cabanas have ocean views; all are air-conditioned. The restaurant is a popular night spot among Belizeans and tourists. The staff arranges diving and snorkeling trips, extended charters, glass-bottom boat rides, and catamaran sails. $$–$$$

Victoria House Resort

P.O. Box 1549, Decatur, GA 30030; tel: 800-247-5159 or 011-501-262067.

This full-service resort on Ambergris Caye occupies 19 acres of tropical palms and beaches. Two private villas and 29 rooms, suites, and *casitas* are available. A restaurant and complete dive and water-sports center are on the premises. $$$–$$$$

DIVE OPERATORS

Belize Aggressor

Aggressor Fleet Limited, P.O. Box 1470, Morgan City, LA 70381-1470; tel: 800-348-2628 or 504-385-2628.

The live-aboard tour, in addition to providing dive opportunities, makes scheduled stops at a bird sanctuary, a caye with iguanas, and the Half Moon Caye lighthouse. Staterooms have VCRs and private baths. Services include film processing, dive deck, and nitrox; training includes open water, advanced, and nitrox diver certification. Weeklong cruises, including meals, cost from $1,695 to $1,895.

Blue Marlin Lodge

#15 Mahogany Street, P.O. Box 21, Dangriga, Belize; tel: 800-798-1558 or 011-501-522243.

This PADI dive center, part of an all-inclusive resort, operates 30- to 42-foot-long dive boats. Trips to dive sites are 5 to 25 minutes away from the dock; dives are mostly drift-style. Services include equipment rental and guided dives; training includes resort, referral, and open-water certification.

Excursions

Bay Islands, Honduras

Honduras Tourism Office, 2100 Ponce de Leon Boulevard, Suite 1175, Coral Gables, FL 33134; tel: 800-410-9608.

Nearly every type of Caribbean coral grows here, making this an excellent spot to slip on a mask. A one-hour flight from Belize City delivers travelers to these waters, where diversity is the keyword. Indeed, divers can see just about any Caribbean marine species here, including more sizes and types of sponges than elsewhere.

Fantasea Scuba School and Watersports Center

P.O. Box 32, San Pedro Town, Belize; tel: 011-501-262576.

Located on the Victoria House pier, Fantasea has a fleet of 24-foot dive boats. Six-passenger excursions are made to nearby dive sites as well as offshore islands and Blue Hole locations. Equipment rental and private instruction are available.

Rum Point Divers

Placencia, Belize; tel: 888-235-4031 or 504-466-7888 or 011-501-623239.

Based at Rum Point Inn, this dive shop operates trips on a 42-foot jet boat. Activities such as fishing trips, sailing, and tours of Mayan ruins can be arranged. Services include equipment rental and guided dives; training includes PADI certification and referral courses.

Sea Horse Guides

Placencia Village, Belize; tel: 800-991-1969 or 510-832-1531 or 011-501-623166.

This guide service offers fishing and jungle tours as well as dive trips aboard two 33-foot boats. Equipment rental, guided dives, and training for all levels of certification are offered.

South Water Caye

International Zoological Expeditions, 210 Washington Street, Shevron, MA 01770; tel: 800-548-5843 or 011-501-522119.

South Water Caye is a great place to combine learning and leisure. The exquisite, 14-acre islet, 12 miles from central Belize, entices divers with its clear water and perfect position on the barrier reef. South Water Caye is ideal for seeing underwater caverns with stalagmites. International Zoological Expeditions conducts classes in marine ecology. Guests may also arrange naturalist-led dive trips and enjoy evening lectures under palm trees. Skiffs transport divers to the caye from Dangriga, Belize.

Placencia

Belize Tourist Board, 415 Seventh Avenue, New York, NY 10001; tel: 800-624-0686.

Placencia, a 45-minute flight south of Belize City, is the country's last frontier for divers. The barrier reef is about 20 miles off the southern coast, but divers can reach spots like Laughing Bird Caye, 12 miles southeast from Placencia. Steep sides with good wall dives surround this shelf atoll or "faro." The faro encircles a lagoon renowned for its variety of corals, especially elkhorn.

Cozumel
Mexico

C H A P T E R **15**

No one knows how long schools of migratory sailfish have been journeying to the tiny island. Yet each spring, thousands of sleek, tireless swimmers cross vast distances of fluid space to ply the waters around **Cozumel**. Their arrival follows the winter migration of divers who flock to this Caribbean island 12 miles off the **Yucatan Peninsula** to soar on clear currents that sweep across Cozumel's massive submarine wall. ◆ Drift diving, as the practice is known, has no terrestrial counterpart. You are weightless, borne on invisible wings. Degrees of freedom are measured vertically. Inhale and your body rises; exhale and it sinks. Newcomers often describe the experience with an almost religious zeal, one of the reasons, perhaps, that Cozumel has become such a diving mecca. ◆ Humans have been making the pilgrimage to Cozumel **Currents ferry divers** for more than 20 centuries. The ancient Mayans who **past brilliant reefs** first settled the Yucatan Peninsula named the **and walls in the home of** island Ah-Cuzamil-Peten, or Land of Swallows. **the ancient Mayans.** Each year they trekked to the 28-mile-long island to pay homage to Ixchel, the goddess of fertility. The remains of their limestone temples can still be found in the parched scrub jungle and marshy lagoons that cover 90 percent of the island. Rumors of treasure that surfaced more than a millennium later inspired Hernán Cortes and his conquistadors to sail to Cozumel in 1519. The Spanish missionaries who followed seized upon the island as a source of souls. ◆ But judging from the numbers, neither Ixchel nor golden treasure nor the Spaniards' missionary fervor exerted the drawing power of the offshore paradise that lies just beyond the

A Nassau grouper meets eye-to-eye with a diver. These large fish can be up to four feet long and, except during spawning, are solitary creatures.

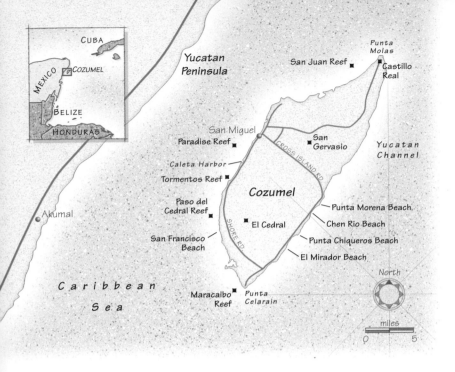

was only one gas station on the island but three bordellos listed on the Internet. There are fewer than five churches but more than 50 dive shops, and no one has counted the bars, eateries, and T-shirt stalls. Whether they serve saint or sinner, all of these engines of economic life depend on the reefs that lie at the heart of the island's ecosystem.

If the ocean's waters were drained away, Cozumel would be seen to rest on a mile-high mesa that rises up from the seafloor and is separated from the mainland to the east by a deep-water strait called the **Yucatan Channel**. Seawater is forced through this passageway, creating the perpetual currents that sweep along Cozumel's protected western flank – a near-vertical submarine wall that runs the length of the island.

jungle-covered isle. Their existence was not revealed until Jacques-Yves Cousteau put Cozumel's reefs on the map with a 1961 film expedition. Today, nearly 60,000 divers undertake the annual trek to Cozumel's protected marine sanctuary, making it Mexico's *numero uno* dive destination.

Sojourn to San Miguel

From the air – a 20-minute hop from Cancun's international airport – the island first appears as a verdant oasis on a shimmering blue desert and gradually fills the horizon. Then the green, pink, and white stucco buildings loom up from the beachhead that separates the low-lying jungle and the sea.

Once a quiet Mexican fishing village, the island's sole town of **San Miguel** today has a bustling tourist economy fueled by air-fills, *cerveza*, and souvenirs. Until 1997, there

Cozumel's reefs spill over the top of the wall in a phantasmagoria of form that defies description. There are majestic coral cathedrals and cavernous reef archways, acres of undulating sea fans, and vertical sponge-covered reliefs that plunge to a depth of over 600 feet. Local divers have christened these individual formations as if to validate their own fleeting impressions. Shallow reefs like **Paradise**, **Paso del Cedral**, and **Tormentos** lie atop the submarine rampart in less than 60 feet of water, and a few of these are even accessible from the beach. The deep reefs – **Maracaibo** to the far south, **San Juan** to the north – plummet into azure vistas beyond the reach of divers. Like a crude map, the names fall short of their ambition as one formation seamlessly gives away to another in water with visibility of up to 150 feet year-round.

The eastern, windward side of the island,

Siesta (left), usually between 1 P.M. and 4 P.M., gives a diver an opportunity to rest up before an evening dive.

accessible by the single two-lane road, remains virtually deserted, with the exception of a few roadside stands. Because of the heavy surf, no one dives there, though it's ideal for a day of sightseeing, exploring the pristine beaches, and communing with Ixchel before returning to town.

The Gospel of Cozumel

There is a natural order to San Miguel, a rhythm as predictable as the annual migration of sailfish, the mating of the endangered sea turtles, and the thousand other cycles that play out on the reefs. In the morning, the first shift of divers makes its way to the docks where the boats are waiting, stowing their gear on board for the passage to the reefs. The flotilla of skiffs and cruisers and yachts – almost anything that floats – motors off to attend to the important business of Cozumel.

Out on the reef, the true gospel of Cozumel is revealed. Divemasters recite chapter and verse of proper drift-diving technique, emphasizing buoyancy control, "don't touch"

Blue-striped grunts (right) may surprise divers by grunting, a sound they make by grinding the teeth in their throats.

Submarine stalactites (below) and other cave formations dazzle snorkelers at Nohoch Nah Chich and other *cenotes*.

Snorkeling in the Giant Bird House

Mention snorkeling and most people think of finning over a multihued reef, but a growing number of adventure seekers are trekking to the Yucatan jungle for the chance to snorkel underground. If you follow their trail, you'll discover **Nohoch Nah Chich**, the world's longest underwater cave. It's like no place you've ever dived before. And scuba tanks are not required.

Located an hour and a half south of Cancun along the sole coastal highway that separates the jungle from the sea, Nohoch Nah Chich – Mayan for "giant bird house" – is part of the vast subterranean river system that drains the Yucatan Peninsula into the Caribbean. The 27-mile-long cave, or *cenote*, flooded more than 13,000 years ago when the surrounding sea level rose.

The Mayans who first settled the peninsula believed that *cenotes* were windows to the underworld, the focal point for their communion with the gods. It's easy to see why when floating beneath the clusters of stalactites and tree roots that reach down from Nohoch's vaulted limestone ceiling. Snorkelers can explore a cavernous area the size of a football field illuminated by the diffuse, verdant light from the *cenote* entrance. The rest of the cave is under water.

Ruinous Existence

Holiday couples planning a romantic interlude at one of Cozumel's two dozen beachside hotels may be surprised to learn they're engaged in a time-honored ritual. Ancient Mayans honoring Ixchel, the goddess of fertility, made the pilgrimage here nearly 2,000 years ago. Instead of booking a suite on the strand, the Mayans erected elaborate stone temples in the low-lying jungle.

Whether the hard limestone surfaces or hoards of bloodthirsty mosquitoes were conducive to their ceremonial rites is one of the questions you may ponder when visiting Cozumel's many ruins. Though most of the vegetation-choked sites have yet to be excavated, the Mexican Institute for Nautical Archaeology and History has trimmed back the bush at the largest ruins to make them more easily accessible.

Located in Cozumel's interior roughly five miles northeast of town, **San Gervasio** attracted worshippers from around the Yucatan Peninsula. The site was connected to more intimate gathering places through a system of jungle thoroughfares called *sacbes* that snaked through dense bush. Today San Gervasio has a main cluster of three-story limestone buildings, pyramids, and archways. Many of the connecting trails have been restored and are well worth the hike – if you slather on insect repellent and watch out for snakes.

Another must-see, provided you rent a sturdy four-wheel-drive vehicle to get there, is **Castillo Real** on Cozumel's north shore near the lighthouse. Unfortunately, much of this five-story tower supposedly used by Mayan navigators was destroyed by Hurricane Gilbert in 1988.

For history's sake, time-travelers may also want to visit **El Cedral**, the site of the island's original Mayan settlement, though all that remain are a few huts and a couple of refrigerator-sized touchstones. Don't overlook the chance to hop the 40-minute flight to the mainland to see the world-class ruins of **Chichen Itza**, once the largest city in the Mayan nation. There you can tour pyramids, old government buildings, and sacred drinking wells, and spend the afternoon at an ancient ball field.

Mayan ruins, like those at Dzibanche (above), are scattered throughout the Yucatan.

Splendid toadfish (opposite, top) are endemic to Cozumel and often hide in crevices in the reef.

Spotted goatfish (opposite, bottom) use barbels below their mouths to dig for food in the sand.

The object is to drift with the current, though "riding" may be a more accurate description. Drifting is easy; you can't prevent it. The current is irresistible. Forceful enough to tug off your face mask at certain times and places, it is barely perceptible at others, just enough to shepherd you lazily across the reef. There are steady currents and capricious ones, gentle eddies and backwaters created by reef topology; on occasion, the current even stops and reverses direction. Local divemasters read these aqueous trails like trackers in the bush. They reserve well-worn paths for novices and fast runs for advanced divers – and save the most perilous waters for themselves.

Riding the currents demands good buoyancy skills and proper weighting. Any deviation from neutrality causes an immediate reaction. If you're riding too heavy, your muscles struggle against the load and burn

reef preservation, and the importance of watching your depth, particularly on the first and deepest dive of the day, which is usually conducted on the wall. In contrast to the practice at many tropical destinations, the divemaster here leads his charges through the dive, deftly guiding them through the reef's many passageways. Because of the current, the boat never anchors but follows the divers' bubbles and picks them up at the end of the dive.

up precious air reserves, and you increase the chance of damaging the coral. Ride too light and you strain to prevent the upward pull, and there's the added risk of missing a safety stop. Be sure to select the proper amount of weight before making the dive. If there's a question, ask the divemaster to assist you. Above all, the key is to relax, breathe, and enjoy the ride.

Once you've mastered the techniques of drift diving, you're ready to explore one of nature's most complex and fragile works of architecture. Spend a lazy afternoon floating through fields of Volkswagen-sized brain corals and cavelike coral structures that are a favorite haunt for skip jacks, eels, and the occasional sleeping nurse shark. Or head to the wall for the blue-water ride of your life and the chance to fin along with some of Cozumel's large pelagics: migratory billfish, sea turtles, wahoo, and white-tipped sharks. You don't have to look for the omnipresent groupers; they'll find you.

At the end of the day, the boats return to harbor. Some refuel and switch crews in preparation for a night dive. Divers who've had their fill meander back to their hotels to recount the blessings of the day's dives over a meal and a bucket of *cervezas* served on ice.

Come One, Come All

Scientists attribute Cozumel's annual migration of sail-fish to biological instinct and analyze the large pelagics that patrol the reef wall in terms of predator-prey dynamics. Economists fall back on the persuasive power of disposable income to explain the motivations of divers and the thousands of seasonal tourists who regularly flood the island's shores. But perhaps humans are too close to the facts to be impartial observers; if there is a similarity between the homing instincts of sea turtles and the romantic flight of starry-eyed couples, we fail to grasp it, though both return to the same beachfront year after year.

Or maybe these parallels just seem closer to the surface in Cozumel. The natural order playing out on the reefs, streets, and sheets of San Miguel is more easily discernible here. One thing, however, is certain: creatures both large and small are drawn to this Caribbean island.

TRAVEL TIPS

DETAILS

When to Go

Temperatures remain in the 80s through much of the year. November to April is the dry season; May is typically the wettest month. College students overrun the island during spring break. November and December winds often interfere with dives. Water temperatures range from 77°F (February through August) to 82°F (September to January).

How to Get There

Commercial airlines serve Cozumel International Airport.

Getting Around

Cozumel has no public transportation. Four-wheel-drive vehicles may be necessary for exploring the island, most of which is undeveloped. Taxis, rental cars, and mopeds are available in town, but most activities are within walking distance.

INFORMATION

Cozumel State Tourism Office

Plaza del Sol, Second Floor, Cozumel, QR 76600, Mexico; tel: 011-52-987-2-09-72.

Cozumel Island Hotel Association

Calle 2 Norte, Cozumel, QR 76600, Mexico; tel: 011-52-987-2-31-32.

Mexico Tourism Hotline

Tel: 800-446-3942.

CAMPING

An adventure company, Aventuras Naturales, specializes in backcountry camping tours, as well as many other guided activities. For information, call 011-52-987-6-09-00.

LODGING

PRICE GUIDE – double occupancy
$ = up to $49 $$ = $50–$99
$$$ = $100–$149 $$$$ = $150+

Cozumel Vacation Homes

4539 South Lewis, Tulsa, OK 74105; tel: 800-742-1563 or 918-742-7070.

If you're looking for more privacy than most large hotels offer, try renting a townhouse or private home on the island. The choices range from five-bedroom, six-bath luxury estates on a private beach to modest homes in a residential neighborhood. Daily maid service is included, and the management arranges activities from custom scuba adventures to tours of the mainland's famous Mayan ruins. $$–$$$$

La Ceiba Beach Hotel

Costera Sur, km 4.5, Cozumel, QR 76600, Mexico; tel: 800-437-9609 or 011-52-987-2-00-65.

This hotel, one of Cozumel's first, has 113 spacious rooms with minibars, televisions, VCRs, and balconies. Enormous palms, a rarity on the island, shade the adjacent beach. On the grounds are two restaurants and a fresh-water pool. Guests snorkel offshore. $$$

Fiesta Americana Cozumel Reef

Carretera a Chankanaab, km 7.5, Cozumel, QR 76600, Mexico; tel: 800-343-7821 or 011-52-987-2-26-22.

Across the highway from the beach, the resort is far south on the luxury hotel strip, close to the best reefs. Deluxe accommodations include 167 commodious rooms with balconies in the main building, and 56 two-story, thatched *casitas* set in a jungle landscape. Tennis courts, a health club, three restaurants, and a dive center are on the premises. $$$$

Plaza Las Glorias Hotel and Villas

Rafael Melgar, km 1.5, Cozumel, QR 76600, Mexico; tel: 800-342-2644 or 011-52-987-2-20-00.

This upscale resort caters to divers. Both PADI- and NAUI-certified dive instructors run the full-service dive shop on the grounds, five blocks from the center of San Miguel. The 170 multilevel junior suites have terraces, and the resort's pool has a swim-up bar. Two restaurants are on the property. $$$$

Presidente Inter-Continental Cozumel

Carretera a Chankanaab, km 6.5, Cozumel, QR 76600, Mexico; tel: 800-327-0200 or 011-52-987-2-03-22.

This 253-room resort complex lies off one of the island's most beautiful beaches. Tennis courts, sailing, windsurfing, and a dive shop are available. A restaurant, café, and swimming pool are on the premises. The resort conducts children's programs during peak seasons. $$$$

DIVE OPERATORS

Aqua Safari

P.O. Box 41, Cozumel, QR 77600, Mexico; tel: 011-52-987-2-01-01.

In operation for 32 years, Aqua Safari has a fleet of modern dive boats equipped with oxygen. An on-site tank is available for divers to review skills and make buoyancy adjustments. Services include equipment rental and a PADI five-star instructor development center.

AquaWorld

Carretera Costera Sur Playa Paraisa, km 3.7, Cozumel, QR 77600, Mexico; tel: 011-52-987-2-12-10.

This PADI dive center, in business since 1989, offers two-tank boat dives at Cozumel's popular reefs with four departures a day. The ratio of divers to divemaster is eight to one. AquaWorld also offers cavern trips for certified divers. Services include dive and snorkel equipment rentals. Multilingual instruction is available, ranging from resort courses and open water to divemaster. Nitrox certification and other specialty classes are also available.

Blue Bubble

P.O. Box 334, Cozumel, QR 77600, Mexico; tel: 800-878-8853 or 011-52-987-2-44-83.

This operation's boats, some of the fastest in Cozumel, carry six divers each. Services include equipment storage and cleaning and one-on-one dive instruction.

Del Mar Aquatics

Costera Sur, km 4.5, Cozumel, QR 77600, Mexico; tel: 888-692-3422 or 011-52-987-2-19-00.

With four 33-foot custom boats, plus three others over 30 feet, Del Mar can handle 150 divers a day. Night dives, snorkeling trips, and deep-sea fishing are also available. Equipment sales, rental, and repair, and certification training are offered. Ask about group specials with La Ceiba Hotel.

Scuba Du

P.O. Box 137, Cozumel, QR 77600, Mexico; tel: 011-52-987-2-03-22 (ext. 6845).

This PADI dive center has five speedy, custom boats. The owners are founding members of the Cozumel Watersports Association, which helps maintain the health of the National Marine Park. Services include equipment sales and rental, guided dives, and training to the instructor level.

Excursions

Akumal

Mexico Tourism Hotline; tel: 800-446-3942.

Akumal, Mayan for "place of turtles," is a diver's gateway to the *cenotes* or caves that honeycomb the Yucatan Peninsula. A 90-minute drive south of Cancun on the coastal highway, this quiet beach community also offers snorkeling, sailboarding, and hiking. Each spring, sea turtles gather here to nest on the palm-lined sandy beaches. Visitors explore ruins in nearby Tulum, a walled Mayan city built between 1,000 and 1,300 years ago.

Cuba

ScubaCuba, 240 Pebble Beach Boulevard, Suite 712, Naples, FL 34113; tel: 800-645-1179.

U.S. citizens are officially discouraged from trekking to Cuba, but a growing number of Yanks, following the lead of Canadian and European divers, are taking the plunge. It's not illegal, though some technicalities exist, and arranging dives can be tricky. Most booking agents rely on daily flights to Cuba from Cancun and the Bahamas. The rewards, however, are well worth the effort – pristine reefs, a plethora of Spanish and Russian shipwrecks, and, of course, world-class cigars.

Cancun

Mexico Tourism Hotline; tel: 800-446-3942.

Luxury hotels, rocking night clubs, long stretches of white, sandy beach, and surf-side bars make Cancun a fine choice for divers who love to party. Situated at the northern tip of the Yucatan's Riviera Maya, Cancun is also a fabulous place for snorkeling, sailing, sail-boarding, and touring the region's many fascinating Mayan ruins. Visitors will do well to remember one of scuba diving's cardinal rules: No drinking and diving.

Flower
Garden Banks
National Marine Sanctuary
Texas

CHAPTER **16**

ike primordial birds looming above the reef top, Atlantic manta rays can startle even a seasoned diver. Surprise turns to wonder as the mantas wing by, then ease into a slow-motion barrel roll. But these antics are not for show; the mantas are feeding, sucking up planktonic nourishment from the semi-tropical waters. In fact, divers at the Flower Garden reefs in the northwestern Gulf of Mexico encounter Atlantic mantas often enough to identify the regulars by their distinctive body blotches, which are as unique as fingerprints. Manta rays are the signature animals of the **Flower Garden Banks National Marine Sanctuary**, twin reefs 100 miles off the Texas coast. ◆ It's amazing that these two tiny coral outposts ever managed to find a foothold hundreds of miles from the nearest reefs in Florida and Mexico. But thanks to Gulf Stream eddies, the conditions here are downright Caribbean. Warm Gulf currents ferry coral larvae to the twin undersea salt domes, which were

Hammerheads, mantas, and spotted eagle rays flock to coral-veiled salt domes a hundred miles off the Gulf Coast.

pushed to within 60 feet of the surface during the late Jurassic period, about 180 million years ago. ◆ It happened like this: Evaporation deposited the salt at a time when the Gulf was a shallow, nearly landlocked sea. Over thousands of years, river silt settled over the salt. Because salt is less dense than water or sediment, it gravitated upward in a sort of geological Lava Lamp effect, pushing the overlying sediments into mountain shapes under the water. Salt domes formed in this manner all over the Gulf of Mexico. The two Flower Garden domes, shallowest of the bunch, formed 12 miles apart in a location that's nearly perfect for coral reef development. ◆ Credit the sun with penetrating the clear water and energizing the hard surface areas as another

A giant manta seems to soar on out-stretched wings. These graceful rays, some more than 20 feet across, are often seen feeding on plankton near the surface.

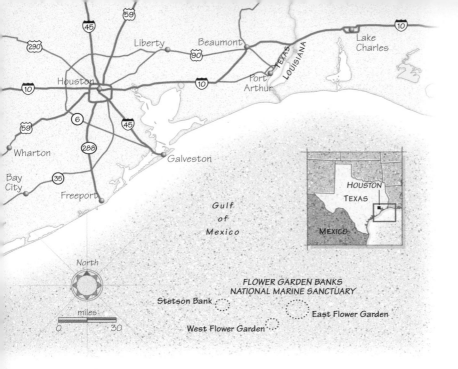

Many of the enormous coral heads have undersides smeared with encrusting sponges in strawberry red, mustard yellow, and sulphur orange. Some of the smaller coral heads have been sculpted into toadstool shapes by a process known as bioerosion, which includes the effects of animals grazing on the coral or digging holes in the formation. Small caverns riddle many of the formations, making the perfect habitat for reef fish like spotfin butterflyfish, yellowfin grouper, sharpnose puffers, and queen angelfish.

piece of the environmental equation that has made these reefs so successful. The **West Flower Garden** reef, a footprint-shaped formation no more than 100 acres in size, caps a bank five miles long and three miles wide. The **East Flower Garden** flaunts a reef cover almost three times the size of its western counterpart. Unlike a typical Atlantic reef with soft and hard coral species, the Flower Gardens are covered entirely in stony corals, mostly brain and star varieties. With depths from 60 to 100 feet, dive sites appear as expansive coral meadows filled with boulder-size coral heads scattered at random.

Only a few patches of sand interrupt the thick blanket of coral. In the narrow sandy alleys between the coral heads, tiny yellowhead jawfish stand vertically at attention above their burrows. Yellow goatfish probe the bottom with catfishlike whiskers called barbels. Schools of blue chromis, which can be quite pugnacious for four-inch-long fish, hover over the coral heads, while schools of two-foot-long, silvery horse-eye jacks rush through the reef. Near the dive boat, barracudas assemble below the safety lines.

More than Mantas

Besides the Atlantic mantas – year-round regulars – two different mobula ray species frequent the Flower Gardens in the spring and summer. And there are more than rays in the megafauna departments. Every summer, divers encounter at least a half-dozen whale sharks. In the late 1990s, sport divers saw these massive filter-feeders on more than 25 occasions during a three-month period. Whale sharks often mosey along, feeding near the surface. Sometimes they hang out in a tail-down position waiting for something tasty to swim overhead – when it does, the shark sucks it in, plankton, small fish, and all. Easy to identify, whale sharks can be up to 60 feet long, with a distinctive polka-dot design.

Every winter, schooling sharks and spotted eagle rays migrate to the Flower Garden reefs. The most fascinating members of the pelagic parade, scalloped hammerhead sharks, congregate here in schools of up to 50 individuals, from December to early April. The eagle rays' unusually long tails and white-ring patterns make them easy to identify. Unlike the leisurely mantas, eagle rays fly through the reef, seldom slowing down. And unlike other rays, spotted eagle rays sometimes join formations of hammerheads. In the fall, winter, and spring, silky sharks congregate en masse at the gas platform known as HI389A, a mile southeast of the East Flower Garden reef. From just below the surface to depths of about 30 feet, groups of these silvery, smooth-skinned sharks circle the metal structure, totally disregarding the thrilled divers.

Sanctuary Status

In the early 1970s, while oil and gas exploration activities increased dramatically in the Gulf of Mexico, government lease stipulations afforded only limited protection to the Flower Gardens reefs. Activists in the diving and scientific communi-

ties lobbied to preserve the Flower Gardens as a marine sanctuary, but their efforts were stymied by bureaucratic inertia. Although the petroleum developers appeared to be the primary threat, the real culprits proved to be the large vessels that caused anchor and chain damage to sections of the reef.

In 1990, a group of sport divers and marine scientists took matters into their own hands and installed 12 permanent boat moorings at the Flower Gardens. These moorings protect the reefs by allowing diveboat operators to tie up without using

Sex and the Single Polyp

Birds do it, bees do it, corals do it. And with impeccable timing. Every year, on the eighth and tenth nights after the full moon in August, the corals of Flower Garden Banks engage in an erotic frenzy. In the case of two full moons in a month, the spawn may happen four times, depending on water temperature and other factors that scientists are still puzzling over.

Star coral polyps first puff up, then withdraw their tentacles, which at night is unusual. The male cavernosa star corals begin "smoking" as they discharge sperm into the water. Female cavernosa colonies spew tiny spherical egg sacs with the regularity and vigor of a popcorn popper. The smaller annularis star corals gently release eggs sequentially in rows. The brain corals develop lines of tiny sex pearls that gradually emerge from the valleys between their convoluted ridges. On a celestial or perhaps chemical cue, hundreds of thousands of BB-sized packets of sperm break free from the coral colonies like a synchronized celebration. Other reef creatures and some fish also join the erotic fray.

To date, scientists have observed seven of the 21 coral species at the Flower Gardens participating in this reproductive orgy. Uncanny as it may sound, the timing of the spawn is predictable to within minutes. Although some spawning occurs earlier or later, the main event starts at 9:15 P.M. Central Daylight Savings Time and lasts about 90 minutes.

During the height of the major eruptions, the normally clear water is transformed into a blizzard of spawn. But unlike snow, the tiny white packets ascend slowly to form a thick mat of biologically active gametes on the surface. This is where most of the fertilization takes place. The young corals – tiny creatures called planulae that resemble flying saucers – drift in the current. Eventually they settle to the bottom and, if conditions are right, attach themselves and start new colonies.

Hawksbill turtles (left) search the reefs for shrimp, sponges, and tunicates to eat.

Star coral polyps (right) release bundles of eggs and sperm, which, in hospitable conditions, will begin a new colony.

In the Company of Sharks

Hundreds of black dorsal fins slice the surface like a scene from a Hollywood movie. But this is not the aftermath of a maritime tragedy; the fins belong to scalloped hammerhead sharks (*Sphyrna lewini*) feeding on fish close to the surface. The divers in the approaching boat know immediately they've hit the pelagic jackpot – a chance to get up close and personal with one of the ocean's great predators.

Flower Garden Banks draw hundreds of scalloped hammerhead sharks every year from December through early April. Some scientists believe the area may serve as a feeding station or mating hub, while others postulate that the animals simply move farther offshore as they seek warmer waters during the winter. The population usually reaches an apex in mid-March, and the animals are gone by the end of April. How they find their way still isn't clearly understood. One possible explanation is the sharks' ability to follow geomagnetic lines using the natural sensors on their heads.

Scalloped hammerheads (above), up to 14 feet long, use serrated teeth to eat fish, crustaceans, and other invertebrates.

Blennies (below) tuck their one- to four-inch bodies into abandoned barnacle shells, crevices, or sandy holes.

Most divers would think twice before jumping into an ocean full of 6- to 10-foot sharks, but these animals aren't aggressive. In fact, getting closer than 30 feet can be a challenge. One technique is to hang at the mooring line about 20 feet above the seafloor. Patience usually pays off. It may take 20 minutes, but to witness a school of these magnificent predators rushing overhead is an adrenaline-pumping privilege.

anchors. In 1992, the Flower Gardens area was designated the nation's tenth National Marine Sanctuary. This precious habitat is now protected by regulations governing fishing, discharges, anchoring, and oil and gas exploration and production.

The charter boats ferrying divers out to the Flower Gardens, usually 90- to 100-foot custom live-aboards, depart from **Freeport, Texas**, making the seven-hour run at night while their passengers sleep. Most trips include two to four days of diving, with a stop at **Stetson Bank**, the third bank welcomed, in October 1996, into the sanctuary's protected status. At this one-acre outcropping 30 miles northwest of the West Flower Gardens, divers find patches of star corals, a few mounds of convoluted brain corals, and a small field of knobby Madracis corals. But there's not enough coral cover to qualify it as a true coral reef. Instead of the limestone base of a coral reef, Stetson, which scientists have determined is geologically younger than the Flower Gardens, has a fine sand and clay base densely packed into sedimentary rock.

An Underwater Moon

Most of the diving at Stetson takes place around a series of sponge-cloaked pinnacles that are randomly spaced on the reef just inside its northern drop-off. Some of these risers are wide and stubby, while others are like pillars more than 15 feet high and rich with sponges, fire coral, and tube worms.

Prudent divers keep their distance from the deceptively smooth-looking fire coral, which is usually beige or mustard colored. Over the hard skeleton of this coral, minuscule hairlike polyps extend from tiny pores. The polyps come in two varieties, sensory/stinging and feeding; it's the stinging polyps that divers remember. Brushing against a fire coral can cause painful welts and a rash that can last for days. Avoid the bristle worms, too. These foot-long crawlers look like fuzzy caterpillars, but the white tufts along their sides pack quite a wallop; they're loaded with stinging cells.

Hard bottom ridges, terraces, and gullies make other areas of Stetson look like the surface of the moon. Unlike the moon, however, Stetson is brimming with life. French angelfish the size of serving plates and at least four varieties of butterflyfish flutter around the pinnacles, while scorpionfish lurk in twos and threes, camouflaged against the algae-covered rocks. Near the pinnacles, neon gobies, small wrasses, and shrimp set up cleaning stations for the rock hinds and blue tangs. The "clean-

Peacock flounders (left) are "left-eyed" fish. As the animal matures, the right eye migrates to the opposite side. Other flounders are right-eyed.

A whale shark (bottom) swims slowly near the surface, filtering plankton and small fish into its huge mouth.

ers" nibble like living toothpicks at parasites and dead tissue stuck to the much larger fishes' gills or mouths; they even enter their clients' mouths without being harmed.

Common invertebrates at Stetson include urchins, sea cucumbers, arrowcrabs, and lobster. Less-common invertebrates, the precious cowries and black sea hares, inundate Stetson every June. Sea hares, cousins of squid and octopus, look like 10-inch snails with rabbit ears. Most Caribbean varieties are pale or olive colored with dark, ringlike spots. The black sea hares emit a purple cloud of ink when distressed. Inside Stetson's drop-offs, patient divers may see tiny sailfin blennies flare their large dorsal fins. Dense schools of creole-fish and chromis fill the water column overhead. At 75 or 80 feet, depth mutes the colors at Stetson, but turn on a dive light or set off a camera strobe and the reef ignites in dazzling colors.

TRAVEL TIPS

DETAILS

When to Go

Diving is best from July to September, when air temperature on the Gulf of Mexico hovers around the upper 80s with high humidity. Sea breezes bring some relief. Coral usually spawns during the full moon in August.

How to Get There

Commercial airlines serve Houston Intercontinental and William P. Hobby Airports. Rental cars are available at the airports. Boats depart from Freeport, Texas, about 90 minutes south of Houston.

Getting Around

The sanctuary is reached only by live-aboard vessels.

INFORMATION

Brazosport Chamber of Commerce

420 West Highway 332, Brazosport, TX 77531; tel: 888-477-2505 or 409-265-2505.

Flower Garden Banks National Marine Sanctuary

216 West 26th Street, Suite 104, Bryan, TX 77803; tel: 409-779-2705.

Freeport Information Center

Parks Department, 500 Brazosport Boulevard, Freeport, TX 77541; tel: 409-233-3306.

CAMPING

Brazoria County Parks Department, 409-849-5711 (ext. 1541), oversees eight county parks with 24 boat ramps, and two RV campgrounds, one with cabins.

LODGING

PRICE GUIDE – double occupancy

$ = up to $49 $$ = $50–$99

$$$ = $100–$149 $$$$ = $150+

Banker's Inn Bed-and-Breakfast

224 West Park Avenue, Freeport, TX 77541; tel: 409-233-4932.

Built as a bank in 1913, the inn features antiques, pressed-tin ceilings, and ornate woodwork. The bed-and-breakfast is within walking distance of the dock. Four guest rooms, two of them suites, share a marble bathroom. All rooms have air-conditioning and a television. The price includes breakfast. A reservation and two-night minimum are required. $$

Country Hearth Inn

1015 West Second Street, Freeport, TX 77541; tel: 888-325-7818 or 409-239-1602.

This standard hotel, situated near the harbor, has 40 rooms. A swimming pool and picnic area with barbecue are on the grounds. The price includes a continental breakfast. $–$$$

Roses and the River

7074 County Road 506, Brazoria, TX 77422; tel: 800-610-1070 or 409-798-1070.

More than 250 rose bushes adorn the grounds of this Texas farmhouse on the Bernard River, about a 20-minute drive from Freeport. Each of the inn's three guest rooms has a private bath, television, VCR, telephone, and whirlpool. Gourmet breakfasts are served. Children age 12 and up are welcome. $$$

DIVE OPERATORS

Greg's, Inc.

4007 North Bolton Avenue, Alexandria, LA 71303; tel: 318-487-4369.

Greg's 55-foot vessel sails out of Sabine Pass, Louisiana, and makes the run to Flower Gardens in about five hours. Most trips include dive stops at an oil rig, wreck, or another coral garden. The boat, which carries six to eight divers, has bunk-style accommodations and one bathroom. Captain Bill Gregory has been diving since 1959 and a scuba instructor since 1976. A weekend trip costs about $325.

Hydrosports Scuba

120 Highway 332 West, Suite A-6, Lake Jackson, TX 77566; tel: 409-284-0600.

This PADI five-star dive center arranges trips aboard the *Sea Searcher II*, a 95-foot boat that accommodates up to 16 passengers. Hydrosports supplies two safety divers, in addition to the vessel's own divemasters. A two-day trip to Flower Gardens includes nine dives, air fills and tanks, snacks, and meals. The cost is about $365 per person. There are three staterooms on board; two rooms sleep four passengers each, and the other is a bunk-room for eight. The boat has two bathrooms, a large dive deck, galley, salon, and a Zodiac chase boat.

Rinn Boats

1203 North Avenue J, Freeport, TX 77541; tel: 409-233-4445.

The 100-foot MV *Fling* and MV *Spree* each accommodate 34 divers and make two-, three-, and four-day excursions to Flower Garden Banks and Stetson Banks National Marine Sanctuaries. Trips also include a dive on at least one oil rig. The vessels are equipped with large dive platforms, sun decks, air compressors, and rinse tanks. There are 30 single bunks and two doubles; passengers share three heads and two showers. Three full meals are served daily. Divers board the vessel on the evening before departure.

MUSEUMS

Brazosport Museum of Natural History

400 College Drive, Lake Jackson, TX 77566; tel: 409-265-7831.

This museum has 14,000 seashells on display, with a special sand dune exhibit highlighting Gulf Coast shells and wildlife. In addition, the museum houses exhibits of regional archaeology, fossils, a replica of an allosaurus, and a large collection of carved antique ivory. Admission is free.

Moody Gardens

One Hope Boulevard, Galveston, TX 77554; tel: 800-582-4673 or 409-744-4673.

At this theme park, visitors can tour a 10-story pyramid called the Aquarium that houses a 1.5-million-gallon tank. Exhibits focus on the north and tropical Pacific, the Caribbean, and the edge of the Antarctic. In addition to experiencing marine life in the aquarium, touch ponds, and tide pools, visitors can observe penguins in a re-creation of their South Georgia Island habitat.

Sea Center Texas

300 Medical Drive, Lake Jackson, TX 77566; tel: 409-292-0100.

With five aquariums, the largest holding 55,000 gallons, Sea Center offers visitors a good look at Gulf Coast marine life, including nurse, black-tip, and bull sharks, red fish, jacks, and more. A touch tank allows youngsters to get their hands on sea anemones, blue crabs, urchins, and sea stars. A state-of-the-art fish hatchery is also open for tours. The center is six miles from Freeport.

Excursions

Gulf Islands National Seashore

1801 Gulf Breeze Parkway, Gulf Breeze, FL 32561; tel: 850-934-2600.

The park encompasses barrier islands strung along the Gulf Coast from the Florida panhandle to Mississippi. Attractions include white, sandy beaches, excellent bird-watching, and several good dive sites. Shore entry is possible at Santa Rosa Island near Fort Pickens, Florida, where a variety of fish, sea urchins, and other marine life is attracted to the jetties. Charter boats will transport divers to a number of sunken barges in the Pensacola area. Florida pompano, sea trout, cobia, sharks, and sheepshead are plentiful in the gulf. Shrimp, crabs, and flounder inhabit the gentler waters of Mississippi Sound.

Oil Rigs

Brazosport Chamber of Commerce, 420 West Highway 332, Brazosport, TX 77531; tel: 888-477-2505 or 409-265-2505.

Because natural underwater shelters are so few, offshore oil rigs constitute the Gulf of Mexico's greatest reef formations, adding acres of hard surface to the water column. Marine life blankets a new rig within months of its construction. Depth monitoring is easy during rig dives, but be prepared to share these sites with boaters and spearfishers. Shallow-set rigs provide fabulous murk-diving for lost items.

Padre Island National Seashore

P.O. Box 181300, Corpus Christi, TX 78480-1300; tel: 361-949-8068.

The largest undeveloped barrier island in the continental United States has more than 130 miles of beach. The main dive site, Seven and One-Half Fathom Reef, is about two miles off the island. The reef may have been the site of an ancient freshwater pond. Divers can explore intricate rock mounds covered in several inches of organic greenery and all kinds of tiny creatures, from mollusks and crabs to brittle stars and pistol shrimp.

Outer Banks
North Carolina

CHAPTER **17**

Flames erupted on the darkened horizon, casting an orange glow over North Carolina's coastal waters as another Allied ship became the casualty of a German submarine. By dawn, charred fragments of the ship littered the beach. It was 1942, just weeks after the bombing of Pearl Harbor, and World War II had undeniably arrived on the eastern shores of the United States. ◆ Shipping traffic along the 300-mile North Carolina coastline was hit hard during the early months of World War II. Tankers and freighters plunged to a watery tomb, joining an untold number of ships downed by nature's fury or human error, or in earlier wars. Today these tragedies provide the rare opportunity for divers to explore a four-century chronicle of maritime history that can't be equaled by museums or books. But it's more than just the urge to touch a piece of history that compels divers to visit these wrecks. Nowhere else in the United States, except southern Florida, does the Gulf Stream sweep so close to shore. This warm ocean current

The Gulf Stream bathes offshore wrecks in warm, clear water, nourishing marine life rarely found at this northern latitude.

flows up the coast from the Caribbean Sea to **Cape Hatteras**, the northern-most of three North Carolina promontories jutting out into the Atlantic. At the cape, the Gulf Stream collides with the chilly, south-moving Labrador Current, then veers out to sea. South of Cape Hatteras, the Gulf Stream brings summer water temperatures in the 80s, visibility of up to 100 feet or more, and the crystal-blue color usually associated with tropical destinations. ◆ As a result of the convergence of currents, North Carolina's waters teem with marine life, both warm- and cold-water species. Vivid carpets of coral and thick schools of silvery baitfish bring life to the rusting hulks of shipwrecks.

A team of divers returns to the surface with tales of coral-encrusted shipwrecks. The Outer Banks are known as the Graveyard of the Atlantic for the abundance of wrecks that litter the seafloor.

amenities and shipwrecks. A word of caution, however: Not all wrecks are created equal. Divers, particularly those with little or no ocean wreck-diving experience, should assess their skill levels before venturing out to deeper, more difficult dive sites.

Remnants of Battle

The adjacent cities of Morehead and Beaufort are located on North Carolina's mainland, west of **Cape Lookout** and just south of the thin ribbon of barrier islands known as the **Outer Banks**. Both towns offer accommodations, from group dive lodges and chain motels to oceanfront condos. Full-service dive shops and a wide selection of charter boats support the large number of divers who visit each year. While novice divers may get their fins wet on shallow, in-shore wrecks, the more experienced are lured to the quintessential North Carolina shipwreck – the German submarine, *U-352*.

On May 9, 1942, while on patrol off the North Carolina coast during the Battle of the Atlantic, the German submarine *U-352* suffered some fatal bad luck when it torpedoed a passing ship. The torpedo malfunctioned and nose-dived to the bottom, 200 yards short of the mark. In retaliation, the intended victim, U.S. Coast Guard cutter *Icarus*, depth-charged the attacking U-boat, killing some of its crew and forcing it to the surface. The surviving German crew members abandoned ship and were transported to Charleston on board the *Icarus*. The *U-352* sank 30 miles southeast of Cape Lookout, a stunning reminder of how close the war came to U.S. shores.

If conditions are good, as they often are here, with visibility reaching 100 feet, divers visiting the *U-352* see its clearly recognizable outline as they descend the anchor line to 115 feet. Beyond the torpedo-shaped wreck, deep blue water stretches into the distance. The sub, listing heavily to starboard, sits on a white-sand bottom, and hundreds of small fish dance in unison over its hull. On occasion, snaggle-toothed sand tiger sharks fin silently around its perimeter.

The most striking feature of the wreck, the conning tower, rises prominently from the

Large jacks and grouper, colorful tropical fish, and solitary creatures like tiny arrow crabs congregate on and around these wrecks. Barracuda are plentiful. Sometimes large sea turtles, stingrays, and sharks glide by in the distance. On the surface, dolphins often accompany dive boats to and from the wrecks, surfing along the bow wake. The presence of marine life depends in part on season, water conditions, and just plain luck.

While marine life may be transient, shipwrecks are not. The coast of North Carolina offers a handful of dive destinations – **Morehead City**, **Beaufort**, and **Hatteras** are the most popular – each with its own

sub's hull. From this vantage point, members of the *U-352* crew once peered out over the dark Atlantic. Today, the hatch remains permanently open, and divers can peek into the narrow vertical cylinder that provided submariners with their principal passageway to fresh air and open sky. Open hatches along the ship's 218-foot hull allow glimpses of the wreck's interior, and pieces of machinery punctuate the deteriorating deck. But the *U-352* is most impressive when viewed from a distance – a German U-boat in its entirety, sitting at the bottom of the ocean.

Another popular dive site is the freighter **Caribsea**, a defenseless casualty of the *U-158* in 1942. Lying in approximately 90 feet of water east of Cape Lookout, the *Caribsea* is renowned for its beauty. An airy lacework of ribs arching above a sandy bottom is all that remains of the forward section. With the sides of the hull broken open, divers peer through the ship, port to starboard. Large deck beams sit atop the remaining vertical structures, forming a canopy. Corals envelop the *Caribsea*, while invertebrates, tropicals, barracuda, and the occasional small shark

A diver (below) inspects the decaying hull of the *U-352*, a German submarine sunk by the Coast Guard cutter *Icarus* in 1942.

An open hatch (left) on the conning tower lets divers glimpse the sub's interior. The wreck lies at a depth of 115 feet about 30 miles from Cape Lookout.

accompany divers. Average visibility is about 65 feet, and because the site is relatively shallow, sunlight often brightens the surrounding water.

Fantastic and ghostly stories abound on the North Carolina coast, but the tale surrounding the *Caribsea* is perhaps one of the most poignant. James Baugham Gaskill, one of the 21 men who lost their lives on the ship, was born on **Ocracoke Island**, the Outer Banks' southernmost barrier island. Not long after the *Caribsea* sank, the sea

swept some of its wreckage north, depositing the jetsam on the shores of Ocracoke. Among the wreckage, a local resident – coincidentally Gaskill's first cousin – found the frame that once held the officers' licenses. Just one certificate remained: James B. Gaskill's. Soon after, the *Caribsea*'s wooden nameplate also floated to Gaskill's birthplace. Today visitors to Ocracoke can see a cross commemorating James Gaskill, carved from a piece of the ship's wreckage and placed on the altar of the United Methodist Church.

Outer Banks Solitude

Hatteras Village, an excellent location for divers who prefer a more isolated destination, is about a five-hour car- and ferry-ride north from Morehead City. The small village is located just north of Ocracoke at the southwestern tip of the Outer Banks' **Hatteras Island**. In the 1990s, Hatteras Village experienced a burst of growth and added its first cluster of stoplights to direct traffic between the ferry dock, the new marina, fancy shops, and the village's first chain motel. Nonetheless, Hatteras still offers the warmth and charm of an island community.

Visiting divers can get their tanks filled in Hatteras but should check with local operators about the availability of rental gear. Several dive boats operate from the local marinas, and although the choice of charters is more limited than in Morehead City and Beaufort, the selection of wrecks is just as appealing.

Bad weather and bad luck teamed up to sink the *F. W. Abrams* in 1942. After losing sight of the Coast Guard vessel that was escorting them to sea, the *Abrams* crew

Ironclad Dive

History loves an innovation, and that's what the U.S. Navy's ironclad ship, the U.S.S. *Monitor*, was on March 9, 1862, when it met the Confederacy's *Virginia* (formerly named *Merrimack*) at Hampton Roads, Virginia, in the most famous naval duel of the American Civil War.

During the brief and inconclusive battle, the *Monitor*, derided by critics as a "cheesebox on a raft," performed admirably against its opponent. In fact, its unique turreted, ironclad construction, teamed with the innovative placement of the majority of the ship's bulk below the waterline, represented several precedent-setting firsts in ship design and prompted revolutionary changes in naval warfare.

Nine months after the *Monitor*'s battle with the *Merrimack* and less than a year after its launch, the ship sank during bad weather – a less than illustrious ending for such a well-known vessel. The ship's location remained a mystery until 1973 when scientists using sidescan sonar discovered it sitting upside down in 235 feet of water about 16 miles southeast of North Carolina's Hatteras Lighthouse. Two years later, the site was designated as the first National Marine Sanctuary, under the management of the National Oceanic and Atmospheric Administration (NOAA).

For more than 20 years, diving the *Monitor* was restricted to official research teams. In 1990, the first private citizens participated in research dives on the *Monitor*, and in subsequent years sport divers were granted special access under NOAA's watchful eye. Sadly, the *Monitor* is rapidly deteriorating. Although NOAA continually works to preserve the ship, the corrosive effects of ocean currents and saltwater may eventually win the long-fought battle.

The U.S.S. *Monitor* (left) is a treasured sight for those with the technical skills and special permits needed to make the dive.

A sand tiger shark (opposite, top) scatters a school of baitfish at the wreck of the *Papoose*, a 412-foot tanker sunk in 1942 by a German U-boat.

Cape Hatteras Lighthouse (right), built in 1870, towers 208 feet above the beach.

mistakenly sailed into the American mine-fields near Hatteras Inlet. The sunken tanker, largely broken up, lies in approximately 90 feet of water. The engine and boilers rise above the rest of the low-profile wreckage.

Compared with the *U-352* or the *Caribsea*, the *Abrams* lacks big-picture appeal, but a close look reveals small creatures nestled in each of the ship's boiler tubes. A small crab peers out over its dainty claws, a tiny tropical darts in and out to guard its domain, and a very small moray eel calls another tube home. Photographers find these captive subjects an excellent reason to charge their strobes and focus their close-up lenses.

Farther offshore lies one of the island's most visually impressive wrecks, the tanker **Dixie Arrow**, sitting in 90 feet of clear water. On the stern section of this U-boat victim, the huge steam engine rises almost 25 feet from the ocean bottom. The intact bow provides an equally striking visual with the ship's large anchor chain still snug in its locker. Amberjacks, groupers, rays, and occasionally turtles frequent this wreck.

More than a dozen wrecks are dived out of Hatteras and other towns such as Nags Head to the north and Wilmington to the south, where divers have access to more chapters of maritime history. Noted dive author Gary Gentile has written an excellent two-volume set, *Shipwrecks of North Carolina*, providing detailed information on more than 80 North Carolina wrecks.

Year after year, hurricanes, nor'easters, and the constant push and tug of the ocean transform the faces of these wrecks. And year after year, divers return to North Carolina to explore its ever-changing underwater landscape.

TRAVEL TIPS

DETAILS

When to Go

June through September is the most popular time to visit both Hatteras and the Morehead City/Beaufort area. Air temperatures hover in the high 70s and low 80s. Water temperature averages 75°F. Hurricanes are always a possibility during these months, and mosquitoes can be voracious in Hatteras, especially after rain.

How to Get There

Commercial airlines serve Norfolk, Virginia. From there, it's 200 miles south to Morehead City and Beaufort, and 130 miles to Hatteras. One carrier serves Dare County Regional Airport in Manteo, about 50 miles from Hatteras. A few carriers serve Craven Regional Airport in New Bern, North Carolina, about 45 minutes from Morehead City. Shuttles run from Norfolk Airport to the Outer Banks.

Getting Around

Rental cars are available in Norfolk, New Bern, and at Dare County Regional Airport. There is no public transportation, but there is a double-decker bus in Beaufort, as much an attraction as a mode of transportation. The Outer Banks have several bike paths, and taxi and limo service is available. For information about ferries to Ocracoke and Hatteras islands, call 800-293-3779.

INFORMATION

Cape Hatteras National Seashore

Route 1, Box 675, Manteo, NC 27954; tel: 252-473-2111.

Cape Lookout National Seashore

131 Charles Street, Harkers Island, NC 28531; tel: 919-728-2250.

Carteret County Tourist Bureau

3409 Arendell Street, Morehead City, NC 28557; tel: 800-786-6962.

Dare County Tourist Bureau

P.O. Box 399, Manteo, NC 27954; tel: 877-298-4373 or 252-473-2138.

North Carolina Travel and Tourism

301 North Wilmington Street, Raleigh, NC 27626-2825; tel: 800-847-4862 or 919-733-4171.

Outer Banks Chamber of Commerce

P.O. Box 1757, 2000 North Mustian Street, Kill Devil Hills, NC 27948; tel: 252-441-8144.

CAMPING

Private and public campgrounds are available along the Outer Banks. For National Park Service information, call 252-473-2111. Reservations are recommended for trips in July and August.

LODGING

PRICE GUIDE – double occupancy

$ = up to $49 $$ = $50–$99

$$$ = $100–$149 $$$$ = $150+

Hampton Inn

4035 Arendell Street, Morehead City, NC 28557; tel: 800-426-7866 or 252-240-2300.

This four-story, 119-room inn is conveniently located on the intercoastal waterway of Bogue Sound, five minutes from Atlantic Beach. Lakeside rooms are available; a restaurant is on the premises. Arrange golfing and charter fishing packages at the hotel's main desk. $$$

Midgett Realty

P.O. Box 250, Hatteras, NC 27943; tel: 800-527-2903 or 252-986-2841.

Midgett Realty represents more than 100 Hatteras rental cottages. Most units sleep 10 or more and have sundecks, central air and heat, four or five bedrooms, and spectacular ocean views. Other amenities include washer and dryer, television, and VCR. $$–$$$$

Thurston House

P.O. Box 294, Ocracoke, NC 27960; tel: 252-928-6037.

Built in the early 1920s, this charming gable-front house is registered in *Historic Places of North Carolina*. The bed-and-breakfast is set on Ocracoke Island, 15 miles south of Hatteras, and offers nine air-conditioned guest rooms with private baths; some rooms have decks. The covered front porch overlooks an ivy-covered yard. $$–$$$

Tranquil House Inn

405 Queen Elizabeth Street, Manteo, NC 27954; tel: 800-458-7069 or 252-473-1404.

Set on Shallowbag Bay in downtown Manteo, the inn was built in 19th-century Outer Banks style. Each of the 25 rooms has its own character; some are mini-suites, with separate sitting rooms and bedrooms. Continental breakfast and evening wine are included. $$–$$$

DIVE OPERATORS

Discovery Diving Co.

414 Orange Street, Beaufort, NC 28516; tel: 252-728-2265.

Open since 1976, this dive operation runs four charter boats, ranging in capacity from 6 to 16 divers. Two lodges adjacent to the shop offer inexpensive accommodations. Services include equipment sales, rental, and repair; guided dives; and training for PADI certification to the instructor level.

Gunsmoke Charters Sightseeing, Snorkeling, and Scuba

Hatteras Landing Marina, P.O. Box 612, Hatteras, NC 27943; tel: 252-995-4021.

The *Gunsmoke*, a 45-foot, custom-built aluminum boat with a temperature-controlled cabin, carries 15 passengers. Arrange custom trips through Diamond Shoals Dive Center, 252-473-3494. Dive charters and underwater camera rentals are available.

Olympus Dive Center

713 Shepard Street, Morehead City, NC 28557; tel: 800-992-1258 or 252-726-9432.

This full-service dive center offers one-day and extended trips on three custom boats – one 65-footer and two 48-footers. Budget accommodations are available in the center's nearby bunkhouse. Services include equipment sales, rentals, and repair; air and nitrox fills; and full PADI and NAUI certification.

Outer Banks Dive Center/Sea Fox Dive Charters

3917 South Croatan Highway, Nags Head, NC 27959; tel: 800-679-6458 or 252-449-8349.

The center's 50-foot customized dive boat visits most of the historic wrecks along the Outer Banks. Services include equipment sales, rentals, and repairs; tank fills; personalized charters; technical diving courses; and training from open water to the instructor level.

Excursions

Bermuda

Bermuda Department of Tourism, 245 Peachtree Centre Avenue N.E., Suite 803, Atlanta, GA 30303; tel: 404-524-1541.

Although this 21-mile-long island is famous for its pink-sand beaches, it's best known to divers for its 450 shipwrecks. The British colony is 600 miles east of Cape Hatteras, and most of its wrecks rest in only 25 to 30 feet of water – great for recreational diving. There are 281 miles of healthy reefs and a wide array of nondiving water sports and activities.

New Jersey

New Jersey State Chamber of Commerce, 50 West State Street, Suite 1310, Trenton, NJ 08608; tel: 609-989-7888.

Countless shipwrecks from steel-hulled freighters to wooden schooners litter the ocean floor just off the Garden State's beaches. These waters, dubbed "Wreck Valley," earned their reputation from weather, war, and navigational mishaps. There are a number of deep-water technical wrecks, including the famous Italian luxury liner *Andrea Doria*, which sank in 1956.

Virginia Beach

Virginia Beach Visitor Information, 2100 Parks Avenue, Virginia Beach, VA; tel: 800-446-8038.

The waters off Virginia Beach claim more than two dozen wrecks, dating from 1888 to 1978. They vary in size from a 189-ton tugboat to a 32,600-ton battleship, and they rest in watery graves from 25 to 420 feet (well beyond the reach of most scuba divers) below the surface. Local operators run diving expeditions.

Lake Superior
Michigan

CHAPTER **18**

Fog wraps the early summer morning in cotton. On a small dive boat, a group of adventurers slips past the **Whitefish Point** breakwater into the waters of **Lake Superior**. At 31,820 square miles, this is the largest freshwater lake in the world, but today, visibility has shrunk to a circle of pond-flat water the size of a swimming pool. For 10 minutes, the captain guides his vessel through this shrouded world, navigating solely by radar and the signals of GPS satellites. It's easy to see why, in the days before radio and electronic navigation, collisions were common here. Whitefish Point marks the beginning of Lake Superior's **Shipwreck Coast**, a treacherous 80-mile stretch extending west to **Munising, Michigan**.   ◆   The boat coasts to a stop within an arm's length of an orange mooring buoy. Nearby, the distinctive chugging of a diesel engine announces the **Divers brave clear, cold** passage of a fishing boat, bringing home **water to explore some** a load of the catch that gives Whitefish Bay its **of the best-preserved** name. After a briefing, neoprene-suited **shipwrecks in the world.** explorers backroll into the water.   ◆   Things may be foggy upstairs, but it's a different story below the surface. As the group pauses at 50 feet to double-check computers and dive lights, every detail on the bottom of the dive boat above is still clear. The divers glide down the mooring line, its bright yellow hue dimming as deep water soaks the colors from the spectrum.   ◆   Farther they go, through thermoclines that place frosty kisses on exposed cheeks, dive lights winking on as blackness closes in. The line angles slightly, and they follow it to a shadowy shape that gradually resolves into the rounded stern of the wooden steamer *Vienna*, topped by a broad, shallow rail. Lower down on the boat's stern, the waterline markings,

Waves break against the eroded coast of Pictured Rocks National Lakeshore, which stretches for some 40 miles along Lake Superior's southern shore.

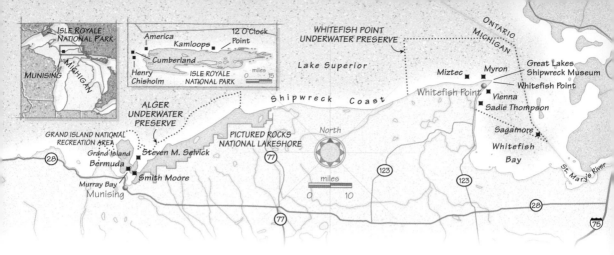

Roman numerals applied with white zinc paint, are still visible. The deck is 115 feet beneath the lake's surface, yet despite the violence of a trip to the bottom, much of the planking lies straight and true. In the hold, close inspection reveals that the wooden "knees" joining hull and deck were made by hand; hundreds of barely visible axe marks attest to hours of labor.

It's hard to believe the *Vienna* has been down here for more than a century.

Liquid Time Machine

Great Lakes diving may not be time-travel, but it's certainly the next best thing. Although there are natural wonders galore here – underwater caverns off **Pictured Rocks National Lakeshore**, near Munising, for instance – it's the shipwrecks that draw

divers from all over the world to the waters of Lake Superior.

All five Great Lakes have brisk, fresh, mineral-free water, which can keep extremely old wrecks in remarkable condition. Ships that went to the bottom during Abraham Lincoln's presidency often look as if they could be raised, repaired, and sailed again. If the Great Lakes have, as their proponents say, the best shipwreck diving in the world, then Lake Superior offers the best of the best – a magic combination of great wrecks, clear water, and a wild-and-woodsy North Country ambiance.

Amazingly enough, many divers living only minutes from the Great Lakes are unaware of their underwater wonders. Temperature is the main deterrent, but it's easily kept at bay with proper protection. Casual divers may settle for heavy-duty wet suits with hoods and mitts, but frequent underwater visitors should probably invest in the gear and training for dry-suit diving. Dry suits afford perfect comfort, even while drifting through the 40°F bottom temperatures that Lake Superior commonly registers in high summer.

Diving Like Royalty

Lake Superior contains the Great Lakes' only national park, 45-mile-long **Isle Royale**, populated by wolves and moose above the waterline and shipwrecks below. The drop-off around the mid-lake island is steep; the steamer *Kamloops*, for example, sits just 225 feet off **12 O'Clock Point**, yet lies 260 feet deep.

Most of the nine wrecks divers visit at Isle Royale are shallower, although all lie at acute angles on sloping bottoms. For instance, on the 183-foot steel-hulled passenger and package freighter *America*, divers – and even snorkelers – can view the bow under eight feet of water, while the stern sits on an 80-foot bottom. In between, divers will find the remains of a piano in the ship's social hall, a Model T truck, and other remnants of the 1920s, when the lakes were cruised in grand style.

The oldest wreck at Isle Royale, the paddle-wheel steamer **Cumberland**, lies near **Rock of Ages Reef** on the southwest end of the island. Bits and wooden pieces of the *Cumberland*, sunk in 1898, are jumbled together with parts of the 270-foot freighter **Henry Chisholm**, which also went down in the late 19th century. Pieces of the *Cumberland*'s paddle wheels are still visible in its watery grave.

While the *Kamloops* is strictly technical-diving country, the rest of the wrecks all have large sections within recreational-diving limits. Eight of the nine are shallow enough, at least in sections, to be explored by beginning

The **America** (opposite, bottom), a schooner sunk in 1880, lies on a steep slope between eight and 80 feet deep.

Dry suits (opposite, top) are essential for serious shipwreck divers in the Great Lakes.

Shallow wrecks like the *Sweepstakes* (right) in Lake Huron are perfect for snorkelers and beginning divers.

divers. The downslope ends of these wrecks tend to be deep, though, usually from 80 to 200 feet. This makes Isle Royale a destination that can grow as a diver gains skills, experience, and training.

Most divers visit Isle Royale on live-aboard charters, although they can also come on a private boat and stay in the lodge, cabins, or campgrounds. There is no dive shop or air station here, so divers need to bring compressors or arrange to buy air from a charter boat. Because of its remoteness (45 miles from the Michigan mainland and more than 20 miles from Grand Portage, Minnesota) and

federal regulations (all divers and private vessels must register with the U.S. Park Service, and charters must obtain a federal license to operate here), an Isle Royale trip is a major undertaking, but there are divers who make it a point to visit every year.

Century-Old Artifacts

Closer in than Isle Royale, Lake Superior offers a full menu of sport-diving options. During calm weather, a 14-foot inflatable is sufficient to reach most of the wreck dives in the **Alger Underwater Preserve**, the submerged portion of Pictured Rocks National Lakeshore, 15 miles northeast of Munising. The steam barge **Smith Moore**, an 1889 wreck, lies at 80 feet on a white-sand bottom, with the heads of its twin-cylinder steam engine visible. Only a 50-foot dive is neces-

sary to explore the **Steven M. Selvick**, a 71-foot tug that was cleansed of pollutants and then intentionally sunk, complete with its huge diesel engine, off **Grand Island**.

In Grand Island's **Murray Bay**, the wooden deck of the **Bermuda** lies only 10 feet beneath the surface, a haven for bass, perch, sculpin, and other freshwater fish. This 145-foot schooner has lain here since 1860, yet only a small portion of her deck is missing. Because the schooner is protected by law as well as by tradition, the only things divers remove are the make-a-wish pennies tossed by sightseers from a glass-bottom boat.

At **Whitefish Point Underwater Preserve**, the **Vienna**, whose mooring buoy is often visible from the Whitefish Point marina one and a half miles away, is the most popular wreck. With her engine intact, this steamer lies where she sank after a collision in 1892. Divers still find artifacts here, but they should be left where they lie. In fact, this wreck is monitored frequently to determine whether visitors are respecting Michigan's look-but-don't-disturb antiquity laws. With her deck at 115 feet and the sandy bottom at 140, the *Vienna* is, for the most part, within sport-diving limits, but it is a relatively advanced dive.

Newer divers will find a shallower option about a mile down the coast. The **Sadie Thompson**, discovered by Great Lakes Shipwreck Museum explorers, is a wooden barge and steam-powered crane lying tipped over on a 100-foot bottom. A bell-shaped work light, winches, and other machinery adorn this wreck, but novice divers should stay out of its interior. This is a good place to see whitefish, perch, and burbot, a deep-water fish that looks like a cross between a catfish and an eel.

Great Lakes Shipwreck Museum

"Penetration" (opposite, top) is the term used by divers for entering a shipwreck. It requires special training and equipment.

Dramatic formations (opposite, bottom) have been carved out of the Great Lakes' rocky shores by glaciers and erosion.

The Whitefish Point Light (right) was built in 1849 to warn ships away from the "Graveyard of the Great Lakes." The building now houses the Shipwreck Museum.

Any number of North Country museums celebrate Great Lakes maritime lore. What makes the Great Lakes Shipwreck Museum different is that, of the 20 ships remembered in its professionally designed exhibits, not one completed its final voyage.

Housed in a historic lighthouse compound on Michigan's lonely Whitefish Point, the museum was founded by scuba divers. All of the wrecks documented in the collection lie in waters within a few miles of the point. Divers can learn about a wreck in the museum and literally see it underwater an hour later.

Documented wrecks range from 19th-century steamers such as the *Vienna* (1892) and the *J. M. Osborne* (1886) to the *Edmund Fitzgerald*, the most recent vessel in the collection. In 1995, 20 years after the *Fitzgerald* sank, a cooperative effort between the museum, the Canadian Navy, National Geographic Society, and the families of the *Fitzgerald* crew recovered the ship's bell and restored it for display in the museum as a memorial to the 29 crewmen who perished. Each museum exhibit includes a scale model of the ship, an oil painting of the moment of its sinking, and actual artifacts recovered from the wreck.

On the other side of Whitefish Point, the *Myron* and the *Miztec*, two 19th-century shipwrecks, lie less than 50 feet deep. In their scattered debris, observers will see pulleys, anchors, chains, deck-machine parts, and other maritime bric-a-brac.

Financed through a variety of avenues, including pennies saved by schoolchildren, the museum opened in 1985. Since then, attractions have expanded to include a video theater and a restoration of the 1849 lightkeeper's quarters.

Curtain Call

Even as Lake Superior water begins its long journey to the sea, it still holds fascinating possibilities for divers. Lake Superior empties into Lake Huron through the **St. Mary's River**, where ships are lowered from one lake to the next via the famous "Soo" locks. Right at the mouth of the St. Mary's River lies the wreck of the *Sagamore*, a well-preserved example of a whaleback steamer-barge.

Metal-hulled whalebacks, vessels unique to the Great Lakes, looked like Jules Verne-era submarines. Their rounded hulls rode low in the water when fully loaded, plowing through and quickly shedding the heavy seas common to these lakes. That low-in-the-water posture proved fatal to the *Sagamore* in July 1901, when the package freighter *Northern Queen* literally overran the whaleback in heavy fog. Weighted with a cargo of iron ore, the whaleback and three of her crew plunged 70 feet to the bottom.

Today, the *Sagamore* sits upright where she sank. Although the deck cabins were blown off in the sinking, and lake perch now swim where the crew once worked, many interesting details, such as the huge tow-guides on the whaleback's bow, survive. On the afterdeck, look for the deck prisms – inverted pyramids of green glass pressed through the metal deck – designed to transmit light to the quarters below.

Since the *Sagamore* is near the shipping lane, divers should notify the Coast Guard when they anchor and again when they leave. In addition, be sure to dive from a vessel large enough to paint a recognizable radar-return. With these precautions, this St. Mary's River site is a fitting curtain call to the world's largest lake and some of the world's best shipwreck diving.

TRAVEL TIPS

DETAILS

When to Go

Unless visitors are prepared for ice diving, they'll have a better time exploring Lake Superior's wrecks in summer, when daytime temperatures range from the mid-50s to the mid-70s.

How to Get There

Whitefish Point is about 70 miles from the Chippewa County International Airport near Sault Ste. Marie, Michigan. The small Houghton County Memorial Airport is about five miles from the Isle Royale Boat Dock.

Getting Around

Visitors may explore the region by car, boat, bus, plane, bicycle, or foot. Rental cars are available at the airports. The Great Lakes Circle Tour, a scenic international road system, covers 6,500 miles and connects the Great Lakes and the St. Lawrence River.

INFORMATION

Great Lakes Information Network

c/o Great Lakes Commission, 400 Fourth Street, Ann Arbor, MI 48103-4816; tel: 734-665-9135.

Isle Royale National Park

800 East Lakeshore Drive, Houghton, MI 49931; tel: 906-482-0984.

Keweenaw Tourism Council

1197 Calumet Avenue, Calumet, MI 49915; tel: 800-338-7982 or 906-482-2388.

Pictured Rocks National Lakeshore

P.O. Box 40, Munising, MI 49862; tel: 906-387-3700 or 906-387-2607.

Travel Michigan

P.O. Box 30226, Lansing, MI 48909; tel: 888-784-7328.

CAMPING

There are thousands of campsites in and around Michigan's state and national forests. Reservations are advisable during summer. For state park information, call Michigan Parks and Recreation, 800-447-2757 or 517-373-1270. For private campground information, call the Michigan Association of RV Parks and Campgrounds, 800-422-6478 or 517-349-8881.

LODGING

PRICE GUIDE – double occupancy

$ = up to $49 $$ = $50-$99

$$$ = $100-$149 $$$$ = $150+

Curley's Paradise Motel

P.O. Box 57, Paradise, MI 49768; tel: 800-236-7386 or 906-492-3445.

The motel's 26 lakeside rooms have new furnishings and televisions. Five cottages near the water have kitchens and one or two bedrooms. A 1,280-square-foot house is available for rent, with two bedrooms, a fireplace, and bay windows. Curley's, which has its own air-fill station, arranges excursions to nearby Whitefish Point with local dive operators. $-$$

Keweenaw Mountain Lodge

U.S. 41, Copper Harbor, MI 49918; tel: 906-289-4403.

Built in 1934, this facility has 34 buildings, including motel-style rooms, a main lodge with a restaurant and bar, and one-, two-, and three-bedroom log cabins. A nine-hole golf course is on the grounds. The lodge, a five-minute drive south of Copper Harbor, is a few miles from the Isle Royale Ferry Dock. $$

Pinewood Lodge Bed-and-Breakfast

P.O. Box 176, Au Train, MI 49806; tel: 906-892-8300.

Ten miles west of Munising, this lodge offers easy access to Pictured Rocks National Lakeshore. Pines surround the log house, set near a sand beach. Six guest rooms are available. Accommodations include a loft, front porch, bridal suite, and lakeside gazebo. The bed-and-breakfast, built in 1989, has been featured in several log-cabin-living publications. $$-$$$

Rock Harbor Lodge

National Park Concessions, P.O. Box 605, Houghton, MI 49931-0605; tel: 906-337-4993 or National Park Concessions, Mammoth Cave, KY 42259-0027; tel: 502-773-2191 (off-season).

This Isle Royale lodge offers 80 units, both self-contained cabins and motel-style rooms (which include three daily meals). A full-service dining room, marina with hook-ups for vessels up to 65 feet, and motorboat and canoe rentals are available. The facility is open from May through September. Visitors arrive via ferry, seaplane, or private boat. The five-hour ferry trip costs about $80 (round trip); children under 12 ride for half price. $$$-$$$$

DIVE OPERATORS

Lake Superior Dive Tours

401 North Armour Street, Chicago, IL 60622; tel: 800-899-7550.

Dive Tours has a Canadian underwater archaeological license, which permits the staff to explore wrecks in nearby Whitefish Underwater Preserve and other Canadian waters. The operator supports divers of all levels. Three- to seven-day packages including lodging, meals, and diving are available from May to September. Services include equipment rental, charters, and technical training.

Narcosis Corner Divers

474 Third Street, Calumet, MI 49913; tel: 906-337-3156.

The only full-service scuba diving company in Upper Michigan's Keweenaw Peninsula uses a 26-foot dive boat. Services include equipment rental, tank fills, charter trips, and both PADI and NAUI instruction.

Shipwreck Tours

1204 Commercial Street, Munising, MI 49862; tel: 906-387-4477.

The operator offers trips for both novice and expert divers to Munising Bay and Alger Underwater Preserve. Two boats carry 6 and 18 divers. Services include equipment rental and tank fills.

Underwater Outfitters

2579 Union Lake Road, Commerce Township, MI 48382; tel: 248-363-2224.

This full-service shop near Pontiac runs charter trips for divers of all levels to Lake Superior and elsewhere in the Great Lakes region. Passengers ride aboard a 25-foot aluminum trihull vessel. Services include equipment sales, rental, and repair, and training to the instructor level. $$

MUSEUMS

Great Lakes Shipwreck Historical Society

111 Ashmun Street, Sault Ste. Marie, MI 149783; tel: 906-635-1742.

The society runs the Great Lakes Shipwreck Museum at Whitefish Point, site of the oldest active lighthouse on Lake Superior.

Excursions

The Dunderburg

Lighthouse County Park, 7420 Lighthouse Road, Port Hope, MI 48468; tel: 517-428-4749.

This three-masted, 187-foot schooner rests in technical diving territory 150 feet below the surface of Lake Huron. The *Dunderburg*, whose 596 tons are marvelously preserved by cold water, sailed her maiden voyage on June 20, 1867. Fourteen months later, she collided with the steamer *Empire State* off the Michigan coast and plunged to the bottom. Below-decks investigation is possible for experienced wreck divers. Many divers say the view of one artifact alone, an intricate carving of a six-foot alligator head, is worth the trip.

Fathom Five National Marine Park

P.O. Box 189, Tobermory, Ontario, Canada N0H 2R0; tel: 519-596-2503.

At Ontario's only national marine park and Canada's first underwater preserve, divers pay a $10 registration fee to gain access to 22 protected shipwrecks. Submerged geological formations such as cliffs and caves also make interesting explorations. Flowerpot Island's hiking trails offer a change of pace during surface intervals.

Voyageurs National Park

3131 Highway 53, International Falls, MN 56649-8904; tel: 218-283-9821.

Fifty-five miles of this 219,000-acre, water-dominated park meander along the Canada/Minnesota border. Named after the French traders and trappers who traveled its waters in birch-bark canoes, Voyageurs encompasses more than 30 glacier-carved lakes, four of which are large enough for boating, canoeing, and diving. Topside and underwater exploration of the hundreds of coves and bays reveal some of the oldest rock formations in the world.

San Juan Islands
Washington

Two divers glide past a submarine wall, trying to comprehend the kaleidoscope of life around them. A jungle of sponges, sea stars, and tunicates blankets the rocky surface; schooling fish shimmer across their field of vision; giant plumose anemones grow like ghostly cauliflower in the dim water below. ◆ Around a stony buttress, the pair tuck into an eddy and move in close to investigate the carpet of creatures on the wall. They backpedal in surprise when two snakelike arms whip out of a crevice. A Pacific giant octopus, just a youngster at four feet across, emerges from its lair. Tentacles writhing, it sheds its camouflage and blushes from khaki to carmine. The divers wiggle their fingers, an attempt at octopus sign language. The cephalopod responds by gingerly probing the alien bubble-blowers, sucking onto dry suits, pulling at a dangling pressure gauge. Then, its curiosity apparently satisfied, the octopus jets backward

Sea life grows large and abundant in the chilly, nutrient-rich currents of the Northwest's Emerald Sea.

and vanishes Houdini-like into an impossibly narrow crack. ◆ This sentry awaits divers in the **San Juan Islands**, made up of about 172 puzzle-like landmasses in Washington's **Puget Sound**. Once an ancient mountain range, the region was overwhelmed by the sea millions of years ago. Today only the highest peaks show above the surface. The four main islands – Orcas, San Juan, Lopez, and Shaw – and their satellite reefs represent an underwater frontier, worlds away from the nearby metropolises of Seattle, Vancouver, and Victoria.

Plumose anemones look like plants, but they're actually carnivorous animals related to jellyfish and corals. Anemones kill their prey with stinging cells in their tentacles.

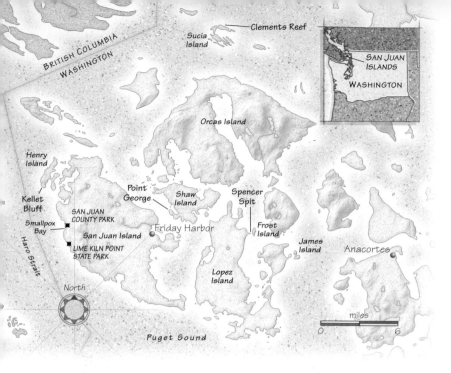

currents. Most dives need to be scheduled for "slack water," the period when water movement is at a minimum. This occurs when the current has stopped flowing in one direction but before it begins running in the other. To determine slack time, refer to current tables, such as *Captain Jack's Tide and Current Almanac*, instead of tide tables. Divers with little or no experience of currents and cold water should buddy up with a local guide, instructor, or veteran. Some dive operators here provide a pre-dive orientation on wearing a full wet or dry suit and adjusting the 25 to 30 pounds of weight necessary to offset the suit's additional buoyancy.

More than 500 dive sites are hidden away in the deep channels – averaging some 600 feet – between the islands. A wide variety of terrain offers divers of all levels interesting and challenging marine exploration. Year-round diving is possible thanks to 300-mile-long Vancouver Island, which shields the

It's no secret that this archipelago has some of the finest cold-water diving anywhere. The late Jacques-Yves Cousteau counted his dives here as some of the most memorable in a lifetime of ocean adventure. The chilly, current-swept waters of this "Emerald Sea" nourish a startling abundance of marine life from orca whales to jeweled snails. Coursing through the glacier-carved passes at up to six knots, the current is the lifeblood of the Pacific Northwest. This conveyor belt loaded with a soup of life-giving plankton is responsible for feeding reefs so lush that they rival the tropics for color and diversity.

Current Events

The ebb and flow of the formidable tides dictate where and when one can gear up and go down. Diving the San Juans safely and enjoyably requires staying within one's limits, knowing how to assess conditions, and having a thorough knowledge of the

Decorated warbonnets
(left) often hide in rocky crevices or camouflage themselves among marine plants.

Octopuses (right) can instantly change the color, pattern, and texture of their skin when they're threatened or looking for a mate.

Loud, misty huffs announce the presence of orcas near a sailboat off Vancouver Island (opposite).

San Juans from the Pacific's ferocious storms.

Most of the top spots here are boat dives. Watercraft enable divers to venture farther afield, reaching sites that promise better visibility and more abundant marine life. "Live-boating," in which the vessel drifts above the divers, following their bubble trail, is widely practiced and makes for easy pick-ups, especially in areas with stiff currents. Setting an anchor is difficult or impossible at many of the sites due to the great depths along the sheer walls.

Boat Dives

On the right tide, novice to intermediate divers find Shaw Island's **Point George** a good beginning. Because of the back eddy formed by the point, divers enjoy a rare situation in the San Juans – a mellow dive with little or no current. Many sites lie within a research reserve, protected from both commercial and sport fishing, and the numerous gargantuan lingcod are evidence of that. Top predators of the reef, the lings sport an impressive arsenal of teeth. Many other fish and invertebrates, including cabezon, scalyhead sculpins, scallops, barnacles, and multicolored nudibranchs, hide in the rocky crannies. Also in Point George's favor is its proximity to **Friday Harbor**. The hub of San Juan Islands' activity, especially in the summer months when thousands of tourists arrive, Friday Harbor is home to the islands' only full-service dive center.

A step up in difficulty, **Kellet Bluff** on the southwest tip of **Henry Island** offers intermediate to advanced divers a premier wall dive. The cliffs above the surface hint at the sheer and deep topography below. The showcase of marine life includes

Christmas anemones, purple and orange ochre stars, fist-sized barnacles, and the classic Northwest creatures – *Metridium* plumose anemones. Puget Sound and quillback rockfish usually make an appearance, along with masterfully camouflaged red Irish lords, a member of the bottom-dwelling sculpin family, and the decorated warbonnet, a reclusive, foot-long, eel-like oddity with growths on its head that resemble a Mohawk haircut. This is also a great spot to find the Puget Sound king crab, an armored tank of a crustacean growing to over one foot across and stunning in its

The Queen Charlotte Islands

Storm-lashed, rugged, and remote, the Queen Charlotte Islands stand alone in the Pacific, about 50 miles off British Columbia's northern coast. For hundreds of generations, this has been the home of the Haida people, about 2,000 of whom still live in this 150-island archipelago. Known in their tongue as "Haida Gwaii," this island wilderness is not only steeped in Haida culture but is rich in wildlife and eco-adventure possibilities. In fact, the Queen Charlottes have a nickname, "The Canadian Galapagos," reflecting their status as a showcase of evolution. The archipelago's isolation has given rise to species of flora and fauna found nowhere else, which include North America's largest black bear subspecies, a pine marten, and a yellow flowering perennial daisy.

Sailing, hiking, fishing, birding, whale watching, sea kayaking, and yes, diving are popular tourist pursuits in the Charlottes, and the roster of marine life is impressive. Marine mammals include gray, orca, and humpback whales, Pacific white-sided dolphins, harbor seals, and Steller sea lions. Beneath the waves, divers often encounter Pacific

Northwest celebrities such as giant octopuses and Muppet-faced wolf-eels, reef fish, and walls as bright as bouquets. Burnaby Narrows has some of the best tidepooling on the entire west coast of North America, with a Monet-like collage of sea stars, anemones, algaes, and other plants and animals on display at low tide.

A trip to the islands is not complete without a visit to Gwaii Haanas National Park Reserve and Haida Heritage Site, which encompasses about 15 percent of the Queen Charlottes. At the Ninstints village site at Skung Gwaii on Anthony Island, mortuary/totem poles have been left to decay slowly in the elements, as is the Haida custom. The fog swirls wraithlike around old-growth forest and fallen, moss-covered longhouses. It does indeed feel as if you've been transported back hundreds of years to the glory days of the Haida people.

Steller sea lions (above) gather in rookeries to socialize, mate, and give birth.

Totem poles (left) and the remains of a few plank houses are all that remain of an abandoned Haida village.

King crabs (opposite) can live for as long as 30 years. Their bodies are about 12 inches across, but their legs can be more than two feet long.

canyon in between. It's an intermediate site best dived at slack tide. Most divers explore the canyon or the inside walls where depths average 30 to 100 feet. Because of the site's protection as a national wildlife refuge, hundreds of black rockfish patrol

red, purple, and yellow shell. About 60 feet is a comfortable depth at Kellet, though one can go much deeper. Because of strong tidal currents and potentially dangerous downdraft currents at peak exchange, this site should be attempted only at slack tide from a dive boat.

At **Clements Reef** off the north shore of **Sucia Island**, two rocky reefs run parallel to each other, with a large, bowl-shaped

the reef in squadron formation. Giant sunflower stars (at some three feet across, the largest starfish in the world) make a meal of spiny urchins. Clements Reef also has harbor seals, which sometimes sneak up under cover of the kelp beds to inspect divers. They usually observe from a distance but occasionally approach, swimming around divers or tugging playfully on a fin.

Sampling of Shore Sites

Much of the waterfront property in the San Juans is privately owned or not easily accessible because of steep cliffs and dense undergrowth. Consequently, boat dives easily outnumber shore sites. However, a handful of popular shore dives are well worth the effort of hauling tanks down to the water.

San Juan County Park overlooks **Haro Strait** on San Juan Island's west side. Camping fans may find this the perfect place to pitch a tent for a few summer days and dive until they drop. There are a number of different novice to intermediate dives, from 10 to 100 feet. For one option, simply walk down the boat-launch ramp, swim out over a sandy bottom, then hug the rocky south shore of **Smallpox Bay**. Or climb down to the cobble beach in **North Bay** and kick out to the boulder piles. Both options yield excellent marine-life observation. Expect to see red sea urchins the size of volleyballs, bright orange sea cucumbers wedged between the rocks with feeding tentacles unfurled, chitons and limpets, and bottomfish such as the optically challenged flounder with both eyes on one side of its head. Shrimp march along the bottom and over tufts of algae while crabs scuttle along the sand, avoiding the lure of well-baited traps.

On Lopez Island, **Spencer Spit** rewards keen observers with a wealth of weird animals: penpoint gunnels, warbonnets, the whiskered bottomfish called poachers, and even grunt sculpins. One of the Pacific Northwest's most unusual fish, grunt sculpins are pig-snouted and wild-eyed, scampering shakily around on long, orange fin spines resembling stilts. If seeing these guys isn't enough motivation to tackle the 500-yard hike down the spit, perhaps the chance to encounter an octopus along the colorful wall of **Frost Island** is. Just remember to make the short channel crossing hugging the bottom at 60 feet to avoid overhead boat traffic.

A Whale Called Killer

Once mistakenly cursed as bloodthirsty monsters, killer whales now enjoy unparalleled popularity. Between May and September, visitors have an excellent chance to experience orcamania firsthand. They also have a good chance to see Dall's porpoises, harbor seals, sea lions, and minke whales, with an occasional humpback or gray whale cruising through. Approximately 100 killer whales make the area their summer home, finning in from the open ocean to feed on salmon and socialize with their pod mates. A thriving whale-watching industry with a fleet ranging from one-person kayaks to 200-foot floating hotels makes it easy to get a good look at this icon of the Pacific Northwest. Landlubbers can settle for a drive to **Lime Kiln Point State Park**. Besides being a thrilling shore dive, Lime Kiln offers terrific orca watching from the rocky shore. Not a bad way to spend a surface interval between dives.

TRAVEL TIPS

DETAILS

When to Go

In summer and early fall, these islands offer pleasant daytime temperatures between 70° and 80°F. The best diving is in spring and fall, periods of greatest visibility. Bear in mind that the water temperature averages about 47°F year-round. Three resident orca pods visit the San Juans from May to September.

How to Get There

There are a number of ways to travel to the San Juans, including car, ferry, seaplane, and conventional airplane. The drive from Seattle to the Anacortes ferry dock is about 85 miles. For information about Washington state ferries, call 206-464-6400.

Getting Around

Car rentals are available at Seattle-Tacoma International Airport and on some islands. On San Juan Island itself, visitors may rent bikes, scooters, and cars.

INFORMATION

Lopez Island Chamber of Commerce

P.O. Box 102, Lopez Island, WA 98261; tel: 360-468-4664.

Orcas Island Chamber of Commerce

P.O. Box 252, Eastsound, WA 98245; tel: 360-376-2273.

San Juan Island Chamber of Commerce

P.O. Box 98, Friday Harbor, WA 98250; tel: 360-378-5240.

San Juan Island National Historical Park

P.O. Box 429, Friday Harbor, WA 98250; tel: 360-378-2240.

San Juan Islands National Wildlife Refuge

33 South Barr Road, Port Angeles, WA 98362; tel: 360-457-8451.

Washington State Parks and Recreation Commission

P.O. Box 42650, Olympia, WA 98504-2650; tel: 800-233-0321.

CAMPING

A county ordinance prohibits off-road camping, but there are plenty of private and public campgrounds on each of the four main islands. For information, call San Juan County Parks, 360-378-1842. Reservations are recommended in summer.

LODGING

PRICE GUIDE – double occupancy

$ = up to $49 $$ = $50–$99
$$$ = $100–$149 $$$$ = $150+

Argyle House Bed-and-Breakfast

685 Argyle, P.O. Box 2569, Friday Harbor, WA 98250; tel: 800-624-3459 or 360-378-4084.

Built in 1910, this bed-and-breakfast is situated on an acre of land, two blocks from downtown Friday Harbor. Lodging includes three upstairs guest rooms with private baths, a two-bedroom suite on the main floor, and a separate guest cottage with a hot tub. Transportation from the ferry to the inn is provided. $$$–$$$$

Lakedale Resort

2627 Roche Harbor Road, Friday Harbor, WA 98250; tel: 800-617-2267 or 360-378-2350.

This San Juan Island resort, about a four-mile drive from the ocean, sprawls over 82 acres. Primarily a campground with 125 tent and RV sites, Lakedale also offers six log cabins. A hot tub is available for cabin guests. The entire compound is tucked between two private lakes. The resort is open mid-March to mid-October. Activities include fishing and boating. $–$$$$

Snug Harbor Marina Resort

2371 Mitchell Bay Road, Friday Harbor, WA 98250; tel: 360-378-4762.

This adventure-oriented resort on the west side of San Juan Island offers a variety of nature tours and rents fishing, sailing, and kayaking equipment. Twelve fully equipped cabins sleep up to six people each. A full-service marina offers scuba tank refills; a general store is on the premises. Accommodation and activity packages, as well as tent camping, are available. $$–$$$$

Trumpeter Inn Bed-and-Breakfast

420 Trumpeter Way, Friday Harbor, WA 98250; tel: 800-826-7926 or 360-378-3884.

Five guest rooms are available at this peaceful, contemporary farmhouse, one mile from town on San Juan Island. Surrounded by a bird sanctuary and acres of meadows, the Trumpeter offers a panoramic view of the valley. Two guest rooms have private decks and fireplaces; all have private baths. There is a hot tub in the garden. Breakfast is included. $$–$$$

DIVE OPERATORS

Emerald Seas Diving and Marine Center

P.O. Box 476, Spring Street Landing, Friday Harbor, WA 98250; tel: 360-378-2772.

This operation specializes in half-day dive charters for groups of two to six people aboard the 30-foot *Emerald Diver*. Diving equipment, kayaks, and underwater photography supplies are available. Training for open-water, advanced, and instructor certification is offered.

Island Dive

One Rosario Way, Eastsound, WA 98245; tel: 800-303-8386 or 360-376-7615.

Set at the Rosario Resort on Orcas Island, the only destination dive resort in the Northwest, this operation runs one 28-foot custom boat for 12 guests. Lodging packages are available. Services include equipment rental, guided dives, and PADI certification to the instructor level.

Anacortes Diving and Supply

2502 Commercial Avenue, Anacortes, WA 98221; tel: 360-293-2070.

The shop offers SSI certification classes from open-water through the instructor level. It rents, repairs, and sells dive equipment and underwater cameras and organizes scuba trips to the San Juans.

Starfire Diving

849 N.E. 130th Street, Seattle, WA 98125; tel: 206-364-9858.

This 54-foot dive boat, active since 1973, operates out of Cap Sante Marina in Anacortes. Two-tank trips are scheduled on weekends and are also available by arrangement. Nondivers are welcome. Training programs can be arranged with advance notice.

Excursions

Edmonds Underwater Park

Edmonds Parks and Recreation Department, 700 Main Street, Edmonds, WA 98020; tel: 425-771-0230.

Octopuses inhabit PVC pipes at the first underwater park in Washington, a 30-minute drive north of Seattle. Wrecks, too, have been introduced as artificial reefs. The popular shore dive is known for its abundant marine creatures, many of which tuck into the nooks and crannies of the human-constructed features. After swimming 150 yards from shore, divers navigate the park along a series of rope "trails."

Keystone Jetty

Fort Casey and Keystone State Park, 1280 Engle Road, Coupeville, WA 98239; tel: 360-678-4519.

Marine fauna – giant ling cod, octopuses, wolf-eels, and anemones – pack the breakwater off the west coast of Whidbey Island. A popular shore dive, Keystone Jetty is raked regularly by strong currents, especially at the end of the breakwater. Divers should consult a tide-and-current table prior to descending, or they risk surfacing a mile down the beach.

Nanaimo

Tourism Nanaimo, 2290 Bowen Road, Nanaimo, BC V9T 3K7, Canada; tel: 800-663-7337.

The 366-foot Canadian Navy destroyer HMCS *Saskatchewan* was sunk in 105 feet of water off this diver-friendly city on the protected east coast of Vancouver Island. The area also offers excellent drift, wall, and boat diving for people at all levels of experience.

Strait of Georgia

Tourism British Columbia, Parliament Buildings, Victoria, BC V8V 1X4, Canada; tel: 800-663-6000 or 250-387-1642.

With more than four submerged Navy vessels, all upward of 300 feet long, the Strait of Georgia, west of Vancouver, is a wreck-diver's wonderland. The Canadian government sunk the vessels deliberately to create artificial reefs and dive destinations. The wrecks are located in 50 to 125 feet of water; some are suitable for experienced divers only.

Monterey Bay
California

CHAPTER **20**

The mother lode for divers in the Golden State is in the kelp forests of **Monterey Bay National Marine Sanctuary**. Like the fabled sequoias of the High Sierra, kelp is the most prominent member of a complex ecosystem that sustains hundreds of interrelated species. Wildly prolific, a single strand of kelp can measure more than 100 feet long and grow at a rate of five to eight inches a day. Anchored to the seafloor and buoyed by air bladders at the base of each blade, the plants sway in the current, forming a leafy green carpet on the surface and filtering the sun into shifting columns of light. ◆ It's a magical place for diving but not necessarily an easy one. Currents are strong, visibility low, and water temperatures usually in the 50s, making a dry suit or quarter-inch wet suit absolutely essential. The kelp itself can be a problem, too, looping around limbs and entangling gear. Avoid wasting precious energy or air at the surface by seeking gaps in the canopy. It may be easier to swim on your back, propelled by wide strokes

Swim with otters, sea lions, and leopard sharks in the kelp forests of the nation's largest marine sanctuary.

of your fins. If the vegetation is too thick, it's time for the kelp crawl: Swim forward on your belly and push the kelp down and aside with your arms as you pull yourself along on top of it. It works, but it's tiring; you'll envy divers zipping by in inflatable boats or kayaks. Should you get snagged, don't panic; slowly work yourself free or cut the offending plants with a dive knife. You can reduce your chances of getting caught by taping down loose mask and fin straps, streamlining the hoses hanging off your body, and wearing a knife on the inside of your calf. ◆ Finally, there's always the option of inserting your regulator and dropping down. You'll find

Shafts of light stream through a dense kelp bed, silhouetting a diver below. Kelp forests are one of the sea's most diverse and productive ecosystems.

much more space beneath the canopy, making the vertical strands much easier to pass through.

Floating through the forest at neutral buoyancy, you can more easily marvel at the natural riches around you and ponder how they developed here. The California Current carries a band of subarctic surface water southward along the coast, but a by-product of the Earth's rotation called the Coriolis effect causes this surface water to veer away from shore. The movement allows colder, nutrient-rich water to move in – water that flows from hundreds of feet below. Monterey Bay happens to sit atop the nation's largest known submarine canyon, which rises from two miles deep to within a hundred feet of the surface. Pushed by wind-driven currents, the upwelling of cold water enters the bay, whipping up the formation of kelp forests.

A kelp forest passes through distinctive seasons. Upwelling occurs from late winter to late summer, and each spring the kelp bed begins to grow from the holdfasts and shorter fronds that have survived the winter. By early summer, the kelp canopy clogs coves and inlets, reducing surface water circulation close to shore. Plants weaken and rot through the summer months. Pounding waves from winter storms thin out the surface canopy and complete the annual cycle. Many giant kelp plants live for just a year; some may last several years.

Divers find the Monterey Bay kelp forest at its most luxuriant in early autumn. Upwelling also declines then, making for consistently clear and slightly warmer water and visibility that can reach 60 or 70 feet – nothing to compare with the clarity of the Caribbean, but rare conditions for central California.

The garibaldi (above), California's state fish, loses its spots as it matures.

Waves (left) crash against the rocky headlands of Cypress Cove at Point Lobos State Reserve.

Market squid females (opposite) pile their egg cases on the seabed. Large numbers of squid arrive in Monterey Bay in May and die soon after spawning.

Beyond the Bay

Some of the region's best diving can be found to the south of Monterey Bay itself. At the southern tip of **Carmel Bay**, **Point Lobos State Reserve** encompasses more than 700 underwater acres that became the nation's first marine preserve in 1960. Nothing can be disturbed here, so the fish are big and tame, and sea otters are commonly encountered (and well fed, judging by the number of empty abalone shells and crab carapaces on the bottom). Only 15 teams of two or three divers can enter the water on a given day, and weekends book up well in advance. Once you enter **Whalers Cove** at the boat ramp, kick out into the kelp and descend, you'll know why.

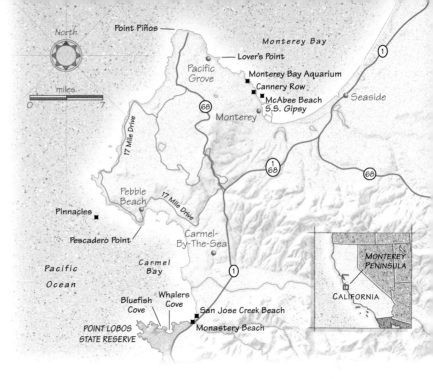

Dense stands of giant and bull kelp rise from rocky reefs encrusted with pale pink, scarlet, and cobalt-blue sponges, orange puffball sponges, and waving ribbons of red algae. A large lingcod sits atop a boulder, unflinching as you come face to face. Swimming around you or lurking under ledges are an array of rockfish: copper, gopher, blue, and China, to name a few. On the rock faces, carefully camouflaged masking crabs scurry away on spidery legs. You will likely see sea lemon nudibranchs or perhaps their delicate, rosette egg cases, so artfully arranged that they might garnish an exquisite plate of sushi.

Divers occasionally spot great white sharks cruising outside the kelp beds – one attacked a diver outside Bluefish Cove here – but much more common are harmless leopard sharks, which spawn every winter in the sandy shallows of Whalers Cove. Spend some time in the sandy patches and you might encounter a cluster of bat stars, stomachs extended, trying to make a meal of a dead but still cumbersome gumboot chiton. Or

hermaphroditic sea hares, odd-looking red-and-black mollusks with boxy snouts and pointy "ears." When bothered, a sea hare squirts a cloud of dark ink from skin flaps along its back. Should you find several forming a circle, with the head of one buried in the back of the one next in line, leave them to their mating.

Adjacent to Whalers Cove but accessible only by boat, the smaller **Bluefish Cove** to the south lays claim to clearer water and up to four times more marine life than its neighbor. Because of the cove's proximity to deeper water and its exposure to waves from many directions, it has a wider variety of open-ocean visitors – jellies, ocean sunfish, and blue sharks. Harbor seals often cruise by, as the beach at the south end of the cove serves as a haul-out spot and rookery. Don't be surprised if a harbor seal or

Monterey Bay Aquarium

When strong surge reduces your dive into a bout of buddy bumping, or underwater visibility vanishes an arm's length from your mask, there's still one way to sample Monterey Bay at its best. Shed those scuba tanks and head down Cannery Row to the Monterey Bay Aquarium. Ever since it opened in 1984, this immensely popular institution has redefined what an aquarium can achieve. And it's a great place to brush up on fish-identification skills.

A focal exhibit features a living, three-story kelp forest inside a 335,000-gallon tank. Shafts of natural light strike the sinewy stipes of giant kelp. Lithe leopard sharks, Day-Glo orange garibaldi, surf perch, and an array of rockfish swim about, while urchins, anemones, and other invertebrates fill the nooks and crannies.

Nearby, seven-gilled sharks cruise between mussel- and barnacle-encrusted pilings that reproduce a Monterey wharf, complete with a litter-laden bottom. Try to coax a bat ray close enough to touch – it's institutionally sanctioned petting – as it glides around a shallow pool.

The Outer Bay gallery offers the illusion of a window to the open sea. The sides and bottom are deliberately obscured by the tanks to represent a watery world without walls. A seemingly endless stream of mackerel streaks by, thanks to the largely hidden doughnut-shaped tank. Pulsating, glittering jellies lure one to look closely, then linger, mesmerized by their diaphanous dance.

Next comes the showpiece: fronted by the world's largest single-pane window, a million-gallon tank for yellowfin tuna, bonito, blue shark, and the bizarre mola, or ocean sunfish. The setting is languid and serene until a tuna tucks its dorsal and pectoral fins and blasts off in a bubble-trailing burst of speed.

A gallery is devoted to the denizens of the vast offshore trough, a formation comparable in depth to the Grand Canyon. Such creatures as ratfish, hagfish, eelpouts, and a predatory tunicate that captures prey like a Venus's-flytrap dwell deeper than scuba divers can descend.

Divers (above) feed the fish in one of the aquarium's enormous tanks.

Sea nettles (left) capture prey with tiny harpoon-like capsules in their tentacles. They can grow to a foot in diameter.

California sea lions (opposite, top) sometimes can be a little too playful; they've been known to nip the fins of passing divers.

A swimming crab (opposite, bottom) peeks out of its hiding place in the sand.

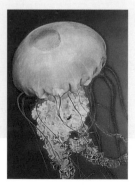

sea lion comes close to investigate while you're submerged at Point Lobos.

The protected inner cove offers calmer diving in a dense kelp bed that grows from a series of reefs. Farther out, the depth rapidly drops to over 100 feet, and this labyrinth of pinnacles, canyons, and sheer walls should be explored only by advanced divers. Here, intimidating gray wolf-eels hunker down among boulders piled at the base of walls coated in sponges, tunicates, tiny strawberry

anemones, and giant green anemones.

Sunflower Stars and Hydrocoral

Just north of Point Lobos, divers gather at **Monastery Beach**, a name uttered in reverent tones not so much for the Franciscan monastery across the highway but for the often rough surf and steep shoreline, which make for a treacherous ocean entry and exit. Many a novice diver winds up foundering in the waves trying to reclaim loose or lost gear, while the successful

emerge from their dives plodding on hands and knees – the Monastery crawl – like some early experiment in amphibious evolution. Even divers who emerge unscathed find plenty of pebbly sand grains coating their gear.

On a calm day, though, the glassy surface here beckons. From the south end of Monastery, also called **San Jose Creek Beach**, divers have easy access to a rich kelp forest that begins in 30 feet of water. Look for the multi-armed sunflower star, the largest and fastest sea star on the coast. A dive light illuminates its true colors: cotton-candy hues of pink and purple. Tiny white pincers protruding from its body fasten like Velcro to your neoprene gloves. Fragile-looking brittle stars and curious sea cucumbers can also be found here.

The rougher north end of Monastery offers divers colorful algae- and sponge-saturated boulders to explore in shallow water, as well as the rare opportunity to drop deep into a sliver of the Monterey

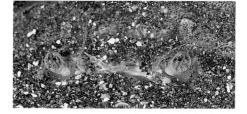

Canyon itself, along a 70-degree wall festooned with sea anemones, sponges, and bryozoans. Venture here cautiously, and adhere strictly to the bottom-time limits on your dive table.

Just north of **Pescadero Point**, less than a mile offshore from the golf courses of Pebble Beach, boat divers frequent an amazing spot called the **Pinnacles**. One pinnacle rises up to a depth of 40 feet, its flat top covered in thick kelp that could easily obscure divers but for their trail of bubbles. Schools of blue rockfish circle the promontory, as do jack mackerel, at certain times of the year. Descend deeper along the sides to see one of the treasures of California diving: pink and purple heads of hydrocoral. Tiny crabs and other animals may perch on the branches for shelter. Though not a true coral, since the anemone-like animals never emerge from their carbonate castle, hydrocoral nonetheless seems somehow out of place on this chilly coast.

Shore Dives

Crescent-shaped Monterey Bay extends northward from Point Piños in **Pacific Grove**, where divers can make a shore entry after wading out carefully through shallow water, or they can anchor a boat offshore. The rugged, rocky bottom offers plenty of terrain to explore without going deep. Nudibranchs and chitons abound. You might glimpse a sea otter probing the rocks for a meal, then gliding by over your head with air bubbles gleaming in its dense fur.

Student and novice divers frequently dive on the east side of nearby **Lover's Point**. Beyond beds of eelgrass, a dense kelp forest rises from patches of rock and sand. Strong sea surge often buffets divers, but Lover's is a likely place to find octopus in cracks or on kelp holdfasts. Impressive bat rays, with a finspan of more than four feet, probe the sandy bottom on the more exposed east side of the point.

John Steinbeck would barely recognize his fabled **Cannery Row**, now that hotels have replaced honky-tonks, but divers can still gain easy access to the water at **McAbee Beach**. It's shallow and sandy here, but one unusual sight is the boiler from the steamship **S.S. *Gipsy***, which ran aground in 1905 and spilled its cargo of kegs and cases of beer. Located about 50 feet out from the point at the south end of McAbee, the boiler sports a coating of pink strawberry anemones inside and may harbor a rockfish or two.

Once you have tried a few of these shore or boat dive sites – a sampling that just skims the surface of what can be found in and around Monterey Bay – ask other divers about their favorite spots. With so much to see in the cold-water world of the kelp forest, you may decide that a tropical diving vacation will just have to wait until next year.

Tidepooling

While divers may face rough conditions along the central California coast, the hardiest souls in Monterey Bay live in the intertidal zone. Twice a day, they endure extremes of wet and dry and the constant crashing of waves. With a little planning, you can enjoy a close look at these sturdy creatures. Consult the tide tables, and when the tide wanes, explore the marine microcosm of tidepools. Watch where you step so you don't squash the local inhabitants, and of course, don't take home anything more substantial than photographs. Wear sturdy shoes or rubber boots, a wind-resistant jacket, and pack an extra pair of warm socks.

Lined shore crabs (above) spend about half their life out of water and are often found in tidepools.

Mola molas (right), or ocean sunfish, feed exclusively on jellyfish, which they suck into their tiny mouths.

In addition, bring a copy of *Between Pacific Tides*. Ed Ricketts, one of the authors of this classic text, achieved immortality as "Doc" in two of John Steinbeck's novels. A noted – and somewhat eccentric – marine biologist, Ricketts was known to taste tidepool critters to test their toxicity. At Ricketts' ramshackle marine lab, which still stands on Monterey's Cannery Row, pay homage to Ed, then continue south to Point Piños in Pacific Grove.

Pick a pool, crouch beside it, and look. Gradually a whole invertebrate world emerges. Anemones unfurl their tentacles – or curl up tight if exposed to air. Hermit crabs tote ungainly snail shells. Sea stars, chitons, and limpets cling tenaciously to any hard surface, while purple-spined sea urchins burrow down into solid rock. Peer behind some pink coralline algae and you may find a small cancer crab or a snubnose sculpin propped up on its pectoral fins.

TRAVEL TIPS

DETAILS

When to Go

Visit in late spring, late summer, and fall, when temperatures are in the 70s and days are mostly sunny. Visibility improves during these periods, and water temperatures rise a few degrees from the winter average of 50°F. Early summer tends to be foggy and cold.

How to Get There

Major airlines serve Monterey Peninsula Airport, three miles from downtown Monterey. San Jose International Airport is a 90-minute drive; San Francisco International Airport is a two-and-a-half-hour drive.

Getting Around

Car rentals are available at all three airports. Automobiles are essential. The highways around Monterey Bay, some of the most beautiful in the country, are worth driving just for the views. The area is also great for biking, especially along Pebble Beach's Seventeen Mile Drive.

INFORMATION

California Department of Tourism

801 K Street, Suite 1600, Sacramento, CA 95814; tel: 800-462-2543 or 916-322-2881.

Monterey Bay Aquarium

886 Cannery Row, Monterey, CA 93942; tel: 800-756-3737 or 831-648-4888.

Monterey Bay National Marine Sanctuary

299 Foam Street, Monterey, CA 93923; tel: 831-647-4201.

Monterey County Travel and Tourism Alliance

137 Crossroads Boulevard, Carmel, CA 93923; tel: 800-555-6290 or 888-221-1010.

Monterey Peninsula Chamber of Commerce

380 Alvarado Street, Monterey, CA 93940; tel: 831-648-5360.

Monterey Peninsula Visitors and Convention Bureau

380 Alvarado Street, Monterey, CA 93940; tel: 831-649-1770.

Point Lobos State Reserve

Route 1, Box 62, Carmel, CA 93923; tel: 831-624-4909.

CAMPING

There are dozens of campgrounds from Marina, north of Monterey, to the southern end of Big Sur. For information, call the State Park Monterey District, 831-649-2836; Monterey County Parks, 831-755-4899; or the U.S. Forest Service, 831-385-5434.

LODGING

PRICE GUIDE – double occupancy

$ = up to $49 $$ = $50–$99

$$$ = $100–$149 $$$$ = $150+

Bay Park Hotel

1425 Munras Avenue, Monterey, CA 93940; tel: 800-338-3564 or 831-649-1020.

Nestled in the trees between Monterey and Carmel-by-the-Sea, this cozy hotel has 80 guest rooms and a restaurant. The hotel is about three miles from the water and a five-minute drive from Fisherman's Wharf. Dive packages are available. $$–$$$$

Carmel River Inn

P.O. Box 221609, Carmel, CA 93922; tel: 800-882-8142 or 831-624-1575.

This secluded inn next to the Carmel River offers 43 rooms with king-sized beds, log furniture, television, and telephones. The inn also offers rustic cottages, some with fireplaces and kitchens. Monastery Beach and Point Lobos are a 10-minute drive away; restaurants are within walking distance. $$–$$$

Casa Munras Garden Hotel

700 Munras Avenue, Monterey, CA 93940; tel: 800-222-2558 or 831-375-2411.

This Monterey hotel, a mile from the harbor, encircles the hacienda of a 19th-century Spanish diplomat. Nine buildings are scattered across four acres of landscaped gardens. Many of the hotel's 150 guest rooms have fireplaces. A heated pool and restaurant are on the premises. $$–$$$$

Lone Oak Motel

2221 North Fremont Street, Monterey, CA 93940; tel: 800-283-5663 or 831-372-4924.

Divers receive a discount at this 46-room motel. The Lone Oak has an indoor spa with sauna and exercise equipment. Some rooms have fireplaces and hot tubs. There are several restaurants within walking distance. $–$$

Monterey Bay Inn

242 Cannery Row, Monterey, CA 93940; tel: 800-424-6242 or 831-373-6242.

This modern inn sits among the historic sites and souvenir shops of Cannery Row, a short walk from the Monterey Bay Aquarium. The 47 guest rooms have king-sized beds, televisions, VCRs, two-line phones, robes, and private balconies overlooking the bay. San Carlos Beach, with great shore diving, is steps away. $$$$

DIVE OPERATORS

Aquarius Dive Shop

32 Cannery Row, Monterey, CA 93940; tel: 831-375-6605.

In business since 1970, this operation has two dive shops. Guides lead up to four divers per excursion. Services include equipment sales, rental, and repairs, and underwater photo needs. Training for open-water, advanced, and divemaster certification is available. Nitrox and rescue classes are offered on request.

Manta Ray Dive Center

245 Foam Street, Monterey, CA 93940; tel: 888-626-8272 or 831-375-6268.

Manta Ray offers shore and boat dives. Guided dives and equipment sales and rental are available. There are extensive certification options, including a wide range of specialty courses.

Monterey Express Diving Charters

P.O. Box 2600, Monterey, CA 93942; tel: 888-422-2999 or 831-659-3009.

This custom-built, 42-foot boat transports up to 20 passengers. There are three hot showers on board. Guided dives are available by arrangement. Services include daily two-tank dives and Saturday night dives. Rental equipment is arranged through local dive shops.

Ocean Odyssey

860 17th Avenue, Santa Cruz, CA 95062; tel: 831-475-3483.

The shop is located 40 miles north of Monterey, but the dive boat, *Xanadu*, leaves from Monterey's "K" dock. Ocean Odyssey's knowledge of diving in the bay is exceptional; it has more than 100 sites in its repertoire. The owner specializes in technical diving. The outfit offers equipment sales and rental, including dry suits; training for all levels of certification; and specialty and technical courses.

Excursions

Jade Cove, Big Sur

Monterey Express Diving Charters, P.O. Box 2600, Monterey, CA 93942; tel: 888-422-2999 or 831-659-3009.

Diving for jade off the Big Sur coast is an adventure – and getting there is half the challenge: a 90-minute, winding drive south of Monterey, then a steep trail down to the cove. The easier method is to hop a charter boat from Monterey for the hour-long trip. There are stringent regulations on collecting the semiprecious stone (check with dive shops for updates); much of it, including a 9,000-pound boulder, has already been removed.

Fort Ross State Historic Park

Box 19005, Coast Highway 1, Jenner, CA 95450; tel: 707-847-3286.

The leaking, 225-foot steamship *Pomona* limped shoreward on March 17, 1908, and sank in 40 to 60 feet of water. Divers can reach the *Pomona* from shore and, afterward, examine artifacts recovered from the wreck at the park's museum. About 85 miles north of San Francisco, the park features a reconstruction of a 19th-century Russian trading post. Twenty campsites are open from April through November. Bring your own dive gear. Water temperatures are 51° to 55°F, and visibility can be poor.

Russian Gulch State Park

P.O. Box 440, Mendocino, CA 95460; tel: 707-937-5804.

More people visit Mendocino for art than diving (dozens of galleries versus three dive shops), but there is some interesting scenery in the 50°F water. At the state park two miles north of town, advanced divers explore the cove's southern end, a marine maze of nooks and rocky crannies. Nondivers roll along the three-mile bike path or explore the tidepools. Thirty campsites are available; the surrounding area features many bed-and-breakfasts.

Channel Islands
National Marine Sanctuary
California

The view from the dive boat is spectacular: a craggy desert island set against the sparkling blue Pacific. Strap on a tank and jump overboard, and the scene below is just as gorgeous: Shafts of sunlight dance through fronds of giant kelp, and a school of silvery anchovies arcs through the underwater forest in perfect synchrony. This cool-water paradise lies off the coast of Southern California in the kelp forests and rocky reefs of the Channel Islands. ◆ Like rough-hewn gems in a sapphire sea, the eight Channel Islands stretch 160 miles from San Diego to Point Conception, just north of Santa Barbara. The five northern islands – San Miguel, Santa Rosa, Santa Cruz, Anacapa, and Santa Barbara – are encompassed by both a national park and a national marine sanctuary, ensuring that the land will remain undeveloped and the surrounding waters pristine for generations to come. In the fall, when the weather is sunny and

Rugged, windswept islands beckon divers to a marine wilderness off the Southern California coast.

calm, there is, some enthusiasts argue, no more beautiful place to dive in the continental United States. The convergence of cool currents from the north and warmer tropical waters from the south creates a unique ecosystem that supports many hundreds of species of fish, invertebrates, plants, and marine mammals. ◆ For divers trained in California's kelp forests, tropical seas seem pleasant and comfortable, yet oddly empty. Sure, the topography of coral reefs can be spectacular and the fish there are colorful and abundant, but a warm tropical sea doesn't support the explosion of life you find in the cool, nutrient-rich waters of the Channel Islands. Differing from the somewhat flattened world of a coral reef, where most of the

Observant divers may spy a *Simnia vidleri*, a brilliantly colored snail less than an inch long that lives on red gorgonians at depths between 30 and 100 feet.

Spiny brittle stars (left) cluster around a purple urchin. Brittle stars are scavengers, cleaning up organic debris on the seafloor, while purple urchins feed on kelp and algae.

Western gulls are opportunistic feeders; this one (bottom) consumes a sea star.

Spiny lobsters (opposite) hide during the day. They search for food with their long antennae at night.

pink-and-black sheephead swimming through the mid-water forest. Giant kelpfish are also common here, but they're easy to miss among the kelp fronds because they change their color to match the background. While you're busy looking for camouflaged fish, a sea lion may zip up and grab one of your fins in a game of tug-of-war.

Pause on your way to the bottom to look up at the sunlight filtering through the canopy: this breathtaking view is like no other underwater scene. Chances are, at some point you'll come face to mask with California's official saltwater fish, the garibaldi. With their garish orange bodies, white lips, and eyes that seem to pop out of their skulls, these fish may look comical, but don't be deceived by appearances: they are fiercely territorial and will boldly charge divers who venture too close to their nests. When you reach the reef, you'll encounter a phantasmagoria of movement, color, and texture. Living organisms blanket every available surface. Colonies of strawberry anemones in hues of pink, orange, and lavender compete for space with giant purple sea stars and spiny red sea urchins.

action is close to the reef, a kelp forest is a full three-dimensional experience with plenty of things to see from the canopy of kelp fronds at the water's surface to the rocky sea bottom 60 or more feet below.

Ambling through an Underwater Forest

On the surface, amber-colored, buglike isopods and frilly bryozoans, colonial animals related to coral and anemones, cling to the kelp fronds, while juvenile rockfish dart about under the canopy. Kicking down, you'll see schools of blue rockfish or a big

The diversity and abundance of invertebrates are especially impressive in the Channel Islands. Search out rock scallops, which are recognizable by the orange or pink

smiles they create when they crack open their two shells to the ocean current. Tunicates, which look like fleshy tulips on a long stalk, are actually a distant relative of all vertebrates, including humans. Nudibranchs, found on the sea bottom and clinging to the kelp, are the showboats of this marine forest, their bright, colorful bodies a warning to predators that these invertebrates make foul-tasting meals.

Peek into holes and crevices and you might catch a glimpse of a lobster or shy octopus. But be warned – you may also come eye to eye with a moray eel. If you look among the gnarled "roots" of the kelp plant, technically known as the holdfast, you'll see brittle stars, snails, crabs, and tiny shrimp. Occasionally, you'll glimpse an abalone clinging to a rocky shelf, but their populations have been decimated by overharvesting and disease. A recent moratorium on collecting these tasty mollusks has been in effect to help them recover, so look but don't touch.

Crossing the Channel

The northern Channel Islands are separated from the mainland by a 40-mile-wide channel, so you'll need to hop on a live-aboard or charter dive boat to get there. Boats leave for the northern islands from the harbors at **Santa Barbara** and **Ventura**. The channel crossing takes from two to four hours, but travelers are often treated to dolphin or whale sightings along the way. Some 27 species of whales and dolphins frequent the area, including gray, blue, and humpback whales, spinner dolphins, and orcas.

Live-aboards are the best way to dive the

Channel Islands. Trip costs include plenty of food and tank fills, and the accommodations are comfortable, if not lavish. Divers share a bunk room and shower facilities; some boats even have a hot tub. During the day, the captains move their boats around, so you can usually dive a number of sites on different islands during the multi-day trip. At each spot, the divemaster or captain gives a brief overview of the underwater terrain and marine life and recommends a dive plan, but the buddy pairs are usually on their own to plan and execute their dives. Because the wind and weather can change from hour to hour, most captains play it by ear when moving around and choose sites in the interest of diver safety.

Diving can be challenging, especially in the winter and spring when wind, swells, and currents kick up. The wind and weather typically blow in from the northwest and

Blue Sharks, Blue Water

The first step is to cast aside a million years of genetic pre-conceptions. The second is even harder. Wait until there are a dozen triangular fins slicing through the water, and take a giant stride off the boat. It's the underwater version of California's favorite come-on – let's do lunch.

Southern California is a feeding ground for dive operators who specialize in shark encounters, offering divers and snorkelers a chance to get personal with blue sharks and the occasional mako looking for an easy meal. Most operations serve up healthy portions of shark ecology and conservation along with a massive helping of adrenaline.

Once the boat has motored to a promising site, the mate begins chumming the water with a bloody mixture of pureed fish – the shark equivalent of a dinner bell – that the predators can smell more than a quarter-mile away. Though some question the ecological merit of this practice, it's the only way to guarantee attendance. The crew members lower the shark cage into the water as soon as the lunch guests begin to arrive.

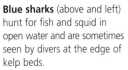

Some operators use a floating cage that people enter from the top, making it ideal for snorkelers. Others suspend the cage in the water column, with the entrance down below. Be prepared for the longest five-yard swim of your life. Divers are escorted into the cage one by one by a chain-mail-clad guide wielding a pointed stick to keep the circling sharks at bay. The chain mail protects the guide from toothy mayhem.

Watching a dozen sharks chow down on chum from the safety of the cage is guaranteed to give you a new perspective on food-chain dynamics. But don't let those cold, black eyes fool you. Human appetites are increasingly threatening these much-maligned predators, which have dominated the seas for nearly 350 million years. A hundred million are killed each year to make shark-fin soup, filets, and imitation scallops. Undoubtedly, your face-to-face encounter will give you a new appreciation of what ironically has been called "evolution's perfect eating-machine." – *Michael Menduno*

Blue sharks (above and left) hunt for fish and squid in open water and are sometimes seen by divers at the edge of kelp beds.

Black and yellow rockfish (bottom) are armed with venom-filled spines on their backs.

Spanish shawls (opposite), a kind of sea slug, are less than two inches long. They swim away from predators by flexing their bodies from side to side.

can hit the exposed northern islands of San Miguel and Santa Rosa pretty hard, especially in the winter. When it's windy, the best spots are on the southeasterly, lee side of the islands. The farther south you go in the island chain, the warmer and calmer the waters are, so winter and spring trips usually stick to Santa Barbara, Anacapa, and the southern Channel Islands.

To dive the Channel Islands, you'll need a full wet suit or dry suit, including hood, gloves, and booties. The water temperatures can be invigorating or shocking, depending on what you're used to and the time of year. During the spring upwelling, when water temperatures dip into the 50s, it may be a little too invigorating for all but the hardiest divers, but have no fear – by late summer and

early fall, water temperatures typically climb into the 70s. The water clarity also tops out in the fall, with visibility of 60 or more feet.

Island Highlights

Each of the islands in the Channel Islands National Marine Sanctuary has its own flavor and sports dozens of distinctive dive spots. There's something for everyone from wreck diving and lobster hunting to photography, snorkeling, and underwater sightseeing. On calm, moonlit nights, consider an after-dinner dive – a mystical experience lit, at certain times of year, by phosphorescent plankton that make tiny blue sparks stream from your fins and fingertips as you swim along.

First in line for south-flowing cold currents is **San Miguel**, the northernmost island. Because of its exposure to wind and weather, getting to San Miguel is more difficult than other islands, but it's worth the trip, since this island supports the highest density of marine life. The invertebrates and fish are larger, and elephant seals, pelicans, and cormorants make it a stopping point. In addition, six species of pinnipeds are found here in the largest rookery in the Channel Islands. Two offshore rocks, **Richardson** and **Wilson**, have sheer rock walls with an abundance of scallops and fish.

Second largest in the chain, **Santa Rosa Island** offers wind-swept sandy beaches, rocky intertidal areas, and grasslands – an especially pretty spot to visit. Explore the good dive sites in the sheltered coves behind **South Point** and the east end **Pinnacles**, where you'll find rocky shelves covered in anemones and scallops.

Santa Cruz Island is the largest and most visited dive spot for liveaboards in the northern Channel Islands. You can snorkel and shore dive off **Scorpion Landing** or visit the wooden wreck of a U.S. Navy minesweeper, the **U.S.S. *Peacock***.

Anacapa is the only rookery in California for the endangered brown pelican. In another area, a mile of the northeast shoreline down to 60 feet is protected from hunting; as a result, the fish, scallops, and lobsters are large and docile. The kelp is also thick in a pristine kelp-forest habitat with hundreds of species of animals and plants.

Santa Barbara supports one of the largest California sea lion rookeries in the state. If you dive here, be prepared for fun and games with the playful pinnipeds, but be careful: Sea lions have sharp teeth. Some, especially mothers with young pups, have been known to nip divers who startle them, so keep your distance. One popular dive spot is **Southeast Reef**, on the protected southeast tip of the island. The kelp is lush and the rocky bottom covered with colorful nudibranchs, anemones, and sea urchins.

TRAVEL TIPS

DETAILS

When to Go

Fall is the best time to visit. The water is calm and clear, and air temperatures are in the mid-70s. Spring and summer are good diving seasons, though wind may interfere in some of the more exposed northern islands. The southern Channel Islands are accessible year-round; the northern islands may be difficult to reach in winter.

How to Get There

Several airlines serve Santa Barbara Airport, and Amtrak, 800-872-7245, stops north- and southbound in Santa Barbara. It's a three- to four-hour drive to Santa Barbara from Los Angeles, and six hours from the San Francisco Bay area. Some dive boats leave from San Pedro and San Diego harbors.

Getting Around

For live-aboard trips, take a taxi from the airport to Sea Landing dock in Santa Barbara. Rental cars are available at the airport.

INFORMATION

California Department of Tourism

801 K Street, Suite 1600, Sacramento, CA 95814; tel: 800-462-2543 or 916-322-2881.

Channel Islands National Marine Sanctuary

113 Harbor Way, Suite 150, Santa Barbara, CA 93109; tel: 805-966-7107.

Channel Islands National Park

1901 Spinnaker Drive, Ventura, CA 93001-4354; tel: 805-658-5700 or 805-658-5730.

Santa Barbara Chamber of Commerce

504 State Street, Santa Barbara, CA; tel: 805-965-3023.

Hot Spots Visitor Information Center

36 State Street, Santa Barbara, CA; tel: 805-564-1637.

Santa Barbara Conference and Visitors Bureau

12 East Carrillo Street, Santa Barbara, CA 93101; tel: 800-927-4688.

CAMPING

There are many state, national forest, and private campgrounds with tent and RV sites in the Santa Barbara area. Reserve state park sites through MISTIX, 800-444-7275. For information about Los Padres National Forest, call 805-967-3481; for Channel Islands National Park, 805-658-5711.

LODGING

PRICE GUIDE – double occupancy

$ = up to $49 $$ = $50–$99

$$$ = $100–$149 $$$$ = $150+

Cheshire Cat Inn

36 West Valerio Street, Santa Barbara, CA 93101; tel: 805-569-1610.

Flower gardens and decks surround the inn, a mile and a half from the harbor. Some of the 17 guest rooms, suites, and cottages have Jacuzzi tubs, fireplaces, and outdoor hot tubs. Rates include a full gourmet breakfast and afternoon and evening refreshments. $$$–$$$$

Coast Village Inn

1188 Coast Village Road, Santa Barbara, CA 93108; tel: 800-257-5131 or 805-969-3266.

This quiet inn has 26 guest rooms and suites, some with partial ocean views and full kitchens. A complimentary breakfast is included; a large heated pool is on the premises. Butterfly Beach is three blocks away, and Montecito, an exclusive shopping and dining area, is nearby. $$

Harbor House

104 Bath Street, Santa Barbara, CA 93101; tel: 805-962-9745.

Away from the bustle of town, yet within one block of beaches and fine restaurants, the inn has nine rooms, each furnished with antiques. All rooms have kitchenettes; some have separate sitting rooms. Bikes are available to the guests at no charge. $$–$$$

Old Yacht Club Inn

431 Corona Del Mar, Santa Barbara, CA 93103; tel: 800-676-1676 or 805-962-1277.

The inn's two restored turn-of-the-century homes lie in a quiet residential neighborhood one block from the beach. Guests use complimentary bicycles, beach chairs, and towels. A full breakfast is included, and several restaurants are within ambling distance. On two Saturday nights a month, the inn offers a five-course gourmet dinner for an additional fee. $$$–$$$$

Villa Rosa

15 Chapala Street, Santa Barbara, CA 93101-3507; tel: 805-966-0851.

This Spanish-style bed-and-breakfast has the casual sophistication for which Santa Barbara is known. One block from both the beach and Stearn's Wharf, the inn offers 18 guest rooms with private baths; four rooms have a fireplace. A walled courtyard encloses a swimming pool and spa. $$–$$$$

DIVE OPERATORS

Dive Boat

1567 Spinnaker Drive, Suite 203-393, Ventura, CA 93001; tel: 805-247-1199.

This 65-foot vessel sleeps 32 people in single and double

bunks. A 12-foot inflatable chase boat carries divers to hard-to-reach sites. The main boat has two bathrooms with showers, plus outdoor freshwater showers. A television, VCR, camera table, sun deck, clothes dryer, and hot tub are on board.

Great Escape Charters
10031 Beatrice Circle, Buena Park, CA 90620; tel: 714-828-9157.

The operator's spacious 80-foot boat, Coast Guard-approved for 49 passengers, carries 35 divers. In addition to bunks, there are six private staterooms, two bathrooms, and four fresh-water showers. The boat departs from San Pedro Harbor, and most trips are in the southern Channel Islands. Guided dives are available, as are meals.

San Diego Shark Diving Expeditions
6747 Friar's Road, Suite 112, San Diego, CA 92108-1110; tel: 888-737-4275 or 619-299-8560.

This operation offers multiday trips to San Clemente Island for cage-diving with sharks. Most of the diving is unanchored. The experience is unequaled, but participants must be prepared for drift dives.

Truth Aquatics
310 West Cabrillo Boulevard, Santa Barbara, CA 93101-3886; tel: 805-962-1127.

Three custom live-aboard dive boats run year-round to the Channel Islands. The one- to five-day excursions include gourmet dining. Non-divers are welcome for fishing, whale watching, and snorkeling. Divers may sleep aboard the boat the night before the trip. $$$

Excursions

Catalina Island

Catalina Island Visitors Bureau, P.O. Box 217, Avalon, CA 90704; tel: 310-510-1520.

Learn to recognize plants and animals on the underwater naturalists' trail in Casino Point Marine Park. Volunteers from the Catalina Conservancy tag plants and invertebrates to inform divers about the diversity of life in the kelp forest ecosystem. The Conservancy changes the trail monthly. An hour's boat ride from San Pedro, California, delivers divers to the remarkably clear water and rich marine life off this privately owned southern Channel Island.

La Jolla Underwater Marine Reserve

San Diego Visitors Bureau, 2680 East Mission Bay Drive, San Diego, CA 92109; tel: 619-276-8200.

At La Jolla Cove, a 20-minute drive north of San Diego, divers edge up to a submarine canyon 100 yards offshore. Fishing and boating

have been prohibited at the cove since 1929. Beautiful kelp forests dazzle snorkelers and divers alike, though only advanced divers should attempt explorations of the canyon's sheer walls.

Coronado Islands

San Diego Visitors Bureau, 2680 East Mission Bay Drive, San Diego, CA 92109; tel: 619-276-8200.

"Want to play?" That's what curious sea lions seem to be saying to divers; rambunctious pups sometimes mimic human swimmers. The pups lounge on the rocks from November to March, a good time to arrange a dive charter to the Coronados, 14 miles south of San Diego in Mexican waters. Divers may also glimpse rare sea creatures like the chestnut cowrie and the white sea urchin. Visibility remains between 50 and 100 feet year-round.

Cabo San Lucas
Baja California Sur
Mexico

CHAPTER
22

Divers off **Cabo San Lucas** find themslves at an ecological crossroad. Here, at the southern tip of Baja California, the sea floor falls away into a submarine canyon some 3,500 feet deep. Tropical fish from the warm Sea of Cortez mingle with large fish and mammals from the Pacific, and creatures that usually inhabit shallow water encounter the denizens of the deep. ◆ Near a wave-battered arch in **Bahía San Lucas**, between a craggy pointer called **Neptune's Finger** and **Anegada Rock** (also known as Pelican Rock), the sheer face of **Middle Wall**, 90 feet below, offers a peek at the drop-off zone. The water is perceptibly colder and darker in the abyss, and full of nourishment. In a process that biologists call upwelling, nutrient-rich water rises from the depths, replenishing the ecosystem. This abundance attracts notable species like the whale shark, a gigantic but gentle fish that tolerates divers as it feeds on plankton and squid. Such impressive residents aside, many of the bay's fish do

Marine life abounds at the southern tip of Baja California, where the tropical Sea of Cortez meets the temperate Pacific.

have a certain well-fed look typical of canyon regions. As if to demonstrate the point, an inordinately fat grouper lingers at the canyon's edge, staring into a mob of angelfish – *big* ones. ◆ A short swim away, the base of Anegada Rock offers an equally robust spectacle at depths to 70 feet. In a moment of interspecies communion, a balloonfish fins slightly to maintain its position 10 inches from a diver's mask, an alien hovercraft with bulging eyes. Wide-mouthed morays bristle at the squadron of tank-bearing strangers in wet suits, while a school of Moorish idols clouds the water with flickering movement, shimmering light.

A school of jacks, one of the most common fish in the Sea of Cortez, swirls around a photographer.

submarine canyon erode the base of the canyon walls, leading to submarine slumps, slides, and avalanches that shape the submarine canyon." At times, the usual trickle of flowing sediments becomes a torrent. Drawn by gravity to the canyon's edge, rivers of sand from Cabo San Lucas beaches tumble like waterfalls in slow motion. As unimaginable as it may seem watching the delicate particles fan out in their descent, experts speculate that millions of years of flowing sand wore the canyon away, much as rivers of water form such gorges on land.

Stationed between gentle slopes and the canyon, Anegada Rock and its environs exemplify the conditions that make Bahía San Lucas one of Mexico's most popular diving destinations. At nearby **Lover's Cove**, novices complete their first dives. Within shouting distance, their more seasoned counterparts explore the **Point** where the bay meets open ocean, the **Sea Lion Colony**, or the edge of the abyss itself. An easy *panga* ride or kayak trip away, a marina with a recompression chamber and a handful of dive shops serves the resort town of

Exploring the Falls and Beyond

Advanced divers descend beyond Anegada Rock into the canyon itself where, at 90 feet, a site called the **Sand Falls** demonstrates how the chasm might have formed. While ancient riverbeds, shifting fault lines, and the violent formation of the Sea of Cortez may have been responsible for an initial trough, many geologists believe that underwater sediment flows actually carved the canyon. "Water currents can be very strong, and sand is a very powerful erosion agent that is capable of creating such spectacular features as the San Lucas Submarine Canyon, cutting through even very hard rocks like the granite at Cabo San Lucas," explains Dr. Mark Legg, a geologist who formerly studied Baja's submarine canyons at the Scripps Institute of Oceanography. "Just as the sand from the beach erodes the base of the sea cliffs, which leads to landslides, the sand flows along the axis of the

Scalloped hammerheads (left) are most often sighted at offshore pinnacles and seamounts such as Gorda Banks.

Balloonfish (opposite, top) inflate their bodies when threatened, making themselves less appealing to predators.

A remote anchorage (right) in the Sea of Cortez promises pristine and secluded diving.

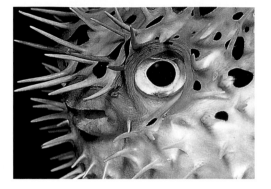

Cabo San Lucas.

Enjoying water temperatures ranging from 65° to 85°F and visibility from 25 to 100 feet (late summer and early fall bring the best conditions), the bay has one main downfall – congestion. Though the region is officially a marine preserve, Cabo San Lucas is the hub of a thriving sportfishing and tourist industry, with a lively nightlife. For a less-frenzied scene, divers explore the entire Los Cabos region, an area that includes Cabo San Lucas, San José del Cabo, and the 18-mile corridor between the two towns.

Between seven and ten miles northeast of Cabo San Lucas, **Bahía Santa Maria**, **Shipwreck Beach**, and **Bahía Chileno** harbor reefs and rocks at depths to 100 feet. Each has easy snorkeling or diving from boat or shore and marine life similar to that found at Bahía San Lucas. Intermediate divers venture onto the deeper finger reefs where, now and then, a Pacific manta ray glides in, its wings spread at lengths to 22 feet. Others take a short boat ride to the **Blowhole**, where walls and ravines between 40 and 100 feet attract the endangered green sea turtle, a graceful swimmer with the reptilian version of a thoughtful stare.

Expert divers head eight miles seaward from San José del Cabo to **Gorda Banks**, an underwater seamount that tops out at 110 feet. In addition to promising a current-raked drop onto bushes of black coral, Gorda Bank is the habitual hangout for schools of scalloped hammerhead sharks. Like sea turtles, hammerheads have fallen victim to irresponsible fishing throughout the Sea of Cortez, and Gorda Banks is one of the few

places you'll still have a good chance of seeing them. Sometimes numbering in the hundreds, the sharks create arresting silhouettes against a backdrop of blue.

Where Desert Meets Reef

For those willing to stage a desert adventure, a 65-mile drive northeast from Cabo San Lucas turns up **Cabo Pulmo National Marine Park**, home to the only living coral reef on North America's western coast. Cabo San Lucas dive operators can organize the trip, but it's easy enough to rent a car and arrange diving and equipment rental yourself in Cabo Pulmo. Along the way, branching cacti called *córdones* tower to heights of up to 60 feet, and

hardy desert plants form the backbone for a landscape of bright flowers and muted terrain. Clear views of the nearby Sierra de la Laguna range hint at the southern peninsula's layout – desert bisected by towering mountains, an ecosystem with coyotes, serpents, bobcats, mule deer, kangaroo rats, and birds.

With only a few dive operators, Cabo Pulmo is a tranquil village with little of the hype that characterizes Los Cabos. The region's prize jewel is **Bahía Pulmo**, a pool of turquoise that sparkles seductively offshore.

Most of Cabo Pulmo's sites are shallow drift dives along the reef, suitable for beginning to intermediate divers. Descending onto one of the eight hard coral fingers that comprise **Cabo Pulmo Reef**, it's easy to see why scientists call the Sea of Cortez a fish trap. With an estimated 3,000 species of fish and invertebrates, the sea contains just about

Cetacean Encounters

Within splashing distance of an inflatable boat, a cetacean blows, the spray bifurcating into the heart shape characteristic of the gray whale. A few blows later, its spine slices the water. The giant mammal's fluke rises to a perpendicular position before it disappears – close enough to count the barnacles and hear it breathe. By standards that astronomer Dr. Allen J. Hynek developed to rate run-ins with aliens and UFOs, the sighting is a close encounter of the first kind. With a bit more communication, it could have been a close encounter of the fifth kind. Alas, while many a whale watcher longs to speak cetacean, the human-whale relationship consists primarily of fascinating facts and heart-stopping sightings.

Fact: More than 50 million years ago, cetaceans' ancestors lived on land. Fact: Between 1864 and the passage of a worldwide whaling ban in 1986, humans hunted some whales nearly to extinction. Decades of conservation efforts are paying off in a resurgence of many species. Tragically, some subspecies are extinct. Fact: Gray whales migrate over 6,000 miles from their summer feeding grounds in the Bering Sea to winter breeding grounds in western Baja. Here they join fin whales, pilot whales, humpbacks, dolphins, and blue whales, which, at lengths up to 110 feet, are the largest animals ever to have inhabited the planet. Fact: Many gray whales give birth in shallow lagoons along Baja's coast every winter between December and April.

While the main breeding lagoons are farther north, the Cabo San Lucas region promises close encounters with several species of cetaceans from December to April. A Zodiac or *panga* is the best viewing platform, and an eco-conscious, respectful guide is a must. A good guide will also know where to find the most whales from day to day. Scan the horizon, and cross your fingers. They will come.

A two-spot octopus (opposite, top) camouflages itself by matching its skin color and texture to the seabed.

A whale shark (opposite, bottom), mouth agape, sieves plankton and other tiny creatures through a modified gill.

A gray whale calf (below) allows itself to be stroked, even kissed, by delighted whale watchers at San Ignacio Lagoon.

every reef fish imaginable and more than a few you wouldn't think up yourself. Many of the fish are endemic, the evolutionary by-products of the peninsula's unique geologic history. Their eclectic heritage reaches far back into the memory of the Pacific and even claims progenitors from the Caribbean. According to Dr. John Minch, author of *Roadside Geology and Biology of Baja California,* the Caribbean flowed to the Sea of Cortez until about three million years ago, when the Central American land bridge closed the link between the Atlantic and Pacific.

Unfortunately, the region's distinguished family tree is invisible to fishing boats, which patrol the sea looking for easy hauls. The Mexican government granted Cabo Pulmo marine park status in 1995, yet locals still struggle to enforce regulations with few resources. For now, thick clouds of fish weave a luminous web. A gray-and-yellow Cortez angelfish dips between clusters of coral, while a trumpetfish sucks prey into its anteater-like snout.

Back at the peninsula's tip, the falling sun sets fire to the **Friars**, the granite stacks that stand sentry over Bahía San Lucas. According to the world atlas, these rocks are the only bits of terra firma you'll see for quite some time should you be moved to hire a schooner and chase the southern horizon. In fact, it'll be just you, water, and the occasional whale until you stumble upon the continent of Antarctica. It's no wonder the rocks are revered here, carefully named like respected residents. They are place markers, symbols of beginnings and

endings, and – if you know how to look at them – historians. Stare closely at the rocks in Baja and you'll often find pale granite infused with dark patches. Those black bits are the birthmarks of the peninsula. Geologists explain that millions of years ago, during the region's turbulent formation, iron-laden, older stones called xenoliths fell into the hot magma. When the fiery soup cooled, the xenoliths retained their sooty color, creating the contrasts visible today.

As solid as they are, the rocks seem a fitting metaphor for southern Baja's diving. Beauty looms in the contrasts, in the unlikely encounters between deep and shallow, tropical and temperate, small and large – and in their extraordinary fusion.

TRAVEL TIPS

DETAILS

When to Go

Temperatures average 78°F year-round. Summer can reach into the 90s, with little humidity except for the occasional tropical storm. Hurricanes are most likely in August and September, but direct hits are rare in the Los Cabos region. October is a serious fishing month with lots of contests and charity events; book hotels well in advance. Several species of whales visit the region from December to April.

How to Get There

Los Cabos International Airport, 30 miles northeast of Cabo San Lucas, is served by commercial and charter planes. Travelers who drive the 1,000 miles from San Diego, California, should purchase car insurance at the border. Follow road advisories, and never drive at night.

Getting Around

Airport shuttles serve many resorts in Cabo San Lucas. Rental cars are available at the airport and in the city. Check availability through a travel agent.

INFORMATION

Mexico Tourism Hotline
tel: 800-446-3942.

Baja Information
7860 Mission Center Court No. 2, San Diego, CA 92108; tel: 800-225-2786 or 800-522-1516 (from California).

CAMPING

There are several camping and RV parks in the Los Cabos area. Call 800-446-3942 for a listing of campgrounds.

LODGING

PRICE GUIDE – double occupancy	
$ = up to $49	$$ = $50–$99
$$$ = $100–$149	$$$$ = $150+

The Bungalows
9297 Siempre Viva Road, Suite 40-497, San Diego, CA 92173; tel: 011-52-114-3-50-35.

Cabo's only bed-and-breakfast is five blocks from downtown Cabo San Lucas. The inn has nine one-bedroom suites, six two-bedroom bungalows, and one honeymoon suite. A freshwater pool lies amid a lush garden. $$–$$$$

Chile Pepper Inn
Abasolo and Avenue 16 de Septiembre, Cabo San Lucas, BCS, CP 23410, Mexico; tel: 011-52-114-3-05-10.

This small inn, four blocks from downtown, offers some of the city's most affordable rates. Rustic Mexican furnishings decorate nine renovated studios, which have air conditioners, queen-size beds, and televisions. $$

Hotel Finisterra
P.O. Box 1, Marina Boulevard, Cabo San Lucas, BCS, CP 23410, Mexico; tel: 800-347-2252 or 011-52-114-3-33-33 or 011-52-114-3-24-60.

On the Pacific beachfront, within walking distance of town, the hotel has 280 spacious rooms and 125 junior suites with terraces, deluxe amenities, air conditioners, and telephones. Two restaurants and bars and three swimming pools are on the premises. Staff members arrange sportfishing trips. $$$–$$$$

Solmar Suites
P.O. Box 8, Avenida Solmar 1, Cabo San Lucas, BCS, CP 23410, Mexico; tel: 800-344-3349 or 011-52-114-3-3535.

This secluded beachfront property is around the point from the famous rocky arches of Land's End, a short cab ride or walk from downtown. Most of the 82 junior suites overlook the Pacific Ocean. There are also 39 studios and 55 condos, as well as two pools (one with a swim-up bar), a restaurant, Jacuzzi, and tennis courts. $$$$

Terra Sol Beach Resort
Avenida Solmar, Cabo San Lucas, BCS, CP 23410, Mexico; tel: 800-524-5104 or 011-52-114-3-27-51.

Serene and private, this low-rise resort on the Pacific Ocean has 42 furnished beachfront studios and a number of one- to three-bedroom condos with full kitchens, private terraces, and air conditioners. A restaurant, pool, Jacuzzi, health spa, and tennis courts are also on the grounds. $$$$

DIVE OPERATORS

Amigos Del Mar
P.O. Box 43, Cabo San Lucas, BCS, CP 23410, Mexico; tel: 800-344-3349 or 011-52-114-3-05-05.

This PADI, SSI, NAUI, and NASDS facility, in operation since the early 1980s, uses a 22-foot *panga*, a small skiff, two 30-plus-foot trimarans, and a 25-foot runabout. Equipment rental, daily natural-history scuba and snorkel tours, sunset cruises, and whale watching are available. The outfit offers training for resort, referral, and open-water certification.

Cabo Acuadeportes
Apartado Postal 136, Cabo San Lucas, BCS, CP 23410, Mexico; fax: 011-52-114-3-01-17.

With locations in Cabo San Lucas and Chileno Bay, this complete service visits famous dive sites around the arches three times a day. Shore dives are conducted from Chileno. Dive sites are within a 10-minute ride. Equipment rental and certification are available.

Solmar V

Cabo Resort Reservations, Inc., P.O. Box 383, Pacific Palisades, CA 90272; tel: 800-344-3349 or 310-459-9861.

A classy live-aboard option, the *Solmar V* runs trips in the Sea of Cortez and to the remote Socorro (or Revillagigedo) Islands about 400 miles southwest of Cabo San Lucas. The luxurious, 112-foot yacht has 12 staterooms with in-suite baths and air-conditioning. The five-day package includes meals, snacks, and diving.

Underwater Diversions de Cabo

P.O. Box 545, San Juan Capistrano, CA 92693; tel: 949-728-1026.

American owned and operated, this PADI five-star dive center runs a 40-foot dive boat with a 20-diver, 50-tank capacity. The largest dive center in the Los Cabos area emphasizes personal service and attention to details. Services include equipment rental, guided dives, and diver certification.

Excursions

Los Islotes and El Bajo

Baja Diving and Service, Paseo Obregón 1665-2, La Paz, BCS, 2300, Mexico; tel: 011-52-11-22-18-26.

These islands in the Sea of Cortez may be visited on day or live-aboard trips from La Paz. Los Islotes features a thriving sea-lion colony and dive sites for both experts and beginners. Be sure to consult local dive operators before venturing out; male sea lions and amorous elephant seals may be a little too aggressive in some seasons. Big creatures frequent El Bajo, too, a spectacular seamount renowned for hammerhead sharks, mantas, and whales. This open-water site is popular with La Paz operators but should be attempted only by experienced divers.

San Ignacio Lagoon

Baja Information, 7860 Mission Center Court No. 2, San Diego, CA 92108; tel: 800-225-2786 or 800-522-1516 (in California).

California gray whales gather in early spring for calving and breeding in this sheltered lagoon on Baja California's Pacific Coast. Although diving and snorkeling are prohibited, visitors can observe the 30- to 40-foot creatures and their offspring from small boats called *pangas*, sometimes at little more than arm's length. It's a long, bumpy ride to the lagoon on a dirt road from the small town of San Ignacio, but for dedicated whale watchers, few experiences are more rewarding.

Socorro Islands

Solmar V; P.O. Box 383, Pacific Palisades, CA 90272; tel: 800-344-3349 or 310-459-9861.

Two words: giant mantas. They're one of the reasons divers travel to these islands 400 miles southwest of Baja. With a wingspan of 20 feet, the mantas are worth the 24-hour trip from Cabo San Lucas. Also known as the Revillagigedo Islands, these volcanic rocks are virtually barren above the surface but teem with underwater life. Sharks, tuna, and schools of jacks also abound, and humpback whales visit in spring. Drift dives are the order of the day, and strong currents limit the trips to advanced divers. Live-aboard trips run from November to May to avoid hurricane season.

Maui
Hawaii

CHAPTER 23

Armed with a magic hook, the Polynesian demigod Maui cast his fishing line into the Pacific and reeled up the Hawaiian archipelago from the depths of the ocean. To this day, a crescent-shaped island, the second largest in the chain, bears the trickster's name. Every year millions of vacationers visit only the terrestrial part of this paradise, but the realm from which Maui pulled the island is equally magnificent.   ◆   The same easygoing aloha spirit that prevails topside also seems to guide the inhabitants beneath the waves. Turtles meander by, often within a few feet of curious divers. Schools of reef fish loiter about, oblivious to errant currents. Adorned with brightly colored patterns, sea slugs of all sizes slink along so slowly it seems they're hardly moving. Hard-to-see anglerfish do their best to remain hidden in plain sight, and octopuses pick out a leisurely path over the seafloor. Armed with nothing more than open eyes, the diver enters a foreign world.   ◆

Fascinating endemic species thrive on the volcanic reefs of the world's most remote archipelago.

Huge, velvety green morays stand sentinel over their hideouts and gnash their razor-sharp teeth. The behavior looks threatening but is meant only to pump water across their gills. More than 35 moray species are found around the islands, making them one of the largest fish families in Hawaiian waters. Conger eels are also Maui citizens, but in contrast to the moray, they appear almost giddy, with pectoral fins protruding close to their faces and big lips frozen in what looks like a smile.   ◆   Green and pink parrotfish patrol the bottom; their constant gnawing on the reef makes a percussive background noise. With their

Endangered green turtles are often seen in areas with plentiful marine vegetation, which they eat. The largest turtles weigh up to 450 pounds.

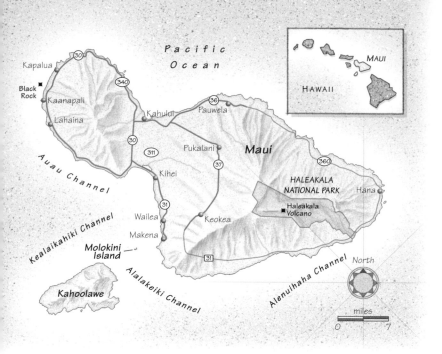

antler, razor, plate, finger, wire, and cauliflower corals. Rare black coral grows at greater depths.

Indigenous Treasures

Perhaps with help from trickster Maui's magic hook, two volcanoes formed the Valley Isle, spilling magma across the divide between them to make what is now a lush valley. This formation lends itself to many different micro-environments across the 729 square miles of Maui. In a trip around the island, visitors encounter rain forests, tropical beaches, ranchland, eucalyptus groves, fields of red earth (magma is rich in iron), deserts, and 40,000 acres of sugar plantations, which yield Maui's number-one crop. This natural contrast overlaps into the inhabited areas as well. High-rise hotels in developed towns such as **Kaanapali** are oases of comfort on the looping highway that traverses miles of untouched land along the perimeter of the island. Maui has more miles of swimming beaches than any other Hawaiian island, and one of the volcanoes, **Haleakala**, is the largest dormant volcano in the world.

As the story goes, it was from the top of Haleakala, which means "house of the

bright colors and beaklike teeth, parrotfish are easy to spot. They produce much of the white sand one finds on the islands; the material they scrape from rocks and coral passes through their digestive systems and emerges as fine sand – something to think about as you lounge on the beach after your dive. A large parrotfish can produce as much as one ton of sand each year.

Colorful little wrasses shift about, hunting for a meal from another fish's dirty scales or teeth. Many wrasses are cleaner fish. Akin to the symbiotic relationship between blackbirds and rhinos, cleaner fish eat parasites off larger hosts in a mutually beneficial transaction. Shortnose, belted, and blacktail wrasses are also found in Hawaiian waters.

Even without the plentiful and colorful marine life, Maui's underwater topography is impressive – intricate lava tubes, dropoffs, caverns, sandy bottoms, and huge basalt boulders. Dozens of hard coral species cling to these formations like visual puns –

sun," that Maui snared the sun and demanded he move more slowly across the sky. The road to the mountain's 10,023-foot summit is the only place on the planet you can climb from sea level to such an elevation in so few miles. Several island entrepreneurs make use of this fact in reverse, renting bikes with beefed-up brakes for the long downhill cruise. For scale, think about this: All of Manhattan could be tucked neatly inside Haleakala's crater. This volcanic Goliath serves as a touchstone on Maui. Residents give directions in terms of *mauka*, toward the mountain, and *makai*, toward the sea.

Some of the island's 2.3 million annual visitors would insist that Maui rates on a few other top-ten lists as well: best wind-surfing spot, Ho'okīpa; best weather, with only a 15-degree fluctuation year-round; most thrilling drive, along the Road to Hana, a 55-mile trek around the rugged eastern coastline. Some would argue that the four islands in Maui County – **Maui, Molokini, Lanai,** and **Molokai** – comprise one of the top ten diving destinations in the world.

Besides bountiful life and intriguing underwater topography, there is another reason why Maui's diving is first-class: Many species are found nowhere else.

Because Hawaii is the most isolated chain of islands on the planet – more than 2,000 miles from the nearest landmass – many of the plant and animal species are isolated from the gene pool. Early explorers found that 95 percent of Hawaii's plants were endemic. Two native mammals, the hoary bat and Hawaiian monk seal (now endangered), and countless birds and insects are found only in Hawaii. Of Maui's 450 species of reef fish, about 25 percent are endemic. Currently no indigenous fish or marine invertebrates are threatened. Unfortunately, the same is not true topside. Native plant and bird populations have declined dramatically throughout the Hawaiian archipelago due to habitat loss and competition from species introduced to the islands.

Dumeril's filefish (opposite, left) raise the long spine on their heads when threatened, making them too large for many predators.

Nudibranchs (opposite, right) are mollusks, usually just a few inches long and without a shell.

Slate-pencil urchins (right) have mouths on the underside of their bodies with which they eat algae on rocks and reefs.

The sea remains a moderate 70° to 80°F year-round. Though swimmers may find it refreshing, most divers opt for a wet suit. There is no thermocline; the water temperature at the top is the same as at the bottom. Visibility on the calm, western side of the island is usually about 100 feet. Maui's many dive operators, most of them clustered around the towns of **Kihei** and **Lahaina**, hit the water at sunrise – often a big surprise to late-rising vacationers. But it's the early bird who enjoys the best diving. Trade winds and surface chop pick up later in the day and make for difficult boating and surface diving. Regardless of conditions topside, those below are invariably wonderful.

Diving the Crater

Only half of Molokini crater's lip breaks the surface, a crescent sliver of land, 150 feet high, around a deep blue pool. A 15-minute boat ride from the Kihei boat ramp, the tiny

landmass is a bird sanctuary, off limits to humans. The surrounding waters are a marine reserve, but divers are welcome. In fact, this is the most popular dive site in all of Hawaii. Though the crater is only 400 feet across, sometimes as many as 20 boats bring snorkelers and divers here. In spite of human enthusiasm for the area, the true inhabitants of Molokini remain healthy and abundant. With a knowledgeable guide, you'll see not only the major marine players, but a supporting cast of creatures as well.

At the crater's center, clouds of reef fish hover over a sandy bottom. In the coral rubble at the crater's edge reside nearly motionless rockfish, and the camouflaged scorpionfish blends seamlessly with the background, pectoral fins spread like steady legs. Only the riffle of fins gives away its presence. The hard-to-find flame wrasse flashes a brilliant red, but only for a moment as it darts quickly between crevices.

The muted black Hawaiian damselfish may be the most plentiful fish in Molokini crater. About the size of a hockey puck, these are the territorial Pomeranians of the fish world; physically tiny, they have an attitude the size of a shark's. Dive guides may point out male damselfish that have lived in Molokini for a while, always staying in the same three-foot radius and bearing war scars along their dorsal fins proving their steadfastness. If an intruder (divers included) violates the territory where they guard eggs,

Whale Song

Underwater, you get used to strange sounds – heavy Darth Vader breathing from your regulator, knives clanking against tanks to get a group's attention, and the shushing of waves across the surface. But in Maui waters between December and May, there is another sound you're not likely to hear anywhere else: the song of the North Pacific humpback whales.

Each year, 500 to 1,200 *Megaptera novaeangliae* – about half the North Pacific population of the endangered humpback whale – trek the 3,500 miles from cold Alaskan waters to the remote Hawaiian Islands, one of the longest trips of any migratory species. Preparation for the trip includes abundant food consumption, as the whales do not feed in Hawaiian waters. What they do is breed, calve, nurse – and sing.

From January to March, the peak whale season, it is nearly impossible to dive off Maui without the accompaniment of the humpbacks. These 40-foot, 40-ton creatures are renowned for their serenades, though the actual purpose of the song remains unclear. Both sexes make various sounds, but only some of the males are "singers."

Since humpbacks have no vocal cords, researchers theorize that the whales produce the songs by circulating air through their complex respiratory systems. Hovering at a depth of 50 to 75 feet, the singing whale assumes a head-down, tail-up position and remains still but for the gentle waving of pectoral fins. His eyes are usually closed.

Whale song, if you're close enough underwater, vibrates your whole body. Even from miles away you can hear it, though it may be difficult to determine the direction of the source. The whales sing in tune with one another, maintaining the same melody, introducing new themes, and adapting accordingly as the song metamorphoses throughout the season. Though they do not sing during the summer, when the whales return the following winter, the singers pick up the prevalent melody from the end of the previous year – and the ever-changing song continues.

Researchers record humpbacks (above) with cameras and hydrophones at Maui's Humpback Whale National Marine Sanctuary.

Titan scorpionfish (opposite, top) camouflage themselves in reef rubble. Their venomous fin spines cause painful wounds.

Butterflyfish (opposite, bottom) swarm a diver at Molokini crater, where the inhabitants are used to being fed. As always, it's best to let fish find their own food.

the fish handle the encroachment with a three-step approach. First they try a few back-ended fin slashes. Then, more perturbed, they swim full speed directly at the eyes of the intruder, veering to the side just before impact. If the intruder remains, they add a menacing growl, sort of a clicking snarl similar to the riffling of a card deck, or a rolled *r*. Okay, they're not all that menacing, but they're serious about their territory and you'll know it. Down the slope of the submerged volcano, lobsters hide in crannies, and schools of indigenous Hawaiian long-fin anthias trail brightly colored pelvic fins above them as they swim upside down under ledges.

Once you're technically up to it, you can venture to the backside of Molokini crater, where the currents bring nutrients, and thus lots of fish, to the wall of a 250-foot drop. Drift dives along the crater's outer rim can be some of the finest in the state. The area is populated with sharks, whales, and other pelagics, including the largest fish in the sea, the gentle, 60-foot whale shark.

Launching from the Beach

Though many divers argue that the best sites must be explored from a boat, there

A Navy PB4Y-1 bomber (right) plunged into the Pacific in 1944. Today fish and coral inhabit the wreck, which lies at a depth of nearly 200 feet.

Harlequin shrimp (below) eat only sea stars, which they flip over to get at the soft underside.

An octopus (opposite) investigates a diver. When threatened, octopuses release a cloud of ink to cover their escape.

are plenty of great shore dives on the southwest coast of Maui. Provided that the surf is calm and access isn't too tricky, most beach-entry sites are suitable for beginner and intermediate divers. The dive profile usually doesn't exceed 40 feet, so there's an extra margin of safety. A brief inquiry at one of the local dive establishments usually reveals the good shore dives in the area.

One of the finest, **Black Rock**, was regarded as a sacred site by ancient Hawaiians, who believed this was a place where the spirits of the dead leaped from this world to the next. This shore dive off the well-developed **Kaanapali** coast is accessible, not too challenging technically, and truly amazing – especially at night. Lying off the point of the largest tourist area on Maui, the entire dive is no more than 35 feet deep, which means plenty of air time to explore the site. A craggy wall meets a sandy bottom riddled with large boulders, rock outcroppings, and plenty of crannies for marine life such as octopus and lionfish.

Scores of free-swimming morays and congers go on the hunt at night. Butterflyfish cloud the water with color. Of the 24 species of butterflyfish in Maui waters, three are endemic to Hawaii – the yellow or milletseed, bluestripe, and multiband. Flitting over the reef, butterflyfish mate for life and often travel in pairs. Blennies poke their heads from crevices, a permanent look of surprise on their faces. Black Rock is the Turtle Dream Inn, with dozens tucked away under ledges and in caverns for the night, breaking their slumber only to snatch breaths periodically at the surface. Colorful nudibranchs are numerous, and the Spanish dancers – in brilliant pinks, reds, and yellows – put on a show. Use a dive light to observe the nudibranchs as they slowly propel themselves upward and then drift, spinning, to the seafloor.

A visit to the Valley Isle – above and below the water– provides ample reason to celebrate the Polynesian trickster's fishing prowess: chittering damselfish, schools of yellow butterflyfish, singing whales, black-sand beaches laced with spindrift, cliff-lined shores hung with veils of water. It's not difficult to see why Maui is one of the world's most popular scuba diving destinations.

TRAVEL TIPS

DETAILS

When to Go

Maui's high season runs from mid-December through March. But the best weather and lowest rates are in spring and fall, when temperatures hover in the mid- to high 80s.

How to Get There

Several commercial airlines fly directly to Kahului Airport on Maui. Other carriers fly to Honolulu, where travelers catch an interisland flight. Flights from the U.S. West Coast are about five hours.

Getting Around

Rental cars are available at the airport. It's about an hour's drive from the airport to Maui's diving hubs, Lahaina and Kihei. Taxis and airport shuttles serve both towns.

INFORMATION

Haleakala National Park
P.O. Box 369, Makawao, HI 96768; tel: 808-572-9306.

Hawaiian Islands Humpback Whale National Marine Sanctuary
726 South Kihei Road, Kihei, HI 96753; tel: 808-879-2818.

Hawaii State Parks (Maui District Office)
54 South High Street, Wailuku, HI 96793; tel: 808-984-8109.

Hawaii Tourism Authority
P.O. Box 2359, Honolulu, HI 96804; tel: 808-586-2550.

Hawaii Visitors Bureau
2270 Kalakaua Avenue, Suite 801, Honolulu, HI 96815; tel: 800-464-2924.

Kalaupapa National Historical Park (on Molokai)
P.O. Box 2222, Kalaupapa, HI 96742; tel: 808-567-6802.

Maui County Parks and Recreation
1580-C Kaahumanu Avenue, Wailuku, HI 96793; tel: 808-270-7380.

Maui Ocean Center
192 Maalaea Road, Wailuku, HI 96793; tel: 808-270-7000.

Maui Visitors Bureau
P.O. Box 580, Wailuku, HI 96793; tel: 800-525-6284.

CAMPING

Plenty of camping opportunities are available in both Haleakala's upcountry and the tropical rain forest surrounding Hana. Some state parks require permits. For information, call 808-572-9306.

LODGING

PRICE GUIDE – double occupancy

$ = up to $49 $$ = $50–$99
$$$ = $100–$149 $$$$ = $150+

The Guest House
1620 Ainakea Road, Lahaina, HI 96761; tel: 800-621-8942 or 808-661-8085.

This five-room bed-and-breakfast is situated in a quiet Lahaina neighborhood, two blocks from the beach and a stroll from the historic district. Each room has a ceiling fan, air conditioner, television, and VCR; four rooms have a private lanai and hot tub. The intimate setting includes a sun deck, swimming pool, and fully equipped kitchen. The owner, a divemaster and tour operator, helps guests organize activities. $$

Kaanapali Beach Hotel
2525 Kaanapali Parkway, Lahaina, HI 96761; tel: 800-262-8450 or 808-661-0011.

Among the high-rises lining Kaanapali Beach, this hotel has 422 air-conditioned rooms with lanais that overlook the beach and lovely courtyard. Stays include snorkeling and/or scuba lessons, plus an extensive Hawaiiana program, with hula, music, cuisine, and lessons in traditional island trades. $$$$

Kea Lani Hotel Suites and Villas
4100 Wailea Alanui Drive, Wailea, HI 96753; tel: 800-882-4100 or 808-875-4100.

This resort is set on 22 landscaped, oceanfront acres with views of Molokini, Lanai, and Kahoolawe. Guests walk the grounds to the Royal Fountain Terrace, where seven waterfalls and four fountains cascade nearly 300 feet. Each of the 413 suites has a wrap-around lanai, marble bath, and entertainment center; 37 villas have gourmet kitchens, private plunge pools, and sun decks. $$$$

Maui Eldorado Resort
2661 Kekaa Drive, Lahaina, HI 96761; tel: 800-688-7444 or 808-661-0021.

These 204 condominium units, built in the 1960s, formed one of Kaanapali's first resorts. Each of the studio and one- and three-bedroom condos has a full kitchen, washer and dryer, and view. The resort has three swimming pools, large grassy areas, and a beach cabana. Several dive packages are available through Lahaina Divers. $$$–$$$$

DIVE OPERATORS

Ed Robinson's Diving
P.O. Box 616, Kihei, HI 96753; tel: 800-635-1273 or 808-879-3584.

Ed Robinson, a well-known underwater photographer, has been exploring Maui's waters since 1971. He usually arranges small charters to fill special requests. Custom dives emphasize natural history and marine biology. Training for introductory, open-water, and advanced certification is available.

Lahaina Divers

143 Dickenson Street, Lahaina, HI 96761; tel: 800-998-3483 or 808-667-7496.

Maui's first PADI five-star dive center and PADI instructor development center also operates the largest boats, a 43- and 50-footer. Equipment rental and certification to the instructor level are available.

Maui Dive Shop

1455 South Kihei Road, Kihei, HI 96753; tel: 800-542-3483 or 808-879-3388.

The operator has three shops in Kihei, and one each in Wailea, Kahana, Kahului, Lahaina, and Kaanapali. They're often the most convenient choice for renting tanks for shore diving. Deep-sea fishing, helicopter tours, and kayak excursions can be arranged. Services include equipment sales and rental, guided dives, and certification to the instructor level.

Mike Severns Diving

P.O. Box 627, Kihei, HI 96753; tel: 808-879-6596.

Run by marine biologists, this operation leads dives off a comfortable 38-foot boat. Diving is relaxed, well organized, and educational. Guided dives, specializing in Molokini, are offered.

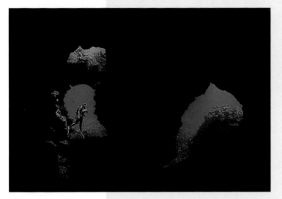

Excursions

Kanaio Coast

Mike Severns Diving, P.O. Box 627, Kihei, HI 96753; tel: 808-879-6596.

Divers with a taste for the rare and remote may appreciate a trip to the Kanaio Coast on Maui's south shore. Since weather conditions often prevent trips to Kanaio, the resident vampire morays and titan scorpionfish have few intruders in their pristine reef environment. From the boat, divers see lava-rock shelters built by ancient Hawaiian communities. Jagged lava flows and arches rise above the surface.

Lanai

Destination Lanai, P.O. Box 700, Lanai City, Lanai, HI 96763; tel: 800-947-4774 or 808-565-7600.

Dive boats travel from Lahaina, Maui, to Lanai in 30 minutes. In addition to acres of pineapples, the island has two high-end resorts and several good beaches. Dive sites run the geological gamut – walls, swim-throughs, caves, lava arches, pinnacles. Signs of human presence are less apparent here than elsewhere in the islands, and marine life flourishes. Most Maui dive operators will go to Lanai if clients plan in advance.

Molokai

Molokai Visitors Association, P.O. Box 960, Kaunakakai, HI 96748; tel: 800-800-6367 or 808-553-3876.

About 15 miles off Maui's northwest coast lies an island best known perhaps for its history as a leper colony. While those days are gone, Molokai remains slightly off the usual tourist track. Hawaii's only barrier reef offers divers plentiful fish and dense populations of turtles and eagle rays. Some Maui dive operators make the trip to Molokai, which has only one operator of its own.

Kona Coast
Hawaii

CHAPTER 24

Newcomers may be surprised by the Big Island. This isn't merely the Hawaii of lush tropical forests and gushing waterfalls but of snowcapped mountains and stark, black lava flows. Two volcanoes – **Mauna Kea** and still-active **Mauna Loa**, each rising nearly 14,000 feet above sea level – dominate the island and shelter the **Kona Coast** from the prevailing trade winds. As a result, divers enjoy calm seas and nearly year-round sunshine, except when the volcano acts up and the island is shrouded in "vog," a dense combination of volcanic ash and fog. Water clarity is exceptional, too, thanks in large part to minimal runoff from freshwater streams. Visibility is often greater than 100 feet and rarely less than 50. ◆ Water temperature in Hawaii dips into the low 70s in winter and warms to the mid-80s in summer. The cooler temperatures prevent coral from growing as robustly as it does in other tropical areas, so the fringing reefs of

In the shadow of two massive volcanoes, a lush fringing reef harbors a colorful cast of tropical fish.

the Kona Coast are relatively compact. Even without massive coral palaces, the topography is dramatic, with lava arches, tubes, and caves creating intricate underwater mazes. Exploring these natural formations is a Kona highlight, and swimming up through a vertical lava tube is an experience every diver should try at least once. ◆ Corals and coralline algae in muted tones of brown, olive, and pale lavender provide a soft background for the showy fish. From the brilliant yellow tang and the classic blue-stripe butterflyfish to the snaggle-toothed moray, more than 680 species are found here, 400 of them in shallow water. Several species of shark and schools of

Lava flows have created a labyrinth of caves, tunnels, and other fascinating volcanic formations along the Big Island's Kona Coast.

spinner dolphins also make their homes off the Big Island, and its reefs harbor the shy octopus and numerous species of colorful nudibranchs and sponges. Deep water just offshore attracts pelagic, or open-ocean, creatures such as humpback whales and manta rays.

Snorkeling or diving the Kona Coast is almost guaranteed to provide encounters with some of the healthiest sea turtles in the Pacific. Spend some time in the water and you'll get to know the spiky Hawaiian turkeyfish, a slipper lobster or two, and schools of slender needlefish that hover just below the waterline. The Hawaiian state fish, the *humuhumunukunukuapua'a*, or Picasso triggerfish, may take a while to pronounce properly, but its vivid, geometrically patterned body is immediately recognizable. The stiff little spotted trunkfish, the classic black-and-yellow-banded Moorish idol, and pairs of elegant, cream-spotted reticulated butterflyfish are also common sights.

Poke your head into the crevices of a reef and you're likely to come within kissing distance of a moray – but be careful of its sharp teeth. Eels, with their long, snakelike bodies, can fit into tight spaces, and during the day all you're likely to see are their gaping mouths. The zebra moray is among the most recognizable eels, with its brown body encircled by yellow-white stripes, but the dwarf moray is by far the most endearing. This six-inch yellow eel sometimes charges out of its hole like a ferocious toy terrier, its tiny white mouth agape.

Along the Kona Coast, rocky beaches are more common than sandy ones, but anywhere you can enter the water generally offers safe snorkeling and shore diving. To beat the crowds and enjoy glassy water and blue sky, head out early – after a cup of Kona coffee. You can enjoy a big breakfast afterward, knowing you've earned the calories.

Some of the best snorkeling

Spiny lobsters (left) avoid intruders by propelling themselves backward. They sometimes make grating noises by rubbing their antennae against their heads.

The Hawaiian lionfish (below) is equipped with venomous fin spines, making it one of the most dangerous fish in the islands.

A dragon moray (right) bears its needle-sharp teeth but poses little threat to divers.

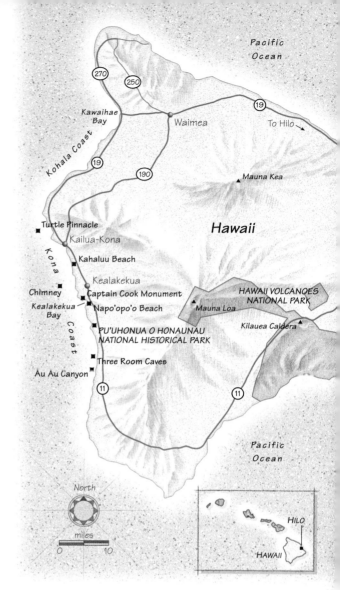

and diving are found around the funky tourist town of **Kailua-Kona** and points south. Most of the island's scuba and snorkeling operations are right in town. Dive boats leave from the main dock, and guides can choose from more than 66 spots between the energy lab to the north and Hookena to the south. Half-day charters ply the 20-plus sites close to town. All-day and multi-day charters opt for pristine spots farther south, where the topography is more dramatic.

Dive boats always welcome snorkelers, who sometimes even outnumber the divers. With its calm conditions and year-round accessibility, the Big Island makes a prime place to learn to scuba, and many dive shops offer certification courses and open-water checkout dives by referral.

Coral, Caves, and Canyons

Among the choice dive spots, **Pu'uhonua O Honaunau** ("City of Refuge") is a protected historical park 20 miles south of Kailua-Kona. The sheltered Honaunau Bay adjacent to the park offers a shallow snorkeling spot close to shore; divers usually head farther out to a 100-foot drop-off. However you experience it, this spot is a beauty, perhaps the best on the island. There's also an ancient Hawaiian temple nearby to explore after diving. Parking can get tight on the weekends, so go early. Snorkelers here are likely to see Moorish idols, the ubiquitous yellow tang, and several species of surgeon-fish sporting razor-sharp natural scalpels on their tails.

Snorkelers of any ability can explore **Kealakekua Bay**, part of a Marine Life Conservation District 12 miles south of

Kona. Hordes of tropical fish swarm the shallows, and a large moray eel keeps a permanent residence just beyond the dock. You can hike down a steep mountain road and jump off the old concrete pier, hop on one of the big snorkel boats in town, or rent a kayak and paddle from **Napo'opo'o Beach** across the bay to the **Captain Cook Monument** (the spot where British explorer James Cook was killed in a scuffle with native Hawaiians in 1779). This shallow, clear lagoon is perfect for beginners but also offers splendid fish-watching for more experienced divers.

At **Kahaluu Beach**, only four miles south

of Kailua-Kona, you can walk right into the shallow bay, which is protected from the surf by an ancient breakwater. Turtles and the coy Picasso triggerfish like this spot as much as snorkelers do. Schools of Achilles tang, with their velvety brownish black bodies, nibble on coral heads among articulated butterflyfish and scribbled filefish.

Turtle Pinnacle, one mile north of the Kona pier, deserves the name. Green sea turtles abound, and they aren't shy. If you look around, you may find a turtle cleaning station, with tangs and sergeant majors picking parasites off the turtles.

If you motor out on a dive charter a couple of hours south of Kailua-Kona, you'll be diving among the underwater lava formations for which the Kona Coast is famous. Along the way, you may spot a hammerhead shark

finning lazily through the water or a school of dolphins hitching a ride on the boat's wake. **Three Room Caves** is a series of lava chambers with steep canyons cut by sand channels. Not for novices, **Au Au Canyon**, between two steep lava walls, is a deep dive that starts at 120 feet. Huge boulders, fields of coral, and black sand channels between lava canyons make a stunning backdrop. Plankton eaters, including pyramid and pennant butterflyfish, damselfish, and fairy basslets, hang out on the walls of these drop-off zones.

At **Chimney** you can swim up through a vertical lava tube. As you pop out the top, you'll be welcomed by tangs and surgeonfish darting around in the surge. Fields of finger corals provide lots of hiding places for little eels and fish.

For larger coral reefs, try the **Kohala**

Coast north of Kona on an older part of the island. The diving is more challenging, with windier conditions, bigger waves, and swifter currents, but the sites are closer – only a 15-minute boat cruise from the harbor at **Kawaihae Bay**.

Ecosystem Worth Protecting

Hawaii is the most isolated group of islands in the world and among the youngest. Farthest south of the chain, the Big Island is also the largest and the newest – only about one million years old and still growing at the rate of an acre a day from active lava flow. Hawaii's remote location and relative youth has prevented many marine species from finding their way here from other parts of the Pacific and has kept the diversity low compared with older, less isolated reef areas such as those in the Philippine Islands. But Hawaii's isolation has also created an underwater environment like no other, with a high percentage of endemic species.

Local and state governments and dive operators have joined forces in recent years to protect Hawaii's underwater treasures. Mooring buoys are now found at most of the established dive sites on the Kona Coast, protecting the fragile reefs from anchor damage. The Big Island has also established underwater sanctuaries to protect the area's 150 species of coral and prohibit or restrict tropical fish collecting. The waters offshore are a humpback whale sanctuary, where you can see mothers and their youngsters on the surface during calving season, usually from December through April.

Night Creatures

Perhaps the transcendent underwater experience on the Kona Coast is night diving – with manta rays. At first, it doesn't sound promising: you sit in 35 feet of water with your dive light pointing up. But soon, clouds of plankton, tiny shrimplike animals, swarm the lights. Then, from out of the darkness, the first 10-foot manta wings in with its huge maw open. You're staring down the gullet of the beast as it filters its plankton dinner and bears down on you. At the last second, the manta arches its wings and executes a perfect gainer somersault above your head. After a graceful turn, it swoops in for another pass through the plankton. For close to an hour, divers sit mesmerized by the manta's elegant feeding dance.

Although they look like marine stealth fighters and are related to sharks, manta rays are as gentle as giant butterflies. Some manta species inhabiting warm water across the Pacific have wing spans surpassing 20 feet. The Kona mantas are about eight to 12 feet across. One of the largest marine animals, manta rays must filter a tremendous amount of food. They do this by scooping water into their throats with the help of special head fins that funnel in the plankton soup. Gills on the undersides of their bodies extract food and oxygen from the water.

Responsible dive operators have established rules to protect the mantas during these interspecies evening visits. Divers stay on the bottom and snorkelers remain at the surface to leave the water column open and give the animals room to maneuver. Although divers may be brushed by a passing manta, they must resist the temptation to reach out and pet one. Mantas have a film on their bodies to help them fight off bacterial infection; stroking them rubs off this protective coating. Above all, don't ride, chase, grab, or otherwise harass the rays, and avoid exhaling bubbles directly into the face of an approaching manta.

Tradewinds (opposite, top) tousle palms on the exposed Kohala coast north of Kailua-Kona.

A day octopus (opposite, bottom) uses its arms to ramble over the seafloor.

A manta ray (right) glides gracefully past a diver. Resist the temptation to touch them, which removes a film on their skin that prevents infection.

TRAVEL TIPS

DETAILS

When to Go

Daytime temperatures range between the low 70s and high 80s year-round. Weather seldom interferes with dives, though conditions are best from May through September.

How to Get There

Commercial airlines serve Keahole Kona International Airport. Most flights require a transfer in Honolulu, but travelers can pay a little more for a direct flight from the mainland to Kona. Flights from the U.S. West Coast are about five hours.

Getting Around

Some taxi service and bus tours are available. Rental cars are available at the airport.

INFORMATION

Big Island Visitors Bureau

75-5719 Alii Drive West, Kailua-Kona, HI 96740; tel: 808-329-7787.

Hawaii Tourism Authority

P.O. Box 2359, Honolulu, HI 96804; tel: 808-586-2550.

Hawaii Visitors Bureau

2270 Kalakaua Avenue, Suite 801, Honolulu, HI 96815; tel: 800-464-2924 or 808-923-1811.

Pu'uhonua O Honaunau (Place of Refuge)

P.O. Box 129, Honaunau, HI 96726; tel: 808-328-2288.

CAMPING

Almost half of the three dozen Big Island parks offer public campgrounds; most require inexpensive camping permits. Facilities range from remote walk-in sites to housekeeping cabins. For information on county parks, call 808-961-8311; for state parks, call 808-974-6200.

LODGING

Aston Royal Sea Cliff Resort

75-6040 Alii Drive, Kailua-Kona, HI 96740; tel: 800-922-7866 or 808-329-8021.

This five-story resort complex perches on a terraced cliff that steps down to the beach. All 150 units have views, air conditioners, full kitchens, and sunny lanais. A swimming pool, sauna, barbecue, tennis court, and laundry facility are available. There's good snorkeling nearby. $$$$

Kona Tiki Hotel

75-5986 Alii Drive, Kailua-Kona, HI 96740; tel: 808-329-1425.

This family-run hotel is a mile south of downtown Kailua-Kona. All 15 rooms overlook the ocean, 30 feet beyond the sea wall that forms one side of the hotel's small swimming pool. Breezy rooms have ceiling fans, mini-refrigerators, and lanais. A breakfast buffet is available. Book well in advance, and note the three-night minimum. $$

Manago Hotel

P.O. Box 145, Captain Cook, HI 96704; tel: 808-323-2642.

Run by the Manago family since 1917, this no-frills hotel, 11 miles south of Kailua-Kona, offers a taste of old Hawaii. The new three-story wing has 42 rooms with private baths and superb views of the ocean and a Japanese garden. A restaurant serves basic meals for reasonable prices. Kealakekua Bay, a winding eight-mile drive away, offers excellent diving and snorkeling. $

Outrigger Waikoloa Beach

69-275 Waikoloa Beach Road, Waikoloa, HI 96738-5711; tel: 800-922-5533 or 808-886-6789.

This full-service resort, completely renovated in 1999, offers splendid views of a palm-fringed bay, fabulous for snorkeling. An ancient Hawaiian fishing pond and petroglyphs are within walking distance of the 545-room resort. Golf, tennis, a variety of dining options, and shopping are available. $$$–$$$$

DIVE OPERATORS

Dive Makai Charters

P.O. Box 2955, Kailua-Kona, Hawaii 96745; tel: 808-329-2025.

In business since 1977, this small operation offers dive charters for 4 to 12 that emphasize unusual marine animals. Equipment rental (including required dive computers) and PADI referral training are available.

Eco Adventures

P.O. Box 2639, Kailua-Kona, HI 96745; tel: 800-949-3483 or 808-329-7116.

This full-service operation offers trips aboard three custom boats. Night dives, manta dives, and multisport packages are available. Services include dive and photo equipment rentals; on-board videographer; rebreather courses, and PADI and Handicapped Scuba Association certification.

Jack's Diving Locker

75-5819 Alii Drive, Kailua-Kona, HI 96740; tel: 800-345-4807 or 808-329-7585.

This PADI five-star dive center and NAUI dream resort has three vessels: two 38-footers and a 23-footer. The outfit offers dive and photo equipment rentals, certification to the instructor level, and children's snorkeling courses.

Kohala Divers

P.O. Box 44940, Kawaihae, HI 96743; tel: 808-882-7774.

Night dives are available at this PADI five-star dive center, which focuses only on Kohala. Snorkelers are also welcome. Equipment rentals and PADI certification are available.

Kona Coast Divers

74-5614 Palani Road, Kailua-Kona, HI 96740; tel: 800-562-3483 or 808-329-8802.

The full-service retail shop runs two custom dive boats and offers both multidive and accommodation packages at reduced rates. Services include equipment rentals; an on-site pool for optional predive checks; and PADI, NAUI, SSI, and TDI training.

Ocean Eco Tours

P.O. Box 2901, Kailua-Kona, HI 96745; tel: 808-937-0494.

This tour company specializes in dive, surf, and other adventure tours. PADI underwater-naturalist instructors take four divers on multiday excursions, conducting lessons and leading shore dives. Packages are available.

Excursions

Kauai

Kauai Visitors Bureau, 4334 Rice Street, Lihue, HI 96766; tel: 800-262-1400 or 808-245-3971.

Descend through geologic time and explore the volcanic origins of Kauai below the water's surface. Divers find black coral arches, caves, lava ridges, and tunnels on all sides of the island. Summer, when the water is calm, is the best season to take the 20-minute flight from Honolulu to Kauai.

Midway Atoll National Wildlife Refuge

Midway Phoenix Corporation, 100 Phoenix Air Drive, Carters, GA 30120; tel: 888-643-9291.

Open to the public since 1996, this remote atoll and former military base is a four-hour flight northwest of Honolulu. The stars of the refuge are the gooney birds and 18 other seabird species that breed here. The atoll lies within a fringing reef, with an infinite number of dive sites to explore and even more abundant sea life than the Hawaiian Islands. Adrenaline addicts will appreciate the abundance of sharks – tiger, gray, white-tipped, and Galapagos.

Oahu

Oahu Visitors Bureau, 733 Bishop Street, Suite 1872, Honolulu, HI 96813; tel: 808-524-0722.

Wrecks transformed into reefs make for good diving adventures on this bustling Hawaiian island. A 15-minute boat ride out of Waikiki brings divers to a double-header: the 175-foot World War II yard oiler *YO257* and the 60-foot fishing vessel *St. Pedro*. The wrecks are surrounded by a natural reef 90 feet below the surface, and both are inhabited by ample marine life.

Resource Directory

FURTHER READING

Nature, Ecology, and the Environment

If you're interested in marine ecology and conservation, the way ocean currents shape the weather, essays on some of the sea's diverse communities, or reflections on the environmental challenges the oceans face in the 21st century, check these titles for educational and entertaining reads.

Among Whales, by Roger Payne (Scribner, 1995).

Blue Meridian: The Search for the Great White Shark, by Peter Matthiessen (Penguin USA, 1997).

Caverns Measureless to Man, by Sheck Exley (Cave Books, 1994).

A City Under the Sea: Life in a Coral Reef, by Norbert Wu (Atheneum, 1996).

The Conservation of Whales and Dolphins: Science and Practice, Mark P. Simmonds and Judith D. Hitchinson, eds. (John Wiley and Sons, 1996).

Creeps from the Deep: Life in the Deep Sea, by Norbert Wu and Leighton R. Taylor (Chronicle Books, 1997).

Discovery Travel Adventures: Whale Watching, Nicky Leach, ed. (Discovery Communications/Insight Guides, 1999).

Dolphin Societies: Discoveries and Puzzles, Karen Pryor and Kenneth S. Norris, eds. (University of California Press, 1998).

The Ecology of Fishes on Coral Reefs, Peter F. Sale, ed. (Academic Press, 1994).

The Ecology of Whales and Dolphins, by D. E. Gaskin (Heinemann, 1982).

Ecoregions: The Ecosystem Geography of the Oceans and Continents, by Robert G. Bailey and Lev Ropes (Springer Verlag, 1998).

Elements of Marine Ecology, by R. V. Tait and Frances Dipper (Butterworth-Heinemann, 1998).

The Emerald Sea: Exploring the Underwater Wilderness of the Pacific Northwest and Alaska, by Diane Swanson and Dale Sanders (Alaska Northwest Books, 1993).

The Enchanted Braid: Coming to Terms With Nature on the Coral Reef, by Osha Gray Davidson (John Wiley and Sons, 1998).

Gift from the Sea, by Anne Morrow Lindbergh (Pantheon Books, 1991).

The Hawaiian Spinner Dolphin, by Kenneth S. Norris (University of California Press, 1994).

The Living Ocean: Understanding and Protecting Marine Biodiversity, by Boyce Thorne-Miller (Island Press, 1998).

The Log from the Sea of Cortez, by John Steinbeck and Edward Flanders Ricketts (Penguin USA, reprinted 1995).

Sea Change: A Message of the Oceans, by Sylvia Earle (Fawcett Books, 1996).

Ships and Shipwrecks of the Americas: A History Based on Underwater Archaeology, George F. Bass, ed. (Thames & Hudson, 1996).

Underwater Wilderness: Life in America's National Marine Sanctuaries and Reserves, by Charles Seaborn (Roberts Rinehart Publishers, 1996).

Regional Titles

Choosing a guidebook for the region where you intend to travel and dive is an important aspect of preparing for and enjoying a trip. Many of these guides provide more than just descriptions of dive sites and lists of accommodations and restaurants; they also introduce the area's culture and holidays, plants and animals, parks and museums.

Adventure Guide to the Florida Keys and Everglades National Park, by Joyce Huber (Hunter Publishing, 1997).

Adventure Guide to the Virgin Islands, Harry S. Parker (Hunter Publishing, 1994).

Adventuring in Belize: The Sierra Club Travel Guide to the Islands, Waters, and Inland Parks of Central America's Tropical Paradise, by Eric Hoffman (Sierra Club Books, 1994).

Beneath the Waves: Exploring the Hidden World of the Kelp Forest, by Norbert Wu (Chronicle Books, 1997).

Best Dives' Snorkeling Adventures: Bahamas, Bermuda, Hawaii, Caribbean, Turks and Caicos, Florida, by Joyce and Jon Huber (PhotoGraphics Publishing, 1998).

Cabo Handbook: La Paz to Cabo San Lucas, by Joe Cummings (Moon Travel, 1998).

Cayman Islands, by Paris Permenter with John Bigley (Hunter Publishing, 1997).

Channel Islands National Park, by Susan Lamb and George H. H. Huey (Southwest Parks and Monuments Association, 1999).

Coral Reefs of Florida, by Gilbert L. Voss (Pineapple Press, 1988).

Dive Sites of the Bahamas, by Lawson Wood (Passport Books, 1999).

Dive Sites of the Cayman Islands, by Lawson Wood (Passport Books, 1997).

Dive Sites of Cozumel and the Yucatan, by Lawson Wood (NTC Publishing Group, 1997).

The Diver's Guide to Maui, by Chuck Thorne (Chuck Thorne, 1985).

Diving Baja California, by Susan Speck (Aqua Quest Publications, 1995).

Diving Belize, by Ned Middleton (Aqua Quest Publications, 1994).

Diving Bonaire, by George S. Lewbel and Larry R. Martin (Aqua Quest Publications, 1991).

Diving British Virgin Islands, by Jim Scheiner (Aqua Quest Publications, 1995).

Diving Cayman Islands, by Jesse Cancelmo (Aqua Quest Publications, 1997).

Diving Cozumel, by Steve Rosenberg (Aqua Quest Publications, 1992).

Diving Offshore California, by Darren and Stacey Douglass (Aqua Quest Publications, 1992).

Diving and Snorkeling Guide to Bonaire, by Jerry Schnabel (Pisces Books, 1991).

Diving and Snorkeling Guide to the British Virgin Islands, by Linda Sorensen (Lonely Planet Publications, 1991).

Diving and Snorkeling Guide to Cozumel, by George S. Lewbel and Larry R. Martin (Lonely Planet Publications, 1998).

Diving and Snorkeling Guide to the Hawaiian Islands, by Doug Wallin (Pisces Books, 1992).

Diving and Snorkeling Guide to Northern California and the Monterey Peninsula, by Steve Rosenberg (Pisces Books, 1992).

Diving and Snorkeling Guide to the Pacific Northwest: Puget Sound, San Juan Islands, and Vancouver Island, by Edward Weber (Pisces Books, 1993).

Diving and Snorkeling Guide to Southern California, by Darren Douglass (Pisces Books, 1994).

Diving and Snorkeling Guide to the Turks and Caicos Islands, by Stuart and Susanne Cummings (Lonely Planet Publications, 1993).

Diving and Snorkeling Guide to the U.S. Virgin Islands, by Stuart and Susanne Cummings (Lonely Planet Publications, 1993).

Exploring Wild South Florida: A Guide to Finding Natural Areas and Wildlife of the Southern Peninsula and the Florida Keys, by Susan D. Jewell (Pineapple Press, 1997).

The Exuma Guide: A Cruising Guide to the Exuma Cays – Approaches, Routes, Anchorages, Dive Sites, Flora, Fauna, History, and Lore of the Exuma Cays, by Stephen J. Pavlidis (Seaworthy Publications, 1997).

Fodor's The U.S. and British Virgin Islands (Fodor's Travel Publications, 1998).

Frommer's Cancun, Cozumel, and the Yucatan 2000, by Arthur Frommer and David Baird (Macmillan General Reference, 1999).

Graveyard of the Atlantic: Shipwrecks of the North Carolina Coast, by David Stick (University of North Carolina Press, 1989).

Hidden Maui, by Ray Riegert (Ulysses Press, 1997).

Lake Superior's North Shore and Isle Royale, by Kate Crowley and Mike Link (Voyageur Press, 1989).

Lonely Planet: Bahamas, Turks and Caicos, by Christopher P. Baker (Lonely Planet Publications, 1998).

Monterey Bay Shoreline Guide, by Jerry Emory (University of California Press, 1999).

Ned DeLoach's Diving Guide to Underwater Florida, Ned DeLoach (New World Publications, 1997).

Northwest Boat Dives: 60 Ultimate Dives in Puget Sound and Hood Canal, by Dave Bliss (Sasquatch Books, 1997).

The Outer Bay, by Michael Rigsby (Monterey Bay Aquarium Foundation, 1996).

Pisces Guide to Shipwreck Diving: New York and New Jersey, by Henry C. Keatts (Pisces Books, 1992).

Shipwrecks: Diving the Graveyard of the Atlantic, by Roderick M. Farb (Menasha Ridge Press, 1991).

Shipwrecks of Isle Royale: The Archaeological Survey, by Daniel J. Lenihan, Larry E. Murphy, and C. Patrick Labadie (Lake Superior Port Cities, 1994).

Shipwrecks of Lake Superior, by James R. Marshall (Lake Superior Port Cities, 1987).

Snorkel Hawaii: The Big Island, by Judy Malinowski and Mel Malinowski (Indigo Books, 1996).

Snorkel Hawaii: Maui and Lanai Guide to the Underwater World, by Judy Malinowski and Mel Malinowski (Indigo Books, 1996).

Natural History and Field Guides

Carry a field guide or book about a region's natural history to help you identify fish, invertebrates, coral, or any of the other creatures or plants you see above or below the surface. Look for guides that have color illustrations and information about habitat and behavior.

Animals of the Oceans, by Stephen Savage (Raintree/Steck Vaughn, 1997).

Between Pacific Tides, by Edward F. Ricketts and Jack Calvin (Stanford University Press, reprinted 1992).

Caribbean Reef Fishes, by John E. Randall and John R. Randall (TFH Publications, 1992).

Coastal Fish Identification: California to Alaska, by Paul Humann (New World Publications, 1996).

Dangerous Marine Creatures, by Carl Edmonds (Best Publishing, 1995).

Field Guide to Coral Reefs: Caribbean and Florida, by Eugene H. Kaplan (Houghton Mifflin, 1988).

Fishes of the Atlantic Coast: Canada to Brazil, Including the Gulf of Mexico, Florida, Bermuda, the Bahamas, the Caribbean, by Gar Goodson and Phillip J. Weisgerber (Stanford University Press, 1986).

Fishes of the Gulf of Mexico: Texas, Louisiana, and Adjacent Waters, by H. Dickson Hoese and Richard H. Moore (Texas A&M University Press, 1998).

Intertidal Invertebrates of California, by Robert H. Morris, Donald Putnam Abbott, and Eugene Clinton Haderlie (Stanford University Press, 1980).

Marine Invertebrates of the Pacific Northwest, by Linda H. Price and Eugene N. Key (University of Washington Press, 1996).

Marine Plants of the Caribbean: A Field Guide from Florida to Brazil, by Diane Scullion Littler and Mark M. Littler (Smithsonian Institution Press, 1992).

National Audubon Society Field Guide to North American Fishes, Whales, and Dolphins, by Herbert T. Boschung and David K. Caldwell (Alfred A. Knopf, 1983).

National Audubon Society Field Guide to North American Seashore Creatures, by Norman A. Melnkoth (Alfred A. Knopf, 1981).

National Audubon Society Field Guide to Tropical Marine Fishes: Of the Caribbean, the Gulf of Mexico, Florida, the Bahamas, and Bermuda, by C. Lavett Smith (Alfred A. Knopf, 1997).

Natural History of Baja California, by Miguel Del Barco (Dawsons Book Shop, 1980).

Pisces Guide to Caribbean Reef Ecology, by William S. Alevizon (Pisces Books, 1994).

Pisces Guide to Watching Fishes/ Understanding Coral Reef Fish Behavior, by Roberta Wilson and James Q. Wilson (Pisces Books, 1992).

Reef Coral Identification: Florida, Caribbean, Bahamas, Including Marine Plants, by Paul Humann and Ned Deloach (New World Publications, 1993).

Reef Creature Identification: Florida, Caribbean, Bahamas, by Paul Humann and Ned Deloach (New World Publications, 1990).

Reef Fish Identification: Florida, Caribbean, Bahamas, by Paul Humann and Ned Deloach (New World Publications, 1994).

Reef and Shore Fauna of Hawaii, by Donald P. Abbott, A. Todd Newberry, and Kendall M. Morris (Bishop Museum Press, 1997).

Reef Watchers Hawaii: Reef Fish and Critter I.D. – Snorkel Skills and Professional Tips, by Astrid Witte and Casey Mahaney (Blue Kirio, 1996).

Sea of Cortez Marine Animals: A Guide to Common Fishes and Invertebrates, Baja California to Panama, by Daniel Gotshall (Sea Challengers, 1998).

Sealife: A Complete Guide to the Marine Environment, Geoffrey Waller and Richard Hull, eds. (Smithsonian Institution Press, 1996).

The Sierra Club Handbook of Seals and Sirenians, by B. Stewart (Sierra Club Books, 1992).

The Sierra Club Handbook of Whales and Dolphins, by Stephen Leatherwood and Randall R. Reeves (Sierra Club Books, 1993).

The Superior North Shore: A Natural History of Lake Superior, Northern Lands and Waters, by Thomas F. Waters (University of Minnesota Press, 1999).

Tropical Seashells, by Pauline Fiene-Severns, Mike Severns, and Ruth Dyerly (Periplus Editions, 1998).

Whales, Dolphins, and Porpoises, by Mark Carwardine and Erich Hoyt (Time-Life Books, 1998).

The Whale-Watcher's Guide, by Patricia Corrigan (Northword Press, 1994).

Preparation and Equipment

Reading about diving can expand your awareness of scuba-diving issues that may not have been covered in an open-water certification class. When you're thinking about adding a new specialty like underwater photography, ice diving, or cave exploration to your scuba repertoire, the information in a book can help you pick up the basics before you take the class. Also, if you get in the water only twice a year on vacation, a little reading may help refresh some rusty skills.

Cold Water Diving: A Guide to Ice Diving, by John N. Heine (Best Publishing, 1996).

DAN Pocket Guide to First Aid for Scuba Diving, by Dan Orr and DAN Medical Staff (Greycliff Publishing, 1998).

Darkness Beckons: The History and Development of Cave Diving, by Martyn Farr (Cave Books, 1991).

Dennis Graver's 100 Best Scuba Quizzes, by Dennis Graver (Aqua Quest Publications, 1996).

The Diver's Handbook, by Alan Mountain (Lyons Press, 1997).

Diving on the Edge: A Guide for New Divers, by Michael Bane (Lyons Press, 1998).

The Essential Guide to Live-Aboard Dive Travel, by Casey Mahaney and Astrid Witte (Best Publishing, 1996).

The Hennessey Guide to Live-Aboard Dive Boats – Worldwide, by R. L. Hennessey (Hennessey Group, 1998).

How to Photograph Underwater, Volumes 1 and 2, by Norbert Wu (Stackpole Books, 1994).

Jeppesen's Open Water Sport Diver Manual, by Richard A. Clinchy (Mosby-Year Book, 1992).

Jim Church's Essential Guide to Composition: A Simplified Approach to Taking Better Underwater Pictures, by Jim Church (Aqua Quest Publications, 1998).

Jim Church's Essential Guide to Nikonos Systems, by Jim Church (Aqua Quest Publications, 1998).

Scuba Diving, by Dennis K. Graver (Human Kinetics, 1993).

Underwater Navigation, by C. Royer (International Marine Publications Systems, 1997).

Wonders of the Reef: Diving with a Camera, by Stephen Frink (Harry N. Abrams, 1996).

Magazines

Still want to read more? Pick up one of these magazines. A few also maintain extensive websites on which they archive past articles and host online chat groups. The latter can be excellent places to post questions on a particular destination or get the latest information about new equipment.

Alert Diver Magazine
Magazine of the Diver's Alert Network, Peter B. Bennett Center, 6 West Colony Place, Durham, NC 27705; tel: 919-684-2948.

Dive Girl
64 Essex Road, London N18LR England; tel: 011-71-226-9925.

Dive Training
P.O. Box 14236, Parkville, MO 64152-9901; tel: 800-444-9932 or 816-741-5151.

Ocean Realm
4067 Broadway, San Antonio, TX 78209; tel: 800-746-2326 or 210-824-8099.

Rodale's Scuba Diving Magazine
6600 Abercorn Street, Suite 208, Savannah, GA 31405; tel: 800-666-0016 or 912-351-0855.

Skin Diver Magazine
6420 Wilshire Boulevard, Los Angeles, CA 90048; tel: 323-782-2760.

Sport Diver Magazine
330 West Canton Avenue, Winter Park, FL 32789; tel: 800-879-0478 or 407-628-4802.

SCUBA CERTIFICATION AGENCIES

This list includes most of the agencies that provide scuba certifications in North America.

Handicapped Scuba Association (HSA International)
1104 El Prado, San Clemente, CA 92672; tel: 949-498-6128.

International Association of Nitrox and Technical Divers (IANTD)
9628 N.E. 2nd Avenue, Suite D, Miami Shores, FL 33138-2767; tel: 305-751-4873.

International Diving Educators Association (IDEA)
P.O. Box 8427, Jacksonville, FL 32239-8427; tel: 904-744-5554.

National Association of Scuba Diving Schools (NASDS)
999 South Yates, Memphis, TN 38119; tel: 901-767-7265.

National Association of Underwater Instructors (NAUI)
9942 Currie Davis Drive, Suite H, Tampa, FL 33619-2667; tel: 800-553-6284 or 813-628-6284.

Professional Association of Diving Instructors (PADI)
30151 Tomas Street, Rancho Santa Margarita, CA 92688-2125; tel: 800-729-7234 or 949-858-7234.

Scuba Schools International (SSI)
2619 Canton Court, Fort Collins, CO 80525; tel: 800-821-4319 or 970-482-0883.

Women's Scuba Association (WSA)
6966 South Atlantic Avenue, New Smyrna Beach, FL 32169; tel: 904-426-5757.

YMCA Scuba
5825-5A Live Oak Parkway, Norcross, GA 30093-1728; tel: 888-464-9622 or 770-662-5172.

Diving Insurance and Medical Information

Divers Alert Network (DAN)
Peter B. Bennett Center, 6 West Colony Place, Durham, NC 27705; tel: 800-446-2671; 919-684-2948 (medical information); 919-684-4DAN (emergencies).

EQUIPMENT MANUFACTURERS

This list reflects the major manufacturers of scuba equipment. Contact the company's headquarters to find a retailer in your area. Remember, it's always a good idea to examine equipment personally and try it on – even take it in a pool, if possible – before you buy.

Apollo Sports USA
12322 Highway 99 South, Unit 102, Everett, WA 98204; tel: 800-231-0909.
Fins, masks, snorkels, underwater vehicles, regulators, BCs, and dry suits.

Aqua Lung America/Sea Quest/U.S. Divers
2340 Cousteau Court, Vista, CA 92083; tel: 760-597-5000.
Dive computers, gauges, regulators, masks, snorkels, fins, BCs, and wet suits.

Atomic Aquatics, Inc.
17942 Georgetown Lane, Huntington Beach, CA; tel: 714-375-1433.
High-performance regulators.

Body Glove
201 Herondo Street, Redondo Beach, CA 90277; tel: 310-374-3441.
Wet suits, dive undergarments, and neoprene accessories (booties, gloves, hoods).

Cressi-sub USA
10 Rueten Drive, Closter, NJ 07624; tel: 201-784-1005.
Masks, fins, snorkels, regulators, gauges, BCs, equipment bags, knives, wet suits, and swim goggles.

Dacor Corporation
One Selleck Street, Norwalk, CT 06855; tel: 800-323-4166 or 800-323-0463.
Regulators, alternate air sources, masks, snorkels, fins, computers, BCs, pressure gauges, underwater vehicles, wet suits, dry suits, accessories, and underwater lights.

Diving Unlimited International
1148 Delevan Drive, San Diego, CA 92102-2499; tel: 800-325-8439 or 619-236-1203.
Dry suits, dive undergarments, BCs, weight systems, and accessories.

Harvey's Skindiving Supplies
2505 South 252nd Street, Kent, WA 98032; tel: 800-347-0054.
Wet suits, dry suits, boots, hoods, gloves.

Henderson Aquatics
301 Orange Street, Millville, NJ 08332; tel: 856-825-4771.
Dry suits, wet suits, gloves, booties, hoods, mitts, and dive wear.

International Divers, Inc.
14747 Artesia Boulevard, Unit F, La Mirada, CA 90638; tel: 800-257-2822 or 714-994-3900.
BCs, regulators, masks, snorkels, and fins.

Mares
One Selleck Street, Norwalk, CT 06855; tel: 800-874-3236 or 203-855-0631.

Masks, fins, snorkels, regulators, BCs, wet suits, computers, neoprene accessories (gloves, hoods, booties), and gauges.

Marine Sports Designs/Guppy Gear
1517 Elmhurst Road, Elk Grove Village, IL 60007; tel: 800-924-1564 or 847-357-1813.

Children's snorkeling and swimming gear.

Nikon, Inc.
1300 Walt Whitman Road, Melville, NY 11747; tel: 800-645-6687 or 516-547-4200.

Underwater cameras.

Oceanic
2002 Davis Street, San Leandro, CA 94577; tel: 510-562-0500.

Wet suits, dry suits, computers, fins, snorkels, masks, BCs, regulators, thermal wear, boots, gloves, weight systems, accessories (lights, belts, knives), equipment bags, and propulsion vehicles.

O'Neill
1071 41st Avenue, Santa Cruz, CA 95063; tel: 831-475-7500.

Wet suits, undergarments for wet suits, neoprene accessories, and equipment bags.

ScubaPro/UWATEC
1166-A Fesler Street, El Cajon, CA 92020; tel: 800-467-2822.

Regulators, BCs, wet suits, masks, snorkels, fins, tanks, accessories, and computers.

Sea & Sea Underwater Photography
1938 Kellogg Avenue, Carlsbad, CA 92008; tel: 800-732-7977.

Underwater camera equipment.

SeaLife/Pioneer Research
97 Foster Road, Suite 5, Moorestown, NJ 08057; tel: 800-257-7742.

Underwater cameras.

SeaVision USA
4399 35th Street North, St. Petersburg, FL 33714; tel: 800-732-6275 or 727-525-6906.

Prescription lenses for masks and swim goggles.

Watermark Scuba
2801A Academy Drive, Auburn WA 98052; tel: 800-939-5510.

Buoyancy systems, including weight belts, ankle weights, traveling weight bags, sea bags, boots, gloves, and hoods.

Zeagle Systems
37150 Chancey Road, Zephyr Hills, FL 33541; tel: 813-782-5568.

BCs, regulators, fins, masks, snorkels, dry suits, undergarments for dry suits, and equipment bags.

GOVERNMENT AGENCIES

Centers for Disease Control and Prevention
tel: 404-639-3311; fax response: 877-394-8747; website: www.cdc.gov/travel/travel.html

For information about health conditions and disease outbreaks in a particular country, required and recommended immunizations, malaria and E. coli information, whether you can drink the freshwater and/or swim in it, and how to stay healthy, check out this website or fax-response system.

National Marine Sanctuaries
1305 East-West Highway SSMC4\ 11425, Silver Spring, MD 20910; tel: 301-713-3125 (ext. 173); website: www.sanctuaries.nos.noaa.gov

This website, administered by the National Oceanic and Atmospheric Administration, provides information about the national marine sanctuary program, as well as links to the specific sites for each sanctuary. In addition, you can call the number listed above for a referral to local marine sanctuary numbers.

National Park Service
1849 C Street N.W., Suite 1013, Washington, D.C. 20240; tel: 202-208-4747; website: www.nps.gov

At ParkNet, Gateway to the National Park Service, you can find a list of all the national parks, monuments, historic sites, recreation areas, national seashores, preserves, and wildlife refuges. In addition to cultural and historical information about park areas, you can find interpretive tips, read about air quality and water resources, and learn more about the geology, biology, and social sciences of the regions where you're planning a trip. You can also call the Park Service to request information.

U.S. State Department
2201 C Street N.W., Washington, D.C. 20520; tel: 202-647-4000; www.travel.state.gov/travel_warnings.html (travel information); www.state.gov/www/services.html (general information).

The U.S. State Department maintains a very useful and comprehensive website and voicemail system through which travelers have access to travel advisories and consular information for other countries. The information includes health issues and medical facilities, unusual immigration practices, currency and entry requirements, crime information, traffic safety and road conditions, and more. The website also contains a link to the Federal Emergency Management Administration (FEMA) site for tropical storm and hurricane watch information. You can even sign up to receive regular travel safety information by e-mail.

TOURISM INFORMATION

To receive information about a country or region, contact one of the tourism offices listed here. In addition to providing lists of accommodations, these offices can also recommend restaurants and advise you on local holidays, customs, and exchange rates. And since many offer free packets of information, these are the logical places to start planning a trip.

Bahamas Tourist Offices
One Turnberry Place, 19495 Biscayne Boulevard, Suite 312, Aventura, FL 33180; tel: 305-932-0051 or 242-322-7500.

Bonaire Tourism Corporation
Adams Unlimited, 10 Rockefeller Plaza, Suite 900, New York, NY 10020; tel: 800-266-2473 or 212-956-5912.

British Virgin Islands Tourist Board
1804 Union Street, San Francisco, CA 94123; tel: 800-835-8530 or 415-775-0344 or 212-696-0400.

California Division of Tourism
P.O. Box 1499, Sacramento, CA 95812-1499, tel: 800 862 2543 or 916-322-2881.

Florida Division of Tourism
126 West Van Buren Street, Tallahassee, FL 32399; tel: 904-487-1462.

Hawaii Department of Tourism
P.O. Box 2359, Honolulu, HI 96804; tel: 808-586-2423.

Michigan Travel Bureau
P.O. Box 3393, Livonia, MI 48151-3393; tel: 800-543-2937 or 517-373-0670.

Mexico Tourism Hotline
tel: 800-446-3942.

North Carolina Division of Travel and Tourism
430 North Salisbury Street, Raleigh, NC 27603; tel: 800-847-4862 or 919-733-4171.

Texas Tourism
P.O. Box 12728, Austin, TX 78711-2728; tel: 800-888-8839 or 512-462-9191.

Turks and Caicos Tourist Office
11645 Biscayne Boulevard, Suite 302, North Miami, FL 33181; tel: 800-241-0824 or 305-891-4117.

Washington State Tourism
P.O. Box 42500, Olympia, WA 98504-2500; tel: 800-544-1800 or 206-586-2088 or 206-586-2012.

Puerto Rico Tourism Company
575 Fifth Avenue, 23rd Floor, New York, NY 10017; tel: 800-223-6530 or 212-599-6262.

U.S. Virgin Islands Tourism
P.O. Box 6499, Charlotte Amalie, St. Thomas, USVI 00801; tel: 800-372-8784 or 809774-8784.

DIVE TRAVEL SPECIALISTS

More than simply travel agents, these companies understand what divers are looking for – destinations with bountiful reefs, hotels close to the dock, dive lockers on the premises, live-aboard vacations, and more. In addition, they often have special arrangements with airlines, resorts, and dive operators, resulting in the best package deals for travelers.

Aggressor Fleet
P.O. Box 1470, Morgan City, LA 79381; tel: 800-348-2628.

Cathy Church Underwater Photo Tours
390 South Church Street, George Town, Grand Cayman; tel: 345-949-7415.

Dive Discovery
1005 A Street, Suite 202, San Rafael, CA 94901; tel: 800-886-7321 or 415-256-8890.

Dive Safaris Worldwide
900 West End Avenue, Suite 1B, New York, NY 10025; tel: 800-359-0747 or 212-662-4858.

Dive Tours
18219 Strack Drive, Spring, TX 77379; tel: 800-433-0885 or 281-257-1771.

Landfall Dive and Adventure Travel
855 Howe Avenue, Suite 6, Sacramento, CA 95825; tel: 800-525-3833 or 916-563-0164.

Live-Dive Pacific, Inc./Pacific Aggressors
74-5588 Pawai Place, Building F, Kailua-Kona, HI 96740; tel: 800-344-5662 or 808-329-8182.

Maluku Adventures
P.O. Box 22067, San Francisco, CA 94122-22067; tel: 800-566-2585 or 415-731-2560.

Predators, Mammals, and Us
2000 Broadway, Suite 1204, San Francisco, CA 94115; tel: 415-923-9865.

Scuba Voyages
595 Fairbanks Street, Corona, CA 92879; tel: 800-544-7631 or 951-371-1831.

Tropical Adventures
P.O. Box 4337, Seattle, WA 98104; tel: 800-909-7691 or 206-441-3483.

U.S. Dive Travel
P.M.B. 307, 15050 Cedar Avenue South, Suite 116, St. Paul, MN 55124; tel: 206-937-7484 or 651-635-8862.

ENVIRONMENTAL ORGANIZATIONS

These organizations are dedicated to conserving the marine environment – from saving coral reefs to helping resorts become ecologically sustainable. Several, as noted below, offer trips in which the public can participate as expedition divers and snorkelers.

American Oceans Campaign
725 Arizona Avenue, Suite 102, Santa Monica, CA 90401; tel: 310-576-6162.

CEDAM International
1 Fox Road, Croton-on-Hudson, NY 10520; tel: 914-271-4723.

This not-for-profit group is devoted to conservation, education, diving, and archaeology. On expeditions, members participate in scientific and conservation-oriented education projects.

Center for Marine Conservation
1725 DeSales Street N.W., Suite 600, Washington, D.C. 20036; tel: 800-262-2322 or 202-429-5609.

Among other conservation projects, this organization runs the annual International Coastal Cleanup on the third Saturday of September.

Cetacean Society International
P.O. Box 953, Georgetown, CT 06829; tel: 203-431-1606.

Conservation International
2501 M Street N.W., Suite 200, Washington, D.C. 20037; tel: 202-429-5660 or 800-429-5660.

Coral Reef Alliance (CORAL)
64 Shattuck Square, Suite 220, Berkeley, CA 94704; tel: 510-848-0110.

CORAL runs a volunteer diver network and a clearinghouse for conservation organizations and researchers to reach volunteers.

Cousteau Society
870 Greenbriar Circle, Suite 402, Chesapeake, VA 23320; tel: 800-441-4395.

Earthwatch Institute
680 Mount Auburn Street, Box 9104, Watertown, MA 02471; tel: 617-926-8200 or 800-776-0188.

This organization supports scientific research worldwide, including some trips for divers and snorkelers.

Ecotourism Society
P.O. Box 755, North Bennington, VT 05257-0755; tel: 802-447-2121.

Greenpeace USA
1436 U Street N.W., Washington, D.C. 20009; tel: 202-462-1177.

Ocean Futures Society
325 Chapala Street, Santa Barbara, CA 93101; tel: 805-899-8899.

Oceanic Society Expeditions
Fort Mason Center, Building E, San Francisco, CA 94123; tel: 800-326-7491 or 415-441-1106.

This organization protects marine mammals and marine environments and offers expeditions for both divers and nondivers.

Oceanographic Expeditions
4418 Saint Ann Street, New Orleans, LA 70119; tel: 504-488-1573.

Dedicated to protecting habitats and biodiversity, this organization works with volunteer divers on marine research.

Oceanwatch Foundation
P.O. Box 462, Fort Lauderdale, FL 33302; tel: 305-359-7835.

Oceanwatch has volunteer opportunities for divers, boat owners, underwater photographers, and the general public.

Reef Relief
201 William Street, Key West, FL 33040; tel: 305-294-3100.

Sierra Club, Hawaii Chapter
1621 Mikahala Way, Honolulu, HI 96816; tel: 808-734-4986.

AQUARIUMS

While there's no substitute for getting your face wet, sometimes a trip to the aquarium can be a useful – and pleasant – adjunct to the real thing. Well-designed exhibits orient visitors to the survival strategies and hangouts of shy marine creatures, alert them to local environmental issues, and often present historical perspectives on the region. For kids, aquariums may be all the show-and-tell necessary to convince them to learn to scuba dive.

Stephen J. Birch Aquarium
Museum at Scripps Institution of Oceanography, 500 Gilman Drive, Dept. 0207, La Jolla, CA 92093-0207; tel: 619-534-3474 or 619-534-3474.

Monterey Bay Aquarium
886 Cannery Row, Monterey, CA 93940; tel: 800-840-4880 or 831-648-4888.

National Aquarium
Pier 3, 501 East Pratt Street, Baltimore, Maryland 21202; tel: 800-551-7328; 410-481-7328 (Baltimore); 202-432-7328 (Washington, D.C.); 703-573-7328 (Virginia).

New England Aquarium
Central Wharf, Boston, MA 02110; tel: 617-973-5200.

Oregon Coast Aquarium
2820 S.E. Ferry Slip Road, Newport, OR 97365; tel: 541-867-3474.

Sea Center Texas
300 Medical Drive, Lake Jackson, TX 77566; tel: 409-292-0100.

John G. Shedd Aquarium
1200 South Lake Shore Drive, Chicago IL 60605; tel: 312-939-2438.

Texas State Aquarium
2710 North Shoreline Boulevard, Corpus Christi, TX 78402; tel: 800-477-4853 or 512-881-1200.

Vancouver Aquarium Marine Science Centre
P.O. Box 3232, Vancouver, BC V6B 3X8 Canada; tel: 604-659-3474.

PHOTO AND ILLUSTRATION CREDITS

D. Holden Bailey 108

Curtis Boggs/EarthWater Stock Photography 114B, 127B, 135M

Jesse Cancelmo 92T, 109B, 135T, 136, 138, 140T, 140B, 193B

Marc C. Chamberlain 4, 130, 141B, 167MR, 167B, 171, 173B, 175, 182B, 185B, 190

Brandon D. Cole 10-11, 66, 76, 79B, 107

Phillip Colla/Innerspace Visions 199

Collection of Leslie Leaney 22T

Bob Cranston/Innerspace Visions 182T

Chris A. Crumley/EarthWater Stock Photography 38T, 40B, 70, 87T, 115, 116T, 119T, 119M, 147T

Sue Dabritz-Yuen/Innerspace Visions 32T

John Elk III 143B, 177M, 177B, 211T

Dave B. Fleetham/Tom Stack and Associates 12-13, 18-19, 23, 45B, 46T, 160, 162B, 194, 196L, 198T, 201, 203T, 206L, 208B, 209, 211B

Jeff Foott/Jeff Foott Productions 165, 173T, 174, 180B, 183

Jeff Foott/Tom Stack and Associates 189B

Robert Fried/Tom Stack and Associates 135B

Bob Friel/Blue Edge Productions 26T, 35T, 49B, 52T, 72-73, 77, 80, 83, 84, 85, 106, 123B, 124T, 127M, 128, 151T

Gary Gentile 144, 148, 154T, 154B, 156T, 159T

John Gerlach/Tom Stack and Associates 152

Francois Gohier/Francois Gohier Pictures 127T, 170B, 172T, 193M

Peter Gutman 65T

Dennis M. Hanser 157

George H. H. Huey 54B

Jay Ireland and Georgienne E. Bradley/Bradley – Ireland Productions 1, 2-3, 8T, 22B, 26B, 27B, 28BL, 34T, 34B, 38B, 39B, 40T, 41B, 50, 58-59, 87M, 104, 116M, 117, 186

Marilyn Kazmers/SharkSong 27T, 47T, 47B, 55, 116B, 143m, 164T, 164B, 163, 212-213

Thomas Kitchin/Tom Stack and Associates 48B

Bruce Montagne 155, 156B, 159M

Randy Morse/Tom Stack and Associates 5B, 9B, 44, 54T, 57T, 114T, 120, 167ML, 170T, 177T, 178, 180T, 181, 181, 182M, 185T, 185M, 191T

Brian Parker/Tom Stack and Associates 8L, 32B, 42, 62B, 63, 65B, 74L, 74R, 82T, 90, 92B, 93, 95M, 98T, 101B, 131T, 133B, 162T, 172B, 197, 206R

Doug Perrine/Innerspace Visions 48T, 82B, 147B, 149T, 188

Doug Perrine/Mo Yung Productions 139

Ed Robinson/Tom Stack and Associates 200T, 200B, 207

Carl R. Sams II 143T

Mark Severns/Tom Stack and Associates 196R

Bradley Sheard 151M, 151B, 167T

Steve Simonsen/Marine Scenes 5T, 14-15, 16, 20, 28T, 45T, 53, 95T, 95B, 101T, 103M, 103B

Wes Skiles/Karst Productions 35B, 131B

Marty Snyderman/Innerspace Visions 119B

Mark Allen Stack/Tom Stack and Associates 39T

Tom Stack/Tom Stack and Associates 109T, 198B, 204

Tom and Therisa Stack/Tom Stack and Associates 6-7, 24, 29, 33, 41T, 46B, 49T, 57B, 60, 64, 67T, 69T, 79T, 87B, 91, 111M

Clara Taylor 36, 62T, 73T, 79M, 98B, 103T, 112, 123T, 133T, 141T

Ron and Valerie Taylor/Innerspace Visions 56T

Tom Till/Tom Till Photography 132, 159B, 208T

Larry Ulrich/Larry Ulrich Photography 88, 149B

Masa Ushioda/Innerspace Visions 189T, 203M

Greg Vaughn/Tom Stack and Associates 203B

James D. Watt/Jeff Foott Productions 75, 191B

Michele Westmorland/ Westmorland Photography 28BR, 30, 69B

F. Stuart Westmorland/ Westmorland Photography 52B, 67B, 96, 111T, 111B

Doc White/EarthWater Stock Photography 193T

Dave Wilhelm/EarthWater Stock Photography 56B, 69M

Norbert Wu 9T, 99, 100, 124B, 125, 168, 211M

Maps by Karen Minot

Design and layout by Mary Kay Garttmeier

Index by Elizabeth Cook

T–top, B–bottom, M–middle, R-right, L-left

INDEX

Note: page numbers in italics refer to illustrations